REDEFINING THE PARTNERSHIP

The United States and Japan in East Asia

edited by

**Chihiro Hosoya
Tomohito Shinoda**

University Press of America,® Inc.
Lanham • New York • Oxford

Copyright © 1998
University Press of America,® Inc.
4720 Boston Way
Lanham, Maryland 20706

12 Hid's Copse Rd.
Cummor Hill, Oxford OX2 9JJ

All rights reserved
Printed in the United States of America
British Library Cataloging in Publication Information Available

Library of Congress Cataloging-in-Publication Data

Redefining the partnership : the United States and Japan in East Asia
/ edited by Chihiro Hosoya, Tomohito Shinoda.
p. cm.
Includes index.
1. United States—Relations—Japan. 2. Japan—Relations—United States. 3. United States—Foreign relations—1989- 4. United States—Relations—East Asia. 5. East Asia—Relations—United States. 6. Japan—Relations—East Asia. 7. East Asia—Relations—Japan. I. Hosoya, Chihiro. II. Shinoda. Tomohito.
E183.8.J3R36 1998 303.48'273052—dc21 98-17712 CIP

ISBN 0-7618-1141-9 (cloth: alk. ppr.)
ISBN 0-7618-1142-7 (pbk: alk. ppr.)

∞™ The paper used in this publication meet the minimum requirements of American National Standard for information Sciences—Permanence of Paper for Printed Library Materials, ANSI Z39.48—1984

Contents

List of Figures and Tables	v
Preface by Chihiro Hosoya	vii
Acknowledgments	xvii

Security

Chapter 1   **The U.S.-Japan Alliance and the Future of East Asian Security**   1
Michael J. Green

Chapter 2   **Changing Security Environments and their Impacts on U.S.–Japan Relations**   15
Akio Watanabe and Hisayoshi Ina

Trade and Domestic Politics

Chapter 3   **Political Change in the United States and Its Impact on U.S.–Japan Relations**   29
I.M. Destler

Chapter 4   **Japan's Political Changes and Their Impact on U.S.–Japan Relations**   43
Tomohito Shinoda

Economic Developments in East Asia and U.S.–Japan Relations

Chapter 5   **Economic Development in China and her Relations with Japan and the U.S.**   59
Akinori Marumo, Chung-Hsun Yu, Hiroshi Ouchi and Yasuko Ikemoto

| Chapter 6 | U.S.–Japanese Economic Relations and the Southeast Asia Connection: A Boring Analysis
Charles Chang, David Fernandez and James Riedel | 83 |

The Chinese Domestic Situation and U.S.–Japan Relations

| Chapter 7 | The Structure of China's Changing Political Society After Deng Xiaoping: Its Paradoxical Dynamism
Satoshi Amako | 103 |
| Chapter 8 | The United States, Japan and Post-Deng China: A Contextual Approach
H. Lyman Miller | 127 |

Human Rights

| Chapter 9 | Changing U.S. Perspectives on Human Rights
Akira Iriye | 159 |
| Chapter 10 | U.S.–Japanese Relations, Democracy and Human Rights Issues in Asia
Tadashi Aruga | 173 |

International Order

| Chapter 11 | Asia–Pacific Economic Regionalism and U.S.–Japan Relations
Tsutomu Kikuchi | 195 |
| Chapter 12 | The United States, Japan and the Tides of History
Charles F. Doran | 217 |

| Index | | 241 |
| About the Editors and List of Participants | | 255 |

List of Figures and Tables

Figures

6-1	Gross Saving and Investment Rates, Japan and U.S.	98
12-1	Dynamics of Changing Systems Structure: Percent Shares of Power in the Central System for Leading States (1500–1993)	220
12-2	Dynamic Simulation of Absolute and Relative GNP Growth for Four Countries (1986–2030)	229

Tables

5-1	Japan's Trade with China	66
5-2	U.S. Trade with China	67
5-3	Trade with China: Regional Composition (percent of total)	68
5-4	Commodity Composition of U.S. Trade with China (percent of total)	70
5-5	China's Trade Balance	71

Tables *(continued)*

5-6	Japanese Foreign Direct Investment in East Asia	73
5-7	Economic Scale and Per-Capita GDP of each Country and Area in 2020 and 2050 (based on the purchasing power parity as of 1993)	78
6-1	The Share of Imports in Apparent Consumption of Key Raw Materials in Japan and the United States (percentages)	85
6-2	The Destination of Japanese Exports and Relative Market Size	86
6-3	Gravity Model Estimates of Bilateral Trade, 1990–1995	88
6-4	Net Foreign Direct Investment Flows to Selected Asian Developing Countries ($ millions and as percentage of GNP)	93
6-5	The Source of FDI in Selected East Asian Countries, 1986–1992 ($ millions and percentages)	95

Preface

Chihiro Hosoya

This volume contains essays produced by both American and Japanese scholars after two years of joint research work. The Japanese research group, composed of 24 members, was organized by the Center for Japan-U.S. Relations at the International University of Japan. The American group, composed of six members, was organized by the Edwin O. Reischauer Center for East Asian Studies, the Paul H. Nitze School of Advanced International Studies, the Johns Hopkins University.

This joint research project, which was designed to explore and redefine the common issues facing Japan and the United States in the Asia-Pacific region, began its activities in September 1995 with generous financial support from the Japan Foundation Center for Global Partnership. After having engaged in their separate research activities, the two groups got together at the Shonan International Village in Hayama, Japan, July 5–6, 1997, to discuss the essential points of the papers which had been submitted to each member several months earlier.

The members were divided into six subgroups according to the subjects to be addressed. Those subjects were: (1) Security, (2) Trade and Domestic Politics, (3) Economic Developments in East Asia and U.S.-Japan Relations, (4) Chinese Domestic Situation and U.S.-Japan Relations, (5) Human Rights, and (6) International Order.

Security

Despite the ending of the Cold War, there is a widely shared view across the Pacific that there is a need for Japan and the U.S. to maintain their bilateral security arrangements, taking into consideration the lack of stability on the Korean peninsula and uncertainties in the policy direction of China. Both countries reached an agreement reaffirming the validity of the alliance on April 17, 1996.

It was also agreed by both parties that they should start a review of the 1978 Guidelines for the U.S.-Japan Defense Cooperation so as to make them more applicable to the new circumstances. A series of bilateral talks had been in progress before the final agreement on the new Guidelines was reached on September 23, 1997.

In the essay "Changing Security Environments and Their Impacts on U.S.-Japan Relations," Akio Watanabe and Hisayoshi Ina deal with the security problem in regional, bilateral and domestic contexts. In the regional context, their essay sheds light on the responses made by countries in East Asia, including China and South Korea, to the redefined security arrangements. Controversial problems such as "rear area support" or "areas surrounding Japan" are discussed in the bilateral context and the "Okinawa Problem" in the domestic context.

Michael Green highlights the global perspective in his essay, "The U.S.-Japan Alliance and the Future of East Asian Security," arguing "the purpose of these bases and forward deployed forces should be to provide intermediate power projection capabilities to the entire hemisphere and to prevent a power vacuum."

He discusses the question of multilateral forums in this region, such as the ARF (ASEAN Regional Forum) and their relevance to the U.S.-Japan security arrangements, concluding that these might provide "a useful compliment," but "not a substitute" for the alliance. "Multilateral institutions will never replace the alliance" in this region.

Trade and Domestic Politics

The ending of the Cold War led to a decline of socialist ideology in Japan and caused the breakdown of the long-standing 1955 political system. The 38-year-long rule of the Liberal Democratic Party (LDP) was replaced by short-lived coalition governments. Japanese domestic politics under these moderate coalition governments has been characterized by a lack of coordination between the ruling parties and the bureaucrats. As Tomohito Shinoda argues in his essay, "Japan's Political Changes and Their Impact on U.S.-Japan Relations," decision-making has become a "more time-and energy-consuming process to build consensus than under the LDP government."

Lack of confidence among the government officials caused by loss of public support and the coming administrative reform, has been noticeable in recent years and is likely to have an effect on the negotiating process of trade issues. Shinoda identifies some changes taking place in Japan's negotiating style on bilateral trade issues, arguing "Japan did not hesitate to break off the talks or to refuse ambiguous compromises as they once did." Whether this change will be permanent remains to be seen.

In his essay "Political Change in the United States and Its Impact on U.S.-Japan Relations," I.M. Destler argues that American policies had been driven by a perception of "Cold War victory and economic defeat." According to an opinion survey conducted in 1990, more than half the respondents replied that in their view "the economic power of Japan" was "a greater threat to the security of the United States these days" than "the military power of the Soviet Union."

Under these circumstances, President William Clinton, who entered office in January 1993, placed more emphasis on trade issues than security matters in his conduct of Japan policy. He set up a new "National Economic Council (NEC)" designed to coordinate the economic policy-making process, and commissioned its members with the task of taking the initiative in conducting trade negotiations with Japan. Thus, W.B. Cutter of the NEC was given leadership in maintaining a tough stance on the "framework agreement" in collaboration with other agencies concerned. Destler concludes that the Clinton administration "was more successful than most of its predecessors in presenting a united front" in trade negotiations.

The tough trade policy Washington had taken toward Japan in 1993 was sustained in 1994. The "Super 301 executive order" for economic sanctions was issued on March 3 of that year. The target date for implementation was set to September 30. The threat of sanctions was employed again in the spring of 1995 when the trade negotiations on the auto-parts issue came to a deadlock.

By 1996 resurgent American competitiveness had become apparent. In the context of domestic politics, Destler considers, it was better for the Clinton administration "to claim victory in old trade wars than to wage new ones." With the collapse of the "bubble economy," Japan began to reveal its economic weakness and lost its position as a serious American competitor.

Destler concludes, that "national security concerns can no longer be expected to dominate" U.S. foreign relations, but that "economic concerns have not clearly replaced them." What can be said is that the domestic political component is strong in the U.S. foreign policy decision-making process. This is the case with the American trade policy toward Japan.

Economic Developments in East Asia and U.S.-Japan Relations

The emergence of China as one of the largest economic powers in the world has had a significant impact on U.S.-Japan relations. Akinori Marumo, Chung-Hsun Yu, Hiroshi Ouchi and Yasuko Ikemoto, in their joint essay, "Economic Development in China and her Relations with Japan and the U.S.," provide us with an analytical description of the rapid economic growth of China and its future potential. Bilateral relations between China and Japan, as well as the United States, in terms of trade and investment flows are also examined. In their conclusion, the writers make a number of interesting observations.

They argue, for example, that "the rapid increase in the trade deficit of the U.S. against China is expected to divert the trade concerns of the U.S. away from Japan to China," and that "this may contribute to reduce the tension and conflict between the two countries."

They also suggest, on the other hand, that the Chinese market could become a source of conflict and promote rivalry between Japan and the United States, as in the period prior to World War II. "The rapidly expanding market of China will tend to cause a rivalry between Japan and the U.S. in securing the market for its own industrial products, both in terms of commodity exports and direct investments."

The essay also identifies some issues and areas in which Japan and the U.S. can act in cooperation: such as asking China to reduce tariff and non-tariff barriers; to remove various measures of protectionism; to secure intellectual property rights; and to modernize its legal system.

Over the last decade, there has been a striking economic growth in Southeast Asian countries. Both Japan and the U.S. have played a significant role in enabling this region to achieve such high economic growth through providing economic and technological assistance. During the days of the Cold War, John F. Dulles was eager to push Japan toward Southeast Asia to secure markets for Japan's exports and to establish a triangular cooperation designed to contain the expansion of communism. Japan and the U.S. cooperated in 1966 to set up the Asian Development Bank. In the 1970s the debacle of the Vietnam War made Washington's leaders less eager to become involved in the affairs of Southeast Asia.

With the economic development of Southeast Asia, there has been a revival of interest among American leaders, as well as in the business community, in this region. This has brought some competition between Japan and the United States in terms of exporting manufactured goods and investing capital. Because of this, it is sometimes claimed that Japan has been making strategic moves to "regionalize" its developmental policies and to outmaneuver American business in this region.

In their essay, "U.S.-Japanese Economic Relations and the Southeast Asia Connection: A Boring Analysis," Charles Chang, David Fernandez and James Riedel argue that this is not the case, and that characteristics of this triangular system are "largely explained by [a] standard economic model."

The Chinese Domestic Situation and U.S.-Japan Relations

In his essay, "The Structure of China's Changing Political Society after Deng Xiaoping: Its Paradoxical Dynamism," Satoshi Amako explores Chinese internal developments in the post-Deng Xiaoping era. He addresses such questions as the future of Jiang Zemin's leadership, the gap between the center and periphery and political democratization. He concludes that the most sensitive domestic issue will be the internal "establishment of Jiang Zemin's leadership system." In foreign policy the most important issue will be "how to cope with Taiwan's active diplomacy to shake China through tensions and negotiations, and the United States policy which considers Taiwan as the major issue."

H. Lyman Miller, in his essay, "The United States, Japan, and Post-Deng China: A Contextual Approach," examines dissension over Chinese policy in the U.S. Some see China as seeking to establish hegemony over Asia, and presenting "a rising threat to international peace and security." Others predict the collapse of the Beijing regime and the fragmentation of China into separate regions. Miller, opposing these positions, sees China as a system-maintaining power in the international system, and believes that its foreign policy is mainly shaped by external contexts rather than by its domestic situation.

Looking at the domestic situation, he has the view that "trends through the mid–1990s suggest that prospects for full-scale regime collapse and regional fragmentation have receded," and that "the post-Deng leadership around Jiang Zemin remains committed to the basic premise that guided Deng Xiaoping's domestic polities." He concludes, "Prospects for radical political change, sudden collapse, or regional fragmentation and break-up are not high."

Miller is skeptical about the idea of a "Chinese Threat." " Beijing's foreign policies," he argues, "are not adventurist, aggressive and assertive; they are cautious and largely reactive to a dynamic and uncertain international context." "The most serious challenge" in the international context comes from the policies of Washington and Tokyo toward China, in particular, the Taiwan question.

He concludes that "Engagement rather than containment is the policy suited to bring to successful and constructive conclusion the effort began in the 1970s to bring China into the prevailing international order. Both the United States and Japan share an overwhelming interest in bringing such a policy of engagement to bear."

Human Rights

Human rights issues make it extremely difficult for the United States and China to reach full rapprochement. They also reveal important differences between the United States and Japan, as evidenced by the divergent responses of the two countries to the Tiananmen Incident of June 1989.

The importance attached to human rights in the conduct of American foreign policy dates back to the days of President Woodrow Wilson. In the 1970s Henry Kissinger's human rights diplomacy had a strong impact on American policy toward the Soviet Union, and President James Carter attached great importance to human rights.

Akira Iriye, in his essay, "Changing U.S. Perspectives on Human Rights," stresses the growing importance of this issue in the post-Cold War period. He argues that "human rights seemed to provide a vision, an organizing principle, for the world in the wake of the Cold War," and it was natural for the United States, the only super-power which had been the "self-claimed champion of human rights," to look upon the principle as "the key to the new world order."

"It is not surprising," he considers "that China would have emerged as the main opponent of the United States in this regard." From the Chinese perspective, "the United States was seeking to prevent China's emergence as a great power," using this issue as a lever. Moreover, it is impossible for the Chinese "to accept the Western definition of human rights" which has its roots in a different civilization.

Iriye attaches great importance to the role played by individuals and NGOs (non-governmental organizations), rather than governments, in the process of achieving breakthroughs in the seemingly irreconcilable human rights issues.

In his essay, "U.S.-Japanese Relations, Democracy and Human Rights Issues in Asia," Tadashi Aruga deals with human rights diplomacy in Japan, and Asian views of human rights. Aruga argues, "In spite of the basic similarity between Japan and the United States in their human rights philosophy, there was a wide gap between their respective conducts of human rights diplomacy."

"Japan has conducted quiet human rights diplomacy toward Indonesia, mentioning its concern with the human rights condition in East Timor. But Japan has never used its Official Development Assistance (ODA) toward Indonesia as a diplomatic lever to put pressure on Indonesia," he contends. He expresses his sympathy with an "Asian Way" of conducting human rights diplomacy, namely the way of bearing in mind the significance of national and regional particularities and various historical, cultural, and religious backgrounds, while admitting the universality of human rights in nature. He draws the conclusion that "it is desirable to mitigate human rights abuses in an authoritarian regime. Human rights diplomacy is to serve this purpose. Even when Japan will employ quiet diplomacy of persuasion in most cases, it should not shrink from using public diplomacy of open criticism in some cases."

International Order

With the deepening of economic interdependence across national borders, there has emerged a trend toward regionalism in various parts of the world. The European Economic Council (EEC) came into existence in Western Europe with 6 member states in 1958 and developed into the European Union (EU) in 1993. The EU is now moving toward setting up the Economic Monetary Union (EMU) in 1999. In North America, the North American Free Trade Agreement (NAFTA), composed of the U.S., Canada and Mexico, was set up in 1994. The Asia-Pacific Economic Cooperation (APEC) Forum first met in Canberra in November 1989.

Tsutomu Kikuchi, in his essay, "Asia-Pacific Economic Regionalism and U.S.-Japan Relations," gives us a picture of the functioning of APEC as a mechanism for promoting regional dialogue and economic interdependence as well as its historical development.

There are some differences in views between Japan and the United States in terms of their approaches to the economic regionalism embodied in APEC. The United States tends to "politicize" this regional entity, in other words, to exploit APEC for the purpose of promoting its politico-strategic purposes. Japan, in contrast, wants this forum to simply help promote economic cooperation among countries in the region. Unlike the U.S., Japan believes it is too early to set up a formal institution on a contractual agreements basis. Kikuchi emphasizes the importance of APEC for U.S.-Japan relations, arguing that it contributes to "helping maintain harmonious economic relations between Japan and the United States, and providing a convenient regional framework for Japan to take a joint leadership role in regional affairs without causing concerns to Asian neighbors."

Japan's delicate and important task is to cautiously help prevent APEC from turning into a sort of East Asian economic bloc, such as the East Asia Economic Caucus (EAEC), as advocated by Prime Minister M. Mahathir, and at the same time to avoid involvement in the kind of joint politico-strategic leadership envisaged by the United States.

Charles F. Doran examines the entire subject in much broader context, regional as well as global, in his essay, "The United States, Japan, and the Tides of History," introducing a systemic approach for international politics.

Having looked at the changing pattern of power cycles in the central system of world politics, he categorizes Japan as a country in a state of "maturation." "Japanese power," he contends, "is beginning to peak ... but is likely to enjoy a very long flat peak in its power cycle." A most striking structural change is taking place in the context of China's emergence. Doran argues that "the ultra-rapid rise of China is responsible for the slowdown in Japan's upward momentum on its power curve."

In reviewing U.S.-Japan relations in the Asia-Pacific region, he suggests that it suits Japanese strategy to "keep the United States involved in global economic issues and broad-based regional arrangements such as APEC."

"The most compelling Asian foreign policy issue for Japan and for the United States is to adopt a common policy" to handle "the challenge of the integration of North Korea into a stable and peaceful market system," and "of the resolution of the China/Taiwan One-China tangle." He discusses three strategic options for the United States and Japan to take vis-à-vis China: (1) an alliance of the Great Powers, including EU, Russia, Japan and the United States; (2) Collective Security Arrangements, emulating the Conference on Security and Cooperation in Europe (CSCE); and (3) Bilateral security arrangements as seen in the U.S.-Japan Security Treaty.

Doran recommends the third choice, saying that "the U.S.-Japan Alliance remains critical to the defense interests of each state and to political harmony in Asia. ... From a structural perspective, there is no reason why Japan and the United States ought not to continue their strategic partnership since these two 'maritime powers' are not likely to undergo substantial change in their underlying capability and foreign policy outlook." They "can exercise a balancing role" in the face of the new rising power of China even "on the outskirts of the great Eur-Asian land mass." "The U.S.-Japan alliance is a cornerstone of security in the Asia-Pacific region," he concludes.

Acknowledgments

We gratefully acknowledge the generous financial support provided by the Japan Foundation Center for Global Partnership and the efforts of Norio Furushima, who oversaw this project. We have benefited from the collaboration of the Center for Japan–U.S. Relations at the International University of Japan. In particular, it would have been impossible to complete this project without the secretarial assistance of Mrs. Kazumi Imai and the expert editing of Rhonda Stokes.

Our special appreciation is extended to Director George Packard, the Edwin O. Reischauer Center for East Asian Studies, the Paul H. Nitze School of Advanced International Studies, the Johns Hopkins University, for his strenuous efforts to organize the American group and to encourage them to produce these excellent papers.

We highly appreciate the efforts of those Japanese scholars who actively participated in our study group and generously shared their knowledge and opinions during the course of this project. they include: Fumiko Fujita, Haruhiko Fukui, Osamu Ishii, Seigen Miyasato, Katsunori Mori, Takeshi Saito, Takuya Sasaki, Hideo Sato, Noriyuki Shikata, Hirokazu Shiode, Kunio Takahashi, Motoyuki Takamatsu and Kenji Takita. We also express our thankfulness to Kazuyoshi Umemoto, Peter Van Ness, and Ambassador Hiroki Seki, who presented their views and useful suggestions at the study meetings.

Finally, we would like to thank Nancy Ulrich and the rest of the staff at the University Press of America for patiently guiding us in the process of publishing this book.

Chapter 1

The U.S.-Japan Alliance and the Future of East Asian Security

Michael J. Green

Introduction

In the late 1980s numerous scholars on both sides of the Pacific were predicting that the United States and Japan would be unable to sustain a bilateral alliance with the absence of the unifying threat of the Soviet Union. The reasons given for the inevitability of this strategic divorce between the two most powerful countries in the Pacific Rim varied. Structural realists maintained that Japan, as a rational actor, would seek an unacceptable level of relative gains and autonomy from the United States.[1] "Revisionist" Japan experts argued that Japan's unique mercantilist approach to the international system would lead to a rupture with Washington.[2] A new wave of international political economy theorists were then inspired by the revisionists to argue that Japan would turn its mercantilist strategies into a new independent technonationalist security policy that would transform East Asian international relations.[3] In Japan as well, there was no shortage of scholars and journalists predicting the "Asianization" of Japanese foreign policy.[4]

Yet, as Mark Twain might have observed, the rumors of the death of the U.S.-Japan Alliance were "greatly exaggerated." If anything, the most noteworthy development in bilateral relations since the end of the Cold War has been the reaffirmation and enhancement of the alliance in the April 1996 U.S.-Japan Joint Security Declaration. The doomsday pundits, it seems, were wrong. They were wrong, first, because they failed to anticipate structural weaknesses in the Japanese economic model. Second, they overlooked the impact of the globalization of innovation and manufacturing on bilateral trade relations. And perhaps most important of all, they failed to see the uncertainty that changing power relationships would create in regional security calculations in East Asia. As Aaron Friedberg has noted:

> What is unfolding in Asia is a race between the accelerating dynamics of multipolarity, which could increase the chances of conflict, and the growth of mitigating factors that should tend to dampen them and to improve the prospects for a continuing peace.[5]

If the U.S.-Japan Alliance is relevant as a military partnership after the Cold War, it is precisely because the bilateral security relationship provides predictability, reassurance and deterrence in the fluid and uncertain strategic environment described by Friedberg. In a word, the alliance provides stability.

This regional dimension of post-Cold War security cooperation was the theme behind the April 1996 Joint Security Declaration. In the declaration, Prime Minister Ryutaro Hashimoto and President Bill Clinton ordered a revision of the 1978 Guidelines for Defense Cooperation to address responses to regional contingencies—with the unstated but most likely scenario being on the Korean Peninsula. They also reaffirmed support for a continued U.S. military presence in the region and in Japan for the foreseeable future, while agreeing to reorganize U.S. bases in Okinawa to reduce the impact on local communities. In addition, they announced their intention to work together to integrate China into the region. And finally, the two leaders highlighted the importance of multilateral dialogues and institution building for the future of East Asian security.

These are, therefore, the agenda items that will ultimately determine how successfully the U.S.-Japan Alliance makes the transition to the post-Cold War era. To review, they are: (1) managing developments on the Korean peninsula; (2) achieving military cooperation; (3) integrating China; (4) maintaining a U.S. forward presence; and (5) building regional dialogue and institutions. Each is examined in the following.

The Korean Peninsula

The Joint Security Declaration highlighted continued tensions on the Korean Peninsula as an important consideration in the maintenance of a strong U.S.-Japan Alliance. The Korean War defined U.S.-Japan security ties more than any other event during the Cold War. It was the North Korean invasion of South Korea that led the United States to rehabilitate Japanese defense and heavy industrial production, reconstitute Japanese military forces, and sign the first U.S.-Japan Security Treaty. After the Cold War, events on the Korean Peninsula may again prove the single most important defining influence in the U.S.-Japan security relationship.

The United States and Japan share a common interest in the peaceful reunification of the two Koreas. It is sometimes claimed that Japanese fear a reunified Korea, and in some quarters in Tokyo that may be true, given the history of Japanese-Korean relations and uncertainties about the course of reunification. However, the division of the Peninsula has left a far more dangerous and unpredictable threat in Japan's neighborhood, and the Japanese Government's record on supporting Seoul's position on reunification has been blemished only by the occasional (and increasingly infrequent) parliamentary delegation to the North. Japan has played a crucial role in supporting KEDO (the Korean Peninsula Energy Development Organization), and stands ready to back up the four-plus-two talks proposed by Presidents Clinton and Kim Young Sam in Korea in April 1996. An important (indeed, indispensable) vehicle for Tokyo's participation in both initiatives will be the bilateral alliance with the United States.

U.S. Forces and bases in Japan have always played a critical role in deterring North Korea from aggression against the South, and would be at the center of any response to a contingency on the Peninsula. Japan's supporting role in such a crisis was considered in the bilateral review of the 1978 U.S.-Japan Guidelines for Defense Cooperation (described in the next section). This bilateral review will eventually require closer trilateral cooperation with Seoul, both to coordinate operational issues and to build mutual confidence in Japan's role in regional crises.

Intensified dialogues between the United States, Japan and Korea will also be necessary to define the role of both the U.S.-Japan and U.S.-Republic of Korea (ROK) Alliances after reunification. It is likely that

Japan will continue to want U.S. Forces in Korea (USFK) and Korea will want U.S. Forces in Japan (USFJ). Clearly, there would be some significant reassessment of forward presence on the U.S. side, but a combined U.S. force based in both countries is not out of the question. From the U.S. perspective, bases in Northeast Asia would continue to be critically important in protecting regional and global interests. However, if U.S. forces stay in Japan and Korea, their mission would take on more of an expeditionary color (as opposed to the current deterrence and defense missions of USFK), with responsibilities as far away as the Gulf. Hosting such forces would require a significantly different view of alliance cooperation in both Japan and Korea. Moreover, it would probably require a higher degree of trust, coordination and communication on a trilateral basis. A hint of the future came during the 1994 North Korean nuclear crisis, when trilateral security consultations reached an unprecedented level. Consultations and coordination will have to deepen and expand if all three countries are to weather the uncertainties of the transformation to a unified Korea. A first step in this direction was taken in Seoul in March 1997 when senior defense officials met to exchange views on defense planning and regional assessments.[6]

Review of the Guidelines

In his 1969 joint communiqué with President Richard Nixon, Prime Minister Eisaku Sato gave an implicit commitment to cooperate with U.S. Forces in the event of a Korean crisis and attempts were made to outline Japan's role during the bilateral negotiations that led to the first U.S.-Japan Guidelines for Defense Cooperation in 1978. Ultimately, the Japanese Government used the Guidelines only to spell-out bilateral cooperation in the event of a direct attack on Japan. The regional dimension of contingency planning was left largely untouched.[7]

For a time, this approach proved useful to broader U.S. regional strategy—particularly since the expansion of Soviet forces in the Far East in the 1980s meant that robust self-defense for Japan helped to "bottle-up" Soviet ships, submarines and bombers in the Maritime Provinces. With the end of Cold War and the demise of the direct Soviet threat, however, Japan's enhanced capabilities for "exclusively defensive defense" proved less useful in the event of a regional crisis. The Gulf War gave an early hint of the limitations of Japan's approach, and the North

Korean nuclear crisis of 1994 raised even more questions about what useful role Japanese Self-Defense Forces (SDFJ) and facilities could play in the event of a regional contingency other than a direct attack on the Japanese homelands. The need for a clearer definition of Japan's supporting role to the United States led President Clinton and Prime Minister Hashimoto to include a revision of the 1978 Guidelines as part of the April 1996 Joint Security Declaration. The objective of this Guidelines Review was not simply preparation for a Korean crisis scenario, of course. In fact, a significant part of the review was geared towards a definition of supporting U.S. roles for Japanese forces engaged in future peacekeeping or humanitarian missions. When it was completed in the fall of 1997, the review clearly outlined what missions the United States and Japan should attempt to fill in the event of regional crises. These missions range from pre-crisis preventative actions, to crisis response and post-crisis stabilization and humanitarian relief. Rather than preparing for Japanese combat missions on the Korean Peninsula—a politically unrealistic and even undesirable objective considering the strong sentiments in both Japan and Korea against such a role—the U.S. and Japanese sides properly explored cooperative missions in logistics and support. It is conceivable that such missions might include the use of Japan's civilian infrastructure (hospitals, airports, and communications), joint use of SDFJ bases, and SDFJ escort and patrol in the Sea of Japan. In the case of a Korean crisis, this would not mean that Japan would escape danger. In fact, a North Korean attack on South Korea would almost certainly be accompanied by attempts at intimidation, sabotage and assault to undermine Japan as an operational base for U.S. and U.N. reinforcements. Defense of territory and sea lanes and protection of U.S. operations in Japan would be a central mission of Japan's Self-Defense Forces in such a crisis.[9]

It is essential that the results of this Guidelines review be implemented in the form of bilateral operational plans, training and modernization. To some extent this will require new legislation in Japan. It may prove difficult for the current Hashimoto Government to establish the leverage to push through such legislation before the Upper House elections in the summer of 1998 (which might clear out Socialist opponents to contingency planning). Even then, it may take an actual crisis before the legislation moves in the Diet. Nevertheless, considerable preparation can be completed in anticipation of enabling Japanese legislation.

One issue that could make that legislative debate highly charged is the question of whether or not Japan should recognize its rights of collective defense. That the right exists under Japan's Constitution is not debated in the Japanese Government, but the issue has long formed an ideological fault line in the Diet and even within the Liberal Democratic Party (LDP). Most of Japan's supporting missions under the Guidelines Review will probably fall well within the traditional definition of "individual" self-defense. The rest will have to be covered by either a looser definition of "individual" or an explicit recognition of "collective" self-defense. Ironically, a large majority of Japanese politicians favor Japan playing a much broader supporting role in regional crises (the LDP, NFP, Sun Party, DPJ and even the JSDP all include it in party platforms), but the Constitutional issue is sensitive and many are therefore cautious about an explicit reinterpretation. For years the issue has been divorced from legal and operational reality. The right, amplified in the *Yomiuri Shimbun*, wants to use the collective defense issue to define Japan as a normal nation. The left, amplified in the *Asahi Shimbun*, is attacking this dangerous assault on the Constitution. The real problem of planning Japan in for a joint response to a regional contingency will only be solved when the discussion is focused on concrete requirements rather than old ideological divisions. Ultimately, the process is the same. Whether Japan recognizes the right of collective defense or relaxes the definition of individual self-defense, national consensus and majority political support in the Diet are necessary.

China

The Joint Security Declaration has sparked a small explosion of criticism of the U.S.-Japan Alliance in China. Ironically, U.S. and Japanese policymakers took great care to note that Washington and Tokyo look forward to "integrating" China into the region—hardly the language of a strategy of containment. It was the political atmosphere of the time, however, that probably led to criticism in China. U.S. carriers, one of them based in Japan, were deployed in March to signal U.S. concern over Beijing's missile tests over the Taiwan Straits. Japan had also crossed paths with the Chinese side over nuclear testing and other issues. For Beijing, the U.S.-Japan Alliance had long been a useful tool for containing both the Soviet Union and Japan. By April 1996, Chinese strategists appeared to be moving toward the conclusion that the Soviets were less of a problem and the Japanese were using the Alliance to expand their military role. The Taiwan Straits demonstrations suggested that the alliance might even be turned against China in a dispute over Taiwan. Beijing favors the U.S.-Japan Alliance, it seems, as long as the Alliance does not do anything.[9]

Chinese apprehension about the April summit is misplaced. The Guidelines Review does not represent an expansion of Japan's military role in the region. In fact, exercise is aimed at filling-in gaps in Japan's support role that most of the region mistakenly assumed were always there. The non-threatening nature of the Guidelines Review is evident in offers from both the U.S. Department of Defense (DOD) and the Japan Defense Agency (JDA) to brief China and other regional powers on the process and focus of the entire exercise (the first of these took place in Tokyo in October 1996). It is also forgotten that the U.S. and Japan issued the Joint Security Declaration after more than a year of intensive bilateral dialogue aimed at reaffirming the importance of the alliance after the Cold War. All of this began before the difficulties caused by the nuclear testing and Taiwan Straits demonstrations and was aimed not at containing China, but at maintaining close U.S.-Japan security ties into the future. In short, the only nations that should be concerned about the maintenance of a close U.S.-Japan Alliance are those nations intent on altering the status quo.

The U.S.-Japan-China relationship is probably not a "strategic triangle," but it is an increasingly complex trilateral relationship that will require greater transparency and dialogue to stabilize. The Theater Missile Defense (TMD) is one case in point. China amplified its criticism of U.S.-Japan TMD cooperation after the contretemps over the Taiwan Straits appeared to put the U.S.-Japan Alliance in a new perspective. At that point, Chinese analysts and officials began warning that TMD would undermine the Chinese nuclear deterrent. This in turn alarmed the Japanese side, because it implied that Tokyo would be the target of Chinese nuclear attack (in opposition to Beijing's declared policies of no first use and no use against non-nuclear states). Ultimately, Beijing's concern about the principles of the Anti-Ballistic Missile (ABM) Treaty and stable deterrence will have to be tested with a higher order of transparency regarding Chinese nuclear doctrine and force structure. It may also eventually require a new level of dialogue on strategic nuclear issues between Washington and Beijing. Similarly, the U.S. and Japan should continue to offer transparency and explanations regarding the Guidelines Review. Posturing in Sino-U.S. and Sino-Japanese relations must be replaced with reasoned dialogue.[10]

At the same time, U.S. and Japanese policymakers may have to grow used to a certain level of rhetoric from Beijing. Friction may be inevitable, even if conflict is not. Tokyo, Washington, and Beijing all appear on the surface to be status quo powers and this is true for the near term. The difference comes in what vision each has for the future. Washington and Tokyo seem most intent on maintaining the current unipolar system that emerged from the end of the Cold War. Beijing has made it clear in joint statements with Moscow (as part of the new Sino-Russian "Strategic Partnership"), that multipolarity should characterize international relations in the future.[11] No one is willing to press their vision too hard, because all three have a stake in preserving stability in the region. However, on specific issues, ranging from the World Trade Organization (WTO) accession to human rights and arms control, the U.S., Japan and China will be in the same bed, but with different dreams.

U.S. Presence

The Joint Security Declaration reaffirmed President Clinton and Prime Minister Hashimoto's strong support for the U.S. commitment to maintain about 100,000 U.S. troops in the Asia-Pacific Region, including the current force levels in Japan. There is a great deal of speculation in Tokyo that Washington's current Quadrennial Defense Review (QDR) will lead to a reduction of U.S. forces in Asia, and specifically on Okinawa. This speculation is almost certainly off the mark. The QDR will produce cuts. But as departing Defense Secretary William Perry has made clear, these cuts will be aimed primarily at infrastructure in the United States. European deployments could come under pressure, but as long as the North Korean threat is an immediate problem, significant overseas force reductions in Asia are unlikely and would be irresponsible.[12]

However, when deterring North Korea is no longer a requirement, the nature of U.S. presence in Asia can and should change (barring other clear military threats). The need for large ground units on the Peninsula will subside (unless a temporary stabilization force is necessary to ease the integration of the North). At the same time, forward deployed air, naval and marine forces will continue to play a crucial role in the region even after the end of confrontation on the Korean Peninsula. The purpose of these bases and forward deployed forces should be to provide intermediate power projection capabilities to the entire hemisphere and to prevent a power vacuum that would ignite a cycle of mutual mistrust and rearmament in the region.

The shape of U.S. forces in Asia will depend on allied and domestic U.S. attitudes and the impact of technology (the revolution in military affairs). At a minimum, a carrier battle group and amphibious ready group, with at least one Marine Expeditionary Unit (MEU), would be necessary to maintain sea lanes and credible response capabilities to regional crises (military or humanitarian). Air forces have more options, but the availability of air bases and forward deployed fighters, transports and refueling aircraft in Japan will still be crucial to the maintenance of global power projection capabilities. Ideally, these forces could be rotated between Japan, Korea, and Australia and would be supplemented in a larger crisis through propositioned equipment and access to other bases and facilities in the region. Technological change (just the C-17 long range heavy transport, for example) may allow the U.S. to project more power than ever before with relatively less "presence" in the region. However, there is no substitute for muddy ground forces or aircraft carriers in terms of clarifying U.S. commitment to stability in the region or responding to crises on the ground.[13]

Multilateral Security

The Joint Security Declaration also emphasized the importance of multilateral security dialogues between the United States and Japan. Tokyo jumped on the regional multilateral bandwagon several years ahead of Washington. The Ministry of International Trade and Industry (MITI) worked with the Australian Government to realize the Asia-Pacific Economic Cooperation (APEC) forum beginning in the late 1980s and the Foreign Ministry encouraged the Association of Southeast Asian Nations (ASEAN) to develop the ASEAN Regional Forum (ARF) beginning in the early 1990s. After the Bush administration resisted these trends by repeating its preference for a "hub and spoke" approach to regional security cooperation, the Clinton administration came in with a stronger mandate for participation in regional security forums. Still, the U.S. enthusiasm for multilateral dialogue has often been inconsistent and problematic for the region. President Clinton turned the Seattle APEC summit into a major success with his leadership, but then undermined the Japanese Government's APEC leadership debut by skipping the 1995 Osaka summit to resolve a domestic political crisis. Secretary of Defense Perry then probably went too far (from the region's perspective), when he speculated that APEC might someday address regional security issues. The United States and Japan share a common view that multilateral security dialogues are a useful compliment to the bilateral security relationship, but not a substitute. Tokyo is probably somewhat more enthusiastic than Washington for processes such as the ARF, since the Japanese Government has fewer outlets for its global security policy to begin with. At the same time, the Japanese and U.S. governments share the common problem that their explicit leadership in multilateral forums, such as the ARF, could undermine support for regional dialogues among the smaller ASEAN states. U.S. and Japanese diplomats are therefore limited in the extent to which they can openly engage in "bilateral cooperation" aimed at strengthening multilateral dialogue. The April Security Declaration statement of support for the process may be about as far as the two nations can go, at least with the ARF.

In Northeast Asia, there is more room for proactive joint U.S.-Japanese leadership to build substantive multilateral dialogue in the long run. In the near term, however, Japan will have to settle for a supporting role in the Four Power talks aimed at completion of an armistice agreement on the Korean Peninsula. Another important step that must occur before U.S.-Japanese leadership can build a Northeast Asian dialogue is improved Korean-Japanese cooperation. Once the United States, Korea and Japan are sitting down to talk about the future of Northeast Asian stability, China will have strong incentives to participate in the process.

Trilateral dialogues between the United States, Japan and third countries may be a useful building block towards broader and deeper regional forums in Northeast Asia. Thus far U.S.-Japan-Republic of Korea and U.S.-Japan-Russian exchanges on defense issues have taken place (both in the spring of 1997). These were important opportunities for the United States and Japan to reduce suspicion by explaining the objectives of the Joint Security Declaration and the review of the Guidelines. In April 1997, the LDP reflected prevailing sentiment in both the U.S. and Japanese governments by calling for a U.S.-Japan-China trilateral strategic dialogue, but Beijing has demonstrated little enthusiasm for such a process thus far.[14]

For the time being then, the multilateral dimension of U.S. and Japanese security cooperation will consist of quiet support for the incremental ARF process, forward movement on the Four Power talks for the Korean Peninsula, quiet trilateral meetings, and a general effort to stave off Chinese criticism of the alliance in broader second-track forums such as the

Northeast Asian Security Dialogue. Steady movement forward will compliment the alliance, but the slow pace of progress suggests why multilateral institutions will never replace the alliance.

Conclusion: Comprehensive Security

The April 1996 Joint Security Declaration set forth an agenda for incremental enhancements of the alliance to give it the flexibility and credibility to weather near-term crises in the Asia-Pacific Region. Some pundits have called for more dramatic measures, such as recognizing collective defense, expanding the SDFJ's out-of-area combat role or radically reducing the U.S. force structure in Japan. These types of measures might reduce the "asymmetry" in the bilateral relationship that seems to irritate so many critics of the alliance, but would it contribute to greater stability in the region? The answer is clearly "no." Expanding the alliance militarily beyond the current agenda would undermine cooperation with the Republic of Korea and propel U.S. and Japanese relations with China into an openly confrontational direction. Cutting U.S. Forces in Japan would reinforce suspicions in China that time is on the side of multipolarity and greater Chinese autonomy in the region—not to mention the impact of deterrence on the Korean Peninsula and U.S. capabilities for global power projection.

For the near term, then, the agenda of the Joint Security Declaration is probably about right, if it is completed. This does not mean that the alliance relationship is now reaffirmed and redefined in perpetuity. Changes in the strategic environment should be anticipated and U.S.-Japan security cooperation adjusted accordingly. For this longer-term agenda, it is well worth considering the prospects for increased collective security (including multinational standing naval forces, for example), or the impact of the revolution in military affairs (on the shape of U.S. force structure and the interoperability of U.S. and Japanese forces). Redefinition of the alliance is a continuous process, after all, if one recalls the primitive state of U.S.-Japan security cooperation three decades ago.

If radical restructuring of the alliance makes sense anywhere at the present time, however, it is in the interaction of the bureaucracies on both sides of the Pacific. Two decades ago the Japanese Government began exploring the concept of "comprehensive security." The notion was that Japan's security policy was influenced by more than traditional military threats, and that Japan had unique non-military instruments to shape its security environment, including: Official Development Assistance (ODA), technology, and proactive diplomacy. Comprehensive security has had some impact on the thinking of Japanese government agencies since that time, but its most important impact was probably to legitimize discussions of security in Japan by moving them beyond the politically divisive debate about pure military power.[15] As rhetoric, comprehensive security also found its way into bilateral alliance cooperation, but the concept never took root in the way it should have. The reason was simple: the Ministry of Foreign Affairs and the State Department did not want newcomers from MITI, the Science and Technology Agency or Treasury interfering with the management of the alliance. In the post-Cold War era this sort of bureaucratic stovepiping of the bilateral security relationship no longer makes sense. It only reinforces frustration over the asymmetries in the alliance and limits our mutual ability to shape our common strategic environment in Asia. A truly comprehensive bilateral security relationship is long overdue.

Notes

1. This prospect does not bother some structural realists, who see even a nuclear Japan as more "normal" and stable. See, for example, Kenneth Waltz, *The Spread of Nuclear Weapons: More May Be Better*, Adelphi Paper No.171 (London: International Institute for Strategic Studies, Autumn 1981).

2. The classic revisionists are Chalmers Johnson, Clyde Prestowitz, Karel Van Wolferen, and James Fallows. The most concise presentation of their general arguments can be found in Fallows, "Containing Japan, *Atlantic* 263, no. 5 (May 1989).

3. See for example, Wayne Sandholtz, Michael Borrus, *The Highest Stakes: The Economic Foundations of the New Security System (Berkeley Roundtable on the International Economy)* (London: Oxford University Press, 1992).

4. Yoichi Funabashi, "The Asianization of Asia," *Foreign Affairs* 72, no. 6 (November/December 1993): 75–85.

5. Aaron L. Friedberg, "Ripe for Rivalry: Prospects for Peace in a Multipolar Asia," in *East Asian Security,* ed. Michael E. Brown, Sean M. Lynn-Jones, and Steve E. Miller (Cambridge: MIT Press, 1995), 25–26.

6. See *Asahi Shimbun* (Tokyo) or *Hanguk Ilbo*, 22 March 1997.

7. For details see, Michael J. Green, *Arming Japan: Alliance Production, and the Post-War Search for Autonomy* (New York: Columbia University Press, 1995), 72–85.

8. For details see Barbara Wanner, "Okinawa Base Controversy Dominates U.S.-Japan Security Discussions," *JEI Report*, no.14A (April 11, 1997).

9. For one expression of this viewpoint see Ding Bang Quan, "Issues Regarding Asia Pacific Security into the Twenty-First Century," *Washington Japan Journal* (Japan America Society of Washington) VI, no. 1 (Winter-Spring 1997).

10. For details see Michael J. Green and Benjamin L. Self, "Japan's Changing China Policy: From Commercial Liberalism to Reluctant Realism," *Survival* (Summer 1996).

11. Lee Hockstater, "Russia, China Sign New Friendship Pact," *Washington Post*, 24 April 1997.

12. Secretary of Defense William Cohen made this point in Tokyo on April 11, 1997, *Nikkei Shimbun*, 12 April 1997.

13. On RMA (revolution in military affairs), see Joseph Nye and William Owens, "The Information Edge," *Foreign Affairs* 75, no. 2 (March/April 1996); on the impact of RMA on the alliance see Michael Green, "Gunji Gijitsu Wa Nichibei Anpo o Kaeru," *Foresight* (November 1996).

14. *Yomiuri Shimbun*, 11 April 1997.

15. For details on Comprehensive Security see, Richard Samuels, *Strong Nation-Rich Army: National Security and the Technological Transformation of Japan* (Ithica: Cornell University Press, 1994); or Etoh Shinkichi and Yamamoto Yoshinobu, *Sogo Anzen Hosho to Mirai no Sentaku* (Tokyo: Kodansha, 1991).

Chapter 2

Changing Security Environments and their Impacts on U.S.-Japan Relations

Akio Watanabe
Hisayoshi Ina[*]

Introduction

The days when international security issues were predominantly determined by the global conflict between the two superpowers, the United States and the former Union of Soviet Socialist Republics (USSR), are gone. Consequently, the nature of the security environments have changed and still are changing. Security policies of the United States and Japan and their relationship need to be redefined in accordance with these changes.

During the past couple of years, the respective governments have made some efforts to readjust their security policies to the new realities. In particular, the joint declaration between President Bill Clinton and Prime Minister Ryutaro Hashimoto in April 1996 was an important step towards a new and more balanced security relationship in the post-Cold War era. A new robust consensus, however, has not yet emerged, both within each society and between the two nations with regard to new security policies.

The two governments are facing the following three sets of adjustment problems: (1) regional, (2) bi-lateral, and (3) domestic.

U.S.-Japan Security Relationship in the Regional Context

There is an increasing awareness in the importance of the U.S.-Japan security relationship for regional security and stability, though the concept of "region" needs to be further clarified. For the time being, let us use this word in a rather loose way simply to signify a geographical scope which roughly corresponds to that of the ARF (ASEAN Regional Forum).

Admittedly, the function of the U.S.-Japan Security Treaty had always been "regional" in the sense that the U.S. forces stationed on Japanese soil played critical roles in various contingencies in the Far East (e.g., Korea, Vietnam and, if somewhat geographically over-stretched, the Persian Gulf). The treaty designates the "Far East" for whose peace and security the United States is granted the use by its land, air and naval forces of "facilities and areas in Japan" (Article 6 of the U.S.-Japan Security Treaty).

During the Cold War days, it was in these "regional conflicts" that the U.S.-Japan Security Treaty proved useful. One may therefore rightly say that there is nothing new about the regional dimension of the U.S.-Japan Security Treaty. Nevertheless, there are several new developments which require both Washington and Tokyo to think about and act for international security from a regional point of view more than before.

The end of the Cold War (circa 1991) brought at least two important changes to the regional aspect of the U.S.-Japan security relationship. First, due to the fading out of the "Soviet threat," the stabilizing function of the U.S.-Japan Security Treaty in the Asia-Pacific region came to the fore. To put it differently, the Asia-Pacific region is assuming the nature of an autonomous unit of power, balancing on its own rather than being a subsidiary theater of a global power contest between the two superpowers. Any changes in U.S.-Japan relations will inevitably have very important implications for the power configurations of the entire region.

Second, Japan is now required to play a more active role in international security. It can no longer satisfy its obligations simply by providing "facilities and areas in Japan" for the U.S. forces stationed there. It cannot be just a "host nation." Its security role needs to be re-defined in a way such that Japan will act with the United States as a "joint provider" of public goods, i.e., regional stability of the Asia/Pacific as a whole. Cognizance is taken of this fact to some extent by the Japanese government in its New National Defense Outline (November 1995) which refers to Japan's role for peace and security in the "areas surrounding Japan." This certainly represents a departure from the established course of Japan's security policy during the Cold War era.

It is small wonder that all member states in the ARF have shown considerable interest in recent developments and in the mutual relationship between the United States and Japan over security matters, such as, among others, the U.S.-Japan Joint Declaration on Security—an alliance for the twenty-first century signed by President Bill Clinton and Prime Minister Ryutaro Hashimoto on April 17, 1996.

As this declaration said:

> The strong Alliance between Japan and the United States helped ensure peace and security in the Asia-Pacific region during the Cold War. Our Alliance continues to underlie the dynamic economic growth in the region.

Few people would find it difficult to accept the first half of this statement. What about the second half? It is significant indeed to see the word "alliance" appear in official language to be used by the Japanese government *today* while its use had been carefully avoided during the Cold War era. One should only remember the fuss about the "alliance" following the summit meeting between President Ronald Reagan and Prime Minister Zenko Suzuki in May 1981, which led to the resignation of Foreign Minister Masayoshi Ito.

China reacted rather sharply to the reaffirmed alliance between the United States and Japan, indicative of their new position on the U.S.-Japan Security Treaty. Until recently the Chinese tended to welcome what they regarded as a restraint on a resurgent Japan. As long as the chief target of the treaty was Russia and not China, Beijing did not appear overly concerned. Fearful of the wind blowing in a different direction in recent years, they have begun to feel nervous about the U.S.-Japan combination.

The Chinese base their objection on the following two grounds. First, they maintain that the alliance is anachronistic and should end, like the Cold War, advocating instead a rather strange multilateral security regime to replace the U.S.-led alliance network. This argument is linked with a diplomatic strategy that China has been practicing in recent months, namely a strategy of diluting the U.S.-Japan alliance with the ARF. Whether or not they are really serious about the ARF has yet to be shown, however, by the way in which they behave regarding South China Sea disputes with members of the Association of Southeast Asian Nations (ASEAN).

Second, they argue that the U.S.-Japan Security Treaty was designed as a device not for regional security but for Japan's security only. This argument can hardly be supported by history in view of the past role played by U.S. Forces in Japan (USFJ), in Korea, and in Vietnam. It is apparent that the Chinese conveniently pretend to be ignorant of these historical facts for one reason or another. More candid remarks recently made by officials in Beijing reveal, however, the real reason for their concern.[1] They are afraid of the deterrence function of the U.S.-Japan Security Treaty with respect to possible future crises in the Taiwan Straits and over the Spratly Islands.

While they criticize as usual U.S. "hegemonic" behavior in advancing these arguments, most Chinese comments on the Hashimoto-Clinton joint declaration are primarily focused on the expanded role of Japan in regional security. "The core of the core" of the matter is, as one Chinese commentator put it, the ongoing review of Guidelines of the U.S.-Japan Defense Cooperation.[2] They see a danger in that Japan, rather than remaining a "protectorate" of the United States, is now emerging as an active "participant" in regional security. According to them, this is a road towards a nuclear-armed Japan which has stockpiled sufficient uranium to produce 100 atomic bombs within six months once Japan has decided to do so.[3]

Despite a seemingly unanimous reaction by the Chinese to the strengthened U.S.-Japan security relationship, careful analysis of Chinese opinion leads us to conclude that China is still internally divided on this subject and has not yet consolidated its position.[4] It seems certain, however, that China sees the U.S.-Japan alliance more in terms of a restraint of China rather than of Japan. The nature and degree of their reaction to the U.S.-Japan alliance will be determined by its implications for the Taiwan dispute, and, to a lesser extent, for the South China Sea disputes.

Interestingly enough, as for the implications of the U.S.-Japan alliance for the Korean contingencies, China remains silent. It is very likely, however, that China will use its veto if the U.N. Security Council proposes to send troops to Korea. Then the only available option for the United States and Japan would be to defend their ally, the Republic of Korea, and protect their interests there, if necessary, by force in accordance with Article 51 of the U.N. Charter.

The Republic of Korea (ROK) occupies a central place in the contemporary debates on the U.S.-Japan security relationship. Korea is supposed to be one of the two "regions" for whose contingencies the U.S. security planners are prepared. Likewise, leaders of the ROK cannot afford to be unconcerned over a "hollowing out" of the U.S.-Japan alliance, a likely consequence of a cry for "Go-home, America" in Japan (and, especially, in Okinawa). There are also some people in the United States who cry "Come home, America."[5] It may well be that these voices on both sides of the Pacific have synergistic effects resulting in the annihilation of the U.S.-Japan alliance. Such a concern was actually expressed by the Korean Foreign Minister shortly after the 1995 rape incident in Okinawa. He emphasized that the U.S.-Japan security ties were essential for the maintenance of peace and stability in East Asia.[6]

As both Korea and Japan are allied with the United States, security relations between the two countries in Northeast Asia can be regarded as "indirect or virtual allies." Despite the still high level of animosities towards the Japanese, some Korean intellectuals have began to talk about the necessity of creating a constructive security relationship with Japan.[7]

One should not form a hasty judgment, however, about the new thinking of Korean leaders regarding security issues. Korea's response to the Hashimoto-Clinton security declaration (and its follow-up activities by the United States and Japan), can be characterized at best as ambivalent. Seoul is now watching with mixed feelings recent developments in the U.S.-Japan security cooperation with regard to the increased roles which are required of Japan's Self-Defense Forces (SDFJ) in the areas outside Japan's domain (vs. the New National Defense Outline of Japan, the ACSA (Acquisition and Cross-Servicing Agreement), and works underway to rewrite the U.S.-Japan Defense Cooperation Guidelines). They are afraid that Japan is acquiring "greater independence from the United States in the security realm," arguing that "few in Asia would see a rupture in the U.S.-Japan security alliance as anything but a source of instability in the Asia-Pacific region."[8] It is an area of great concern to those who are thinking along this "traditional" line, that the U.S.-Japan security alliance would wither if Japan remains a mere "protectorate" of the United States. The only available solution to this dilemma seems to be the creation of a collaborative security relationship between Japan and Korea.

Most of the ASEAN members and Australia responded more favorably on the whole to the newly developing security relationship between Tokyo and Washington. Australian journalists reported in as "a matter of fact" way about the Hashimoto-Clinton declaration and other related matters, such as the agreement on the closing of Futenma Air Base and the ACSA. For example an Australian foreign affairs commentator wrote as follows:

[These] kinds of moves are likely to require a more liberal interpretation of the constitutional peace clause than Japan has so far been prepared to take, and open the way for Japan to play a greater role in regional security. It is a prospect that should no longer provoke fear in the region, and one which will become increasingly important as Japan's neighbours grow in economic and military strength and US comes under domestic pressure to wind back its Asian defence presence.[9]

Australia-Japan cooperation for regional security was an agenda item in the meeting between Mr. John Howard, the Australian Prime Minister, and his counterpart, Mr. Hashimoto, during the latter's visit to Canberra in April 1997. They agreed on an expanded relationship about security issues, focusing on regional peacekeeping, military exchanges and regional security. The idea of holding regular high-level consultations on security matters between Tokyo and Canberra was adopted although scaled-down to lower level talks.[10]

Southeast Asians remained rather silent probably due to fear of Chinese reaction. However, in view of the ongoing disputes over the South China Sea with the PRC (People's Republic of China), they "welcome at the bottom of their heart" the U.S.-Japan alliance. They can safely be regarded as hidden supporters for the strengthening of the Hashimoto-Clinton joint declaration.[11] Although the reactions of Japan's neighbors have been varied, the very fact that they reacted to new developments in the U.S.-Japan security relations is significant. It has proved that the U.S.-Japan security relationship is a matter of common interest among the regional states. It is no longer a bilateral matter.

In view of the fact that the rationale of the U.S.-Japan security relations is sought in the context of the regional security of Asia and the Pacific rather than that of a bipolar agenda between Washington and Tokyo, one of the necessary tasks that the leaders of the two countries have to tackle is to persuasively explain the purpose of the U.S.-Japan security relationship before regional members as well as their domestic audiences.

U.S.-Japan Defense Cooperation

Prime Minister Hashimoto and President Clinton signed the "U.S.-Japan Joint Declaration on Security" on April 17, 1996. In the declaration, the leaders agreed to start a review of the 1978 Guidelines for the U.S.-Japan Defense Cooperation. In addition, they also agreed to initiate a study on

bilateral cooperation in dealing with situations that may emerge in areas surrounding Japan that will significantly influence Japan's peace and security. Both governments agreed to reconstitute the Subcommittee for Defense Cooperation (SDC) on June 28, 1996. The SDC has adopted the following pillars for organizing the review.
(1) Cooperation under normal situations;
(2) Actions in response to an armed attack against Japan (to include an imminent armed attack); and
(3) Cooperation in situations that may emerge in areas surrounding Japan that will significantly influence Japan's peace and security.

The SDC is scheduled to complete the review by the autumn of 1997. The SDC agreed that this review will proceed in accordance with the following principles. The review will:
(1) not change the rights and obligations under the U.S.-Japan Security Treaty and related arrangements;
(2) not change the fundamental framework of the U.S.-Japan alliance; and
(3) be conducted within the framework of the Constitution of Japan.

These principles mainly stem from domestic politics in Japan. The review is regarded as a most politically sensitive issue as it touches upon the revision of the current interpretation of the Constitution over the right to collective self-defense. Item (3) means that the Government of Japan does not intend to revise the Constitution.

The political situation in Japan poses two questions. The first deals with the time frame for proceeding with the review. The second is with the scale of achievement which both sides should pursue.

As for the former, neither government had started substantial talks before the elections in both countries. It was felt that the election season was not an appropriate time to be conducting diplomatic negotiations in any country. The hesitation for initiating substantial talks on defense cooperation is also related to the situation surrounding Japan. Japan currently has border disputes with both China and South Korea. The relations between Japan-China and Japan-South Korea have been strained as a result. According to a senior official in the Foreign Ministry of Japan, nonconstructive reactions may result if substantial talks are started in this situation.

What should be achieved in the new Guidelines is basically fixed in accordance with the previous Guidelines adopted in 1978. There are, however, missing elements. The 1978 Guidelines are a sort of operation scenario based on the Cold War era. There is no longer a Soviet Union. Hence, regional conflicts are now more likely to occur. The revolution on technology also should be considered in drafting the new Guidelines.

The most serious problem in the 1978 Guidelines is the lack of operation scenarios in the event of a crisis occurring in the areas surrounding Japan. Officials on both sides have been discussing this issue based on the following five cases in an "off-the-record" basis: (1) peacetime operation, (2) pre-crisis cooperation, (3) regional contingency, (4) defense of Japan, and (5) post-crisis operation.

The peacetime operation is relatively easy to study. Both sides have agreed that it includes cooperation in the following areas: (1) intelligence sharing, (2) defense policies and military-postures, (3) bilateral studies, exercises and training opportunities, (4) bilateral policy coordination for international peace and stability, and (5) defense and security dialogues.

Actions in response to an armed attack against Japan have already been studied in the 1978 Guidelines. Dealing with the case of pre-crisis cooperation and regional contingency is politically delicate in Japan. However, both sides have agreed to study the following bilateral cooperation: (1) Humanitarian relief operations, (2) Operations to evacuate non-combatants, (3) Rear area support for U.S. force activities, and (4) Operation of the Japanese Self-Defense Forces and U.S. forces.

The most controversial issue among them is the definition of "rear area support." It does not necessarily mean "logistic support" because the latter sometimes takes place in the front line. The operation in the front line is not permitted in the Constitution of Japan, as noted by a Japanese official. Clarification of the "rear area support" is to be discussed seriously at the political level, before legislation can proceed in this area.

The post-crisis cooperation is less delicate since it involves peacetime operations, such as returning refugees to their homeland or rebuilding areas damaged by war.

Defense cooperation is basically that found in the framework of the U.S.-Japan Security Treaty. However, there are defense cooperations which have no direct relevance in the treaty. For example, during the Gulf War Japan donated $13 billion to the coalition forces. Also it sent a mine sweeper to the Gulf after the war. These cooperations are not based on the treaty but come, in general, from a sense of alliance. Japan is trying to expand its area of defense cooperation using this logic.

The Hashimoto-Clinton summit in Washington on April 25, 1997, was regarded as step in the process for the new Guidelines. The leaders reconfirmed that the two countries would conclude the process in September 1997. Prior to the summit, a working level conference was held in Colorado Springs in the U.S. Both sides discussed the substance of the progress report which was scheduled to be issued in the beginning of June 1997. A Japanese official said that the report would be a "maximum list" of the "rear area support operations" that Japan could provide for the U.S. This comment reflected part of the latest domestic political situation in Japan.

What is most significant is the fact that more than 80 percent of the Diet members agreed to the revision of the special measure law on the land lease for the U.S. bases in Okinawa. The revision was vitally important for the maintenance of the U.S.-Japan security arrangements The revision itself is a sort of "emergency evacuation"—Kadena air base would not be functional without it because the landowners could be staging a "sit in." Even though their lands were small, their contracts regarding parts of the base land expired on May 14, 1997. However, the emergency evacuation was not the only reason for the fact that more than 80 percent of the lawmakers agreed on the revision. The maturing of the U.S.-Japan security arrangements was thought to be the main reason. After the sudden change in the Social Democrats' defense policy in 1994, one party (not the Communist Party) approved the system as a useful means for maintaining national security and stability in the surrounding region of Japan.

According to one rhetoric, the new Guidelines are also an emergency evacuation in the sense that Japan has no choice other than making it satisfactory for both sides, especially for the U.S. side. The new Guidelines assume contingencies in the surrounding area of Japan. If something happens in the Korean Peninsula and Japan's support for the U.S. is ineffective because of the limited contents of the Guidelines, the U.S.-Japan alliance will fall apart. This is quite similar to the Okinawan base issue. There is no way but to maintain and enhance the alliance as an option from the political viewpoint.

One of the most important factors in the decisionmaking process of the security policy is to assure transparency for both the domestic and international audiences. For the domestic audience, transparency is important because the new Guidelines may touch on the current interpretation of the Constitution. "Within the framework of the current constitution or current interpretation" was a key phrase when the two governments started their talks. However, the clarification or re-definition of "individual self-defense right" will be inevitable. One says that it will lead to revisions of the current interpretation. Without the transparent process for such revisions, political frustration will grow and it may lead to distrust of the government.

Frustration and distrust may also appear in the international context if the process lacks transparency. China and South Korea are the countries which, based on history, may have such feelings. There have been meetings with them, said Japanese officials. South Korea understands the importance of the new Guidelines unless Japan's Self-Defense Forces land on Korean soil. China is taking a different position. From China's viewpoint, the reconfirmation of the U.S.-Japan alliance may be seen as a tool to contain China. To effect changes in Chinese perceptions is important and the transparent process is vital to accomplish this goal.

The Guidelines are not a treaty which require approval from the Diet. However, implementation of the actions in the Guidelines probably requires new legislation which is related to not only the Defense Agency but also to the Ministry of Transportation, the Ministry of Construction, the Ministry of Posts and Telecommunications, etc. Politicians have to be involved with this legislative process after the conclusion of the new Guidelines. No one can predict what will happen—a so-called "conservatives-conservative coalition," or a coalition between the Liberal Democratic Party (LDP) and the New Frontier Party (NFP) may take shape in the legislative process. However, one thing which is clear is the fact that discussions on security are no longer ideological but rather are technical in nature. During the Cold War era, the debate on whether the U.S.-Japan security arrangements were good or bad led to the debate as to which camp Japan should join, the Western alliance or the Soviet bloc. Now the Soviet Union no longer exists. This is a main reason why the Social Democrats accepted the U.S.-Japan alliance as a vital instrument for stability in the region. The problem now is how to defend Japan or how to maintain peace and stability in the region. The differences among the security policies of the respective parties are not as serious as generally believed.

The U.S.-Japan alliance is often called a political alliance. This term is actually used to erase the image of a military alliance for the Japanese audience although the term basically stems from a military conception. The political alliance in real terms is an alliance which is based on not only a military foundation but also on a broad political consensus such as the U.S.-U.K. alliance. The new defense cooperation Guidelines are an important examination in this context.

Public Acceptance at Local Level: The Case of Okinawa[12]

Mr. Masahide Ota, Governor of Okinawa, sharply retorted in a recently-held interview with a group of Japanese and American security experts, saying "We, Okinawans, have never enjoyed peace." He made this statement in reply to a question put forward by one of the interviewers to the effect that when speaking of "peace dividend" could it not be argued that peace, which had actually been provided by the American presence, was in itself a dividend. The word "peace" was used in different ways in this dialogue. As was shown in his remarks on other occasions, Governor Ota does not challenge the *raison d'être* of the Alliance. He spoke of peace in the above-quoted discussion in the sense that individual personal security has quite often been endangered by the existence of a huge military complex on Okinawa throughout this period of "long peace."[13]

The question implied by the Governor's response is, therefore, as follows: given the seeming relaxation of military tension after the end of the Cold War, is it not unreasonable for Okinawa to ask for alleviation of these burdens?

In an attempt to answer this question, one must bear in mind that under the provisions of the Security Treaty nearly 75 percent of the facilities and areas that are made available for the U.S. Forces stationed in Japan as a whole are located in the Okinawa Prefecture and that nearly 10 percent of the entire land area of mainland of Okinawa is made available for the same purpose.

This is not the place to present a detailed analysis of the Okinawa problem which has multiple facets. Suffice it to remember that: (1) Okinawa is a unique province in Japan with a very strong sense of local identity deeply rooted in centuries of history; (2) related to the above the psychological distance between Naha (provincial capital) and Tokyo (national capital) has always been greater than an ordinary relationship between the metropolitan and rural areas in other parts of the Japanese body politic; (3) Okinawa became one of the fiercest battle grounds during the Pacific War, costing tens of thousands of lives of the civilian population; (4) after the war Okinawa was treated by the United States in a different way from mainland Japan and continued to remain under the rule of American "military" administration for another twenty years even after Japan regained its independence at the conclusion of the San Francisco peace treaty in 1952; (5) the anti-military culture is a characteristic component of Okinawan tradition, which has been accentuated further by their bitter experiences in recent history; and (6) Okinawa continues to be among the poorest provinces in Japan and its economic disadvantage was even worsened during the American administration.[14]

Taking these facts into account, it is not very difficult to understand the nature and degree of grievance of Okinawa. An especially telling argument is that, if peace is a dividend that the Japanese nation can make from the Alliance, why should the whole nation not be ready to shoulder the burden instead of relying heavily upon only Okinawa? One can answer the question by first referring to the uniquely important location of Okinawa from a geopolitical point of view. And secondly to the probably huge amount of money that would be needed to build a new complex elsewhere, given that any alternative place is available, in order to replace the existing one in Okinawa. Anybody with a practical sense can accept these arguments. Nevertheless, one should not miss the essential point by forgetting that what Okinawa is really asking is whether or not all the Japanese people are ready to pay for the cost of peace.

How can Japan pay that cost? Small steps have been, or are being, taken by transferring some of the facilities from Okinawa to Iwakuni and a couple of locations in Hokkaido. Further efforts should be made along that line. However, even after further reductions and transfers of the military facilities from Okinawa, the island will most likely remain a cardinal stronghold which is necessary for the purpose of international security of the entire Asia-Pacific region.

Two areas of policies are needed for long-term solutions to the Okinawa problem: one is socio-economic and another is politico-military. As for the first, the nation should pay a special dividend as a visible sign of their appreciation of the important contribution made by Okinawa to national and international security. As one commentator suggests, it would not be very unreasonable to exempt the prefectural taxes (which currently amounts to somewhere between 20 and 30 billion yen) in view of the fact that the nation's defense budget (currently 4,800 billion yen) is very much economized thanks to the U.S.-Japan Alliance.[15]

A more direct approach would be to transform the "American" bases into "Alliance" bases. Already some of the facilities and areas in Japan are categorized as those "for joint use" between the USFJ and the SDFJ. If this system can be expanded and more SDFJ bases and more USFJ bases were brought under that system, it might be possible to reduce the number of facilities and areas that have to be maintained for peace. More importantly, it would be of symbolic value in that Japan's alliance is visibly demonstrated. That would entail a closer operational collaboration (even a joint command) between the two nations. This applies not only to Okinawa but also to the other parts of Japan. However, because of the special location and importance of Okinawa, the island may sometime in the future become a stronghold in the Asia Pacific region that could render valuable services to the U.N. peace-keeping activities for the maintenance of regional security.

Okinawa surely is a special case. But it also is representative of the level of public awareness in Japan of the security needs of the nation. In that sense Okinawa is a symptom of the disease that the nation is suffering from: security impotence. A remedy has to be found. Redefinition of the U.S.-Japan alliance seems a promising step towards this goal.

Notes

* We wish to acknowledge our fellow group member, Prof. Seigen Miyasato, who actively participated in the preceding discussions.

1. *Asahi Shinbun* (Tokyo), 28 July 1997.
2. "Why do the US and Japan want to strengthen security relationship?," leading article of the *People's Daily*, 19 April 1996.
3. "Japan's Constitution is to be tested," *People's Daily*, 23 April 1996.
4. Tomoyuki Kojima, "China carefully watches reviewing of U.S.-Japan security relationship" (in Japanese), *Toa*, no. 348 (June 1996): 49–66; this article offers a careful and detailed analysis of Chinese opinion on this subject.
5. Eugene Gholz, Daryl G. Press, and Harvey M. Sapolsky, "Come Home, America: The Strategy of Restraint in the Face of Temptation," *International Security* 21, no. 4 (Spring 1997): 5–48.
6. *Yomiuri Shinbun* (Tokyo), 15 October 1995.
7. A notable example is, "The time has come to think about Japan-Korea security relationship," *This is Yomiuri* (December 1996): 191–201. See also an article written by the same author in *Yun Dukmin*, 13 November 1996 (in Korean language).
8. Young-Sun Song, "Korean Concern on the New U.S.-Japan Security Arrangement," *Korea and World Affairs* 20, no. 2 (Summer 1996): 197–220. See also Kim Tae-Hyo, "Preparing for Standing on Its Own: Japan's Changing Security Policy," *New Asia* 4, no. 1 (Spring 1997): 142–161. Professor Kim envisages a more autonomous security policy of Japan which cannot rely on American protection after the Cold War.
9. Robert Garran, "Japan extends military role," *The Australian*, 15 April 1996. See also Tony Boyd, "Japan to expand military roles," *The Financial Review*,

18 April 1996.
    10. Scott McKenzie, "Japan PM announces new defence links," *The Daily Telegraph*, 30 April 1997. Australian newspapers paid more attention to other issues than security, such as Australia's admission to ASEM (Asia-Europe Meeting), special considerations for Australia's situation regarding greenhouse emissions, investment in car industries, access of rice and apples to Japanese market, etc. This makes a sharp contrast to the Japanese press which sharply focused on politico-military issues.
    11. It is reported that the media in some of the ASEAN countries commented unfavorably on the interim report of the new guidelines made public recently. Because the sources are primarily Chinese-language papers in Malaysia and Singapore, they should be regarded as reflecting the feeling of the "Chinese" rather than the entire population of Southeast Asian countries as a whole. See *Yomiuri Shinbun*, 12 June 1997.
    12. Parts of this section were taken from Akio Watanabe, "The Changing Context of U.S.-Japan Relations: Is the New Hard Edge a Long-Term Prospect?," Background Paper for Session 3: Security Issues presented at the Anniversary Roundtables of Japan Society and the America-Japan Society held on April 6, 7 and 8, 1997 in Tokyo.
    13. Governor Masahide Ota, unrecorded interview by author, at the Governor's Office of Naha on 24 January 1997.
    14. See Akio Watanabe, *The Okinawa Problem: A Chapter in Japan-U.S. Relations* (Melbourne: Melbourne University Press, 1970).
    15. Yukio Okamoto, "Okinawa mondai wa kaiketsu dekiruka" (Any solution to the Okinawa Problem?), *Gaiko Forum*, no. 94 (June 1996): 56–67. A similar idea is expressed by Tomohisa Sakanaka, "Possible US Force Structure and Its Impact on Military Bases: A Japanese Perspective," paper presented at Revitalizing the Japanese-Alliance: Workshop III, sponsored jointly by the Research Institute for Peace and Security and the Ralph Bunch Institute at Okinawa on January 24-26, 1997.

Chapter 3

Political Change in the United States and Its Impact on U.S.-Japan Relations

I.M. Destler

For Japan, the political breakpoint is clear: the loss of its Diet majority by the Liberal Democratic Party (LDP) in July 1993, and the enactment of broad electoral reform by the Hosokawa coalition government which succeeded it. The results are hardly all in, and those to date have certainly not fulfilled the hopes of many. But fundamental change there has been—in how Japanese are represented in their national government.

There has been no comparable recent change in United States politics: nothing since court-ordered reapportionment in the 1960s undercut rural domination of state governments, or since the Voting Rights Act of 1965 brought the ballot, finally, to African-Americans in the South. The search for American turning points in the period under study here, therefore, must focus on changes more ephemeral and reversible. This essay finds the general force for change in the perceived combination of Cold War victory and economic defeat, one which shifted, at least temporarily, the predominant emphasis in the politics of U.S. foreign policy. This shift reached its peak during the first administration of President Bill Clinton—the time period covered by this essay. And a good time to begin is the closing months of 1991.

The (Temporary?) Primacy of Economic Issues

In 1989 the Warsaw Pact collapsed. In 1990 President George Bush won a signal victory in Europe, the peaceful uniting of Germany within the North Atlantic Treaty Organization (NATO), on terms acceptable to long-time allies and long-time adversaries. And in 1991 that same President led a broad international coalition to a smashing military victory against a blatant international aggressor.

In November of that same year, this most successful of foreign policy presidents saw his party lose a by-election for a Senate seat in the state of Pennsylvania. And he panicked. Knowing that the Democratic candidate had turned his foreign triumphs against him ("Take the George Bush tour, anywhere but the USA!"), and looking ahead at a schedule with two major international trips before Christmas, he canceled a long-planned, previously-postponed visit to Asia which was to culminate in a stopover in Japan. Compelled by circumstances to reschedule it, he declared a new agenda—"jobs, jobs, jobs" for Americans at home. To underscore this purpose, he invited senior corporate executives to accompany him to Tokyo. American and Japanese officials scurried to put together agreements worthy of this new priority, and significant deals were, in fact, struck. But the trip became a symbol of Bush's alleged fecklessness on economic issues—the exact opposite of the message that the change of agenda had meant to convey.

This author has argued elsewhere that the trip was tailor-made for failure, even had Bush not exhibited his famous stomach illness at the climactic State Dinner in Tokyo.[1] The point here is different though related: that it marked an important turning point in U.S. global policies. Domestic pressures had forced an internationalist President to highlight issues he preferred to leave to others. It marked the end, at least temporarily, of the primacy of national security concerns in U.S. foreign relations.

This end came not just because of the final disintegration of the Soviet Union, which fell apart in the weeks between the old dates for the trip and the new. It came also because Americans' economic anxieties were high— and focused significantly across the Pacific. By 1990, 58 percent of Americans told questioners for a *New York Times*/CBS News/Tokyo Broadcasting System that they found "the economic power of Japan" to be "a greater threat to the security of the United States these days" than "the military power of the Soviet Union," with just 26 percent holding to the long-predominant opposite view.[2] To a nation mired in a persistent (if shallow) recession, and two decades of sluggish productivity growth, Japanese success stood in sharp contrast. And many of the traditionally pessimistic Japanese were beginning to see things the same way, to perceive themselves as surpassing the United States.

In any case, William Jefferson Clinton centered his 1992 Presidential campaign on the economy, as any Democratic candidate would have. His message summoned Americans to economic renewal, which required action on both the domestic and international fronts. "I will elevate economics in foreign policy," Clinton told the Los Angeles World Affairs Council.[3] As an instrument for doing so, he pledged to create a new economic policy coordinating body "similar to the National Security Council [NSC]."

Once elected, he moved to deliver on his promises. Most significant was his naming of his economic officials first, as a team, before the national security group which traditionally had had pride of place. Also important as signal and fact was his delivery on his organizational campaign promise, creation of the National Economic Council (NEC) "to coordinate the economic policy-making process with respect to domestic and international economic issues."[4] His seriousness was underscored by his naming of Robert Rubin, an enormously respected senior executive from Goldman Sachs, as director of the new Council and Assistant to the President for Economic Policy.

The initial focus of Clinton—and the NEC—was on the ballooning federal budget deficit. Getting Congressional action to reduce it became the central test of the new administration's economic credibility. And though the international impact of the budget deficit was not emphasized, it was common economic wisdom that it was the prime cause of the huge U.S. trade deficit. Thus, in this and other ways, getting America's domestic house in order was expected to have an important international spillover.

The budget battle proved excruciatingly difficult. Clinton had called for action in the first 100 days, but it stretched through to July. Not a single Republican vote in either House or Senate was cast in support of the Clinton plan. This reflected increased partisanship in Washington. It was also a reflection of the dominant conservative view that tax increases were bad policy and bad politics: George Bush's compromise on this issue in 1990, after he promised otherwise, was viewed as a prime cause of his defeat in 1992.

On the international economic agenda, most prominent for Clinton were the trade negotiations which he inherited from George Bush. Foremost in the public mind was the North American Free Trade Agreement

(NAFTA), which triggered the most dramatic domestic political struggle over U.S. trade policy since the Smoot-Hawley Act of 1930.[5] Clinton had endorsed NAFTA in his campaign, provided that side agreements could be negotiated with Mexico and Canada on trade-related labor and environmental issues. This negotiation consumed the spring and most of the summer, with U.S. Trade Representative Mickey Kantor seeking language that would satisfy unions and environmentalists without alienating Republicans and the business community. Preoccupation with the side agreements had the unfortunate effect of putting the administration on the sidelines while organized labor and Ross Perot helped build a potent opposition coalition. Meanwhile, Clinton advisers fought over whether the President should commit his prestige to the uncertain fight for Congressional approval.

The other inherited trade negotiation, inaugurated under Ronald Reagan, was the Uruguay Round under the General Agreement on Tariffs and Trade (GATT). This was the most far-reaching trade agreement ever attempted. Bush's trade negotiators sought vainly to bring it to conclusion during the post-election period of 1992–93, and they did reach a breakthrough agreement with the European Union (EU) on agricultural issues. But their time ran out on January 20, and the statutory authorization ran out on March 1. Thus Clinton and Kantor had to seek from Congress an extension of the Uruguay Round deadline. This they achieved, with December 15, 1993, as the new drop-dead date.

On these trade issues, Clinton's convictions and instincts signaled continuity. NAFTA and GATT offered the opportunity to play the "new Democrat" role of centrist politician, confounding the old ideological coalitions. On Japan, however, Clinton's instincts signaled change— rejection of previous administrations' work as inadequate, and a need for a fundamentally new approach. As Clinton summarized their conversations on April 16, 1993, at a joint White House news conference with visiting Japanese Prime Minister Kiichi Miyazawa, "I stressed that the rebalancing of our relationship in this new era requires an elevated attention to our economic relations."

On Japan, Clinton could depart from the Reagan-Bush record without sustaining partisan attack, due to the broad, bipartisan Congressional view that the Japanese market was insufficiently open and that previous U.S. negotiations hadn't changed that fundamental fact. In fact, rhetorical toughness on Japan had become ingrained in U.S. trade policy culture. The U.S. Trade Representative (USTR) had to be demanding vis-à-vis

Tokyo to retain credibility for her/his general trade liberalization posture. And Congress had to push him or her to be tougher still.

Taking the initial Clinton administration lead on Japan policy, however, was not the USTR but the new NEC, and specifically Deputy Assistant to the President, W. Bowman (Bo) Cutter. NEC initiative began with the need to prepare for the Miyazawa visit—that meant, as one official recalled, that "we had to have a Japan policy."[6] So the NEC Deputies Committee met intensively under Cutter's chairmanship to formulate an approach. Once Clinton and Miyazawa agreed in April to work out an agreed framework for negotiations on market access in specific economic sectors, the question became who should lead the U.S. delegation. The NEC staff was not intended to negotiate with foreign governments, but each of the two prime candidates—the Department of the Treasury and the Office of the United States Trade Representative—strongly opposed the other's assuming this responsibility. So Cutter was a logical compromise choice.[7] He led the effort to negotiate a "framework agreement," which was reached in an all-night Tokyo session just after conclusion of the July 1993 economic summit of the Group of Seven. And in the months thereafter, Cutter continued to have the overall lead, though talks of specific sectors, like autos and insurance, were assigned to the appropriate agency.

For most of 1993, the Japan issue dominated the agenda of the NEC Deputies committee. As one of them put it, they "traveled together and negotiated together." It was described by more than one of them as "a bonding experience." They shared in the broad administration stance: the Japanese economy was atypically closed; what previous U.S. administrations had done was inadequate; it was important for Washington to present a united position. In prior administrations, broad internationalist departments like State and Treasury would have preached moderation, but Under Secretary (later Deputy Secretary) of the Treasury Lawrence Summers—a very influential voice—was a forceful critic of Japanese protectionism, and Under Secretary of State Joan Spero had developed similar views from her experience as a senior executive at American Express. The State Department's Bureau of East Asian Affairs was not a regular participant in deputies' discussions, nor was the Pentagon. Sandy Berger of the NSC was sometimes engaged. The U.S. Embassy in Tokyo was home to senior experts who had problems with the practicality of the administration's approach, but they were handicapped through most of 1993 because Clinton's Ambassador, former Vice President Walter F. Mondale, was not yet on the scene. In any case, the administration was more successful than most of its predecessors in presenting a united front. Japanese negotiators later told administration officials it was harder than usual for them to find (and exploit) daylight between agency positions. In part, however, this unity was achieved by keeping the U.S. bottom line vague. Ongoing negotiations inherently contribute to such vagueness, of course. There are always built-in incentives against compromise before it is clear that compromise is necessary. At least as important, however, was the issue that dominated the external face of the negotiations: that of "numerical targets" for Japanese imports. Specific market share goals had been endorsed by Japanese officials in the Semiconductor Trade Agreement of 1986 and the Bush auto talks of 1992. "Revisionist" critics of Japan, and of prior U.S. policy, saw these as silver linings in a generally cloudy sky. And such targets clearly interested President Clinton, who spoke positively of this means of trade expansion in his April 1993 press conference with Miyazawa.[8]

Outside of the USTR and Commerce, U.S. officials were skeptical about whether such targets were any longer negotiable. Japanese officials had always emphasized that they were goals, not binding commitments, and the tendency of their U.S. counterparts to treat them as the latter only increased Tokyo's inclination to resist. Senior Clinton officials exhibited this tendency.[9] This reinforced a burgeoning movement in Japan against "numerical targets" as a new form of "managed trade," one which united government officials and free traders outside government against the American approach. Moreover, this Japanese stance won the support of the European Union and Asian nations as well.

The issue of targets was finessed in the July framework agreement by compromise language, setting forth a joint commitment to "evaluating progress achieved" in the sectoral agreements through use of "objective criteria, either qualitative or quantitative or both as appropriate."[10] Furthermore, the White House stressed on more than one occasion that it was not insisting that Tokyo commit to a specific volume of imports over a specific period of time. By the second half of 1993, even as some U.S. officials seemed to continue the emphasis on targets, others saw them as unattainable and their pursuit an impediment to successful negotiations. But they were hesitant to voice this too strongly, given the administration's general ethos, its posture of determination to conduct a new and different Japan policy. And the consensual NEC process tended to mute such differences rather than surface them for clear argumentation and resolution.

For the administration, of course, the main trade issue that fall was not

Japan but NAFTA. The President entered September having finally committed himself to an all-out fight for Congressional approval, which many pundits felt he would lose. The main debate centered on NAFTA's impact on jobs and the U.S. economy, specifically the consequences of expanded trade with low-wage Mexico. But with trade tensions palpable across the Pacific, the administration was not above "tapping Japan's bogeyman image to save a troubled trade pact," as *The New York Times* worded a headline of October 21. As if to confirm the *Times*'s account, the October 22 edition of NAFTA NOTES, a daily White House circular distributed to NAFTA supporters, exploited comments by a Ministry of International Trade and Industry (MITI) official in Mexico City with this lead: "Japanese Trade Official Blasts NAFTA, Says It Would Make It Harder for Japan to Compete with U.S." And in one of his less credible utterances, Clinton declared more than once that if Congress rejected NAFTA, the Japanese Finance Minister would be in Mexico City "the next day" to cut a deal.

In fact, Congress approved NAFTA in mid-November, by larger than expected majorities. And the trip "the next day" was that by the American President to Seattle, where he hosted the first-ever summit meeting of the Asia-Pacific Economic Cooperation forum (APEC). The NAFTA victory gave Clinton important political momentum, abroad as well as at home. And in turn, the Seattle success created pressure on Europeans to compromise on remaining Uruguay Round issues, which they did in the weeks leading up to the December 15 agreements in Geneva.

By early 1994, however, attention had returned to the ongoing U.S.-Japan "framework negotiations." And the continuing predominance of the hard-liners on the U.S. side was underscored by an episode surrounding the February 1994 visit to Washington by Japan's reform prime minister, Morihiro Hosokawa. The framework agreement had established a goal of concluding sectoral agreements by the time of this visit: it was hoped that the summit could play its venerable political role as an action-forcing process for negotiation and compromise. As the deadline approached with the two sides wide apart, officials on both sides made special efforts to bridge the gap. In one of these efforts, Cutter of the NEC reportedly conveyed some compromise ideas to MITI Minister Hiroshi Kumagai the weekend before the February 11 summit meeting. Cutter had reportedly checked these ideas out with at least one other key member of the NEC Deputies Committee. But USTR Kantor was not pleased, and he carried the day within the administration. When Tsutomu Hata, deputy premier and foreign minister, arrived in Washington for a last-ditch effort to find a compromise, he found instead that Kantor and his cabinet-level colleagues were holding to a hard line.[11] Clinton and Hosokawa confirmed their disagreement at their joint press conference: the former declared it "better to have reached no agreement than to have reached an empty agreement," while Hosokawa stressed the need for each side to "frankly admit what we can and cannot do."

In the weeks thereafter, the White House maintained the position that the talks themselves were suspended pending a more constructive Japanese response. It did not, however, take the dramatic anti-Japan action that some advocated and many predicted. One issue conveniently available was market access for cellular telephones: despite an earlier agreement, official regulation had effectively denied the leading U.S. producer, Motorola, access to the lucrative Tokyo-area market. With Washington threatening retaliation, Ambassador Mondale was able to broker a settlement which changed Japan's domestic rules and gave Motorola the sought-after access. The other tough-seeming administration action was the issuance, on March 3, of a so-called "Super 301 executive order," in which the administration gave itself a target date of September 30 to identify "priority foreign country trade practices" which restricted U.S. exports.[12]

Through the remainder of 1994, the main U.S. trade policy action involved securing Congressional approval of the Uruguay Round, which created the new World Trade Organization (WTO). This it finally won at the end of the year, by a large bipartisan majority, after substantial partisan wrangling in the summer and early fall. And the main policy action for the administration overall was in the field of health care reform, where Clinton's proposals were dealt a humiliating Congressional defeat. The Japan talks remained the most important and prominent U.S. bilateral trade negotiation, however. And in the aftermath of February, there was a clear shift of intra-administration leadership from Cutter's NEC to Kantor's USTR. Talks were resumed in the spring with the new, short-lived Hata government: at this time, the administration formally renounced numerical targets but persisted in its emphasis on quantitative indicators. And after all-night negotiations on the new deadline date, September 30, 1994, agreements were reached on all issues except the most contentious, trade in autos and auto parts. The administration punctuated this non-agreement by initiating a regular (not "super") 301 investigation into the Japanese after-market for auto parts. And that issue carried over into 1995.

In the meantime, President Clinton and his Democrats suffered a crushing defeat at the polls. Voters put Republicans in control of both houses of Congress for the first time since 1953–54, and a large, militant class of seventy-plus freshman marched on Washington determined to implement their electoral platform, the "Contract with America." The immediate White House reaction was shock and demoralization. Soon the administration began to regroup, however. And attention focused overwhelmingly on the need for the President to develop a winning strategy for 1996.

Trade policy was not central to that strategy. Nor was it even mentioned in the Republicans' Contract with America. And U.S.-Japan relations were just one of many second-order issues with marginal impact, at best, on the outcome.[13] Nevertheless, from 1995 onward, much of the U.S. trade policy was effectively put on hold to avoid damage to the 1996 campaign. And Mickey Kantor didn't just play along with this game—he wrote the script. According to a story widely repeated in Washington, Kantor was asked shortly after his appointment, by his Republican predecessor Bill Brock, what his primary goal as USTR would be. He replied, "To get Clinton re-elected." "No, I mean your top trade policy priority." "To get Clinton re-elected."

With this overriding objective in mind, the administration allowed legislation granting new "fast-track authority" for trade to languish in Congress, rather than make the concessions on labor and environmental issues necessary to its enactment. Better to defer serious follow-up to NAFTA and the Uruguay Round, and to Clinton's free trade promises at the APEC summit of November 1994 and the Miami Hemispheric Summit of December 1994, than to risk rubbing salt in the wounds of these important Democratic constituencies.[14] By contrast, trade negotiations with Japan were seen by Kantor (and by Clinton aide Dick Morris) as a political winner—provided the administration came across as tough and (hopefully) was perceived as having won something with this toughness.

There was a broader view in the administration, of course, that the U.S.-Japan auto dispute should not be allowed to fester forever. But as Washington raised the stakes in the spring of 1995, it was Kantor who led the way. With President Clinton's clear support, he forced the action—specifically the threat of sanctions through prohibitive tariffs on Japanese luxury automobiles if an agreement was not reached by late June. Others in the administration inclined to move more slowly got their hearing in the National Economic Council, now headed by Laura Tyson. But Kantor and the USTR were typically one step ahead. The choice of Acura, Infiniti, and Lexus as sanctions targets in May proved to be brilliant two-nation politics: it struck at the profits of the Japanese auto giants, while the market was too limited in the United States to provoke any broad consumer reaction. Nor were Morris and Kantor reluctant to use the issue for domestic advantage, arranging to center a Clinton Saturday radio address on the subject, and pushing what one official involved recalls as quite virulent language for inclusion in the talk.[15]

The sanctions threat appears to have spurred Toyota et al. to cooperate (modestly) in the eleventh-hour resolution of the auto issue reached that June in Geneva. And while the substance of the accord was ambiguous from the administration's vantagepoint—MITI Minister Ryutaro Hashimoto was able to deny, in his agreed joint statement with Kantor, any Japanese government association with the numerical goals which the U.S. side insisted were central—the agreement proved a domestic-political plus for Clinton. A *Journal of Commerce* survey later that summer found his Japan policy winning points with working-class voters skeptical of NAFTA and GATT.[16] It was hardly a major factor in Presidential election: the key policy event was Clinton's winning the public relations of his "battle of the budget" with the Republican Congress. But the perception that Clinton had gone to the mat with Japan and extracted something of value, seemingly confirmed by a sharp rise in U.S. exports to Japan, effectively insulated his Japan policy from attack in the forthcoming campaign.[17]

After the fireworks of May–June 1995 came relative economic calm across the Pacific, at least toward Japan. The rape of an Okinawan schoolgirl by U.S. soldiers brought bilateral security issues back to prominence; so did loud Chinese military maneuvers aimed at influencing the March 1996 Presidential election in Taiwan. The Japanese were not prominently involved in the post-election "scandal" involving Asian money channeled to the Democratic National Committee.

By late 1997 and early 1998, of course, U.S.-Japan economic issues were again in the headlines. The United States threatened sanctions in a conflict over the practices of Japanese ports. A WTO panel made a sweeping preliminary decision *against* the United States in the Kodak-Fuji film case. The bilateral trade imbalance was rising again, driven by a weak yen and an even weaker Japanese economy. Most important, Japan's weakness was undercutting efforts to help East Asia rebound from its worst economic crisis in decades. And the United States was pressing Tokyo to take more forceful action to resolve its banking crisis and jumpstart its economy. But these events take us beyond the first Clinton administration, the time period addressed in this essay.

Reflections

Contrary to conventional wisdom, the end of the Cold War did not initiate the shift toward greater economic emphasis in U.S. international relations. The origins of this movement could be found as early as 1962, when Congress made John F. Kennedy establish the office of Special Trade Representative to keep the State Department from leading the upcoming trade negotiations with a uniting Europe. It was given substantial impetus by Richard M. Nixon, who shook the international economic system with his "new economic policy" of August 15, 1971. Other steps in the same direction included the Trade Act of 1974, the new Reagan trade policy of 1985, and the Omnibus Trade and Competitiveness Act of 1988.[18] Vis-à-vis Japan, the toughening of U.S. policy and attitude began in the 1970s, when emphasis shifted from U.S.-market to Japanese-market issues.[19]

The end of the Cold War, however, removed an important constraint on U.S. policy. Critics had argued that the nation had pulled its economic punches to maintain good U.S.-Japan security relations. Now they would have their chance. They could, to use Clinton's word, work for a "rebalancing" and see how far they could get. And their efforts would be reinforced by a broad national concern that, to paraphrase Clyde Prestowitz, the United States was "losing the future to Japan" and "needed to reclaim it."

How far in fact did they get? The answer seems to be no farther than their predecessors, and perhaps not as far.[20] There were extenuating circumstances, of course. Political reform in Japan, intended to strengthen political responsibility, had in fact created a shortage in strong politicians with whom Americans could deal (to the frustration of Ambassador Mondale, among others). Prior agreements containing numerical targets had poisoned that particular well. And the cumulative, binational use of *gaiatsu*, or external pressure, had generated a reaction in Tokyo, not least among bureaucrats who controlled much of Japanese policy during the Clinton period. The new atmosphere made it possible for one of the stronger politicians, Ryutaro Hashimoto, to underscore his resistance to American demands and to ride his strong stance to the premiership in January 1996.

But there were also particular factors on the American side. Clinton's people began their campaign in 1991–92 as advocates of major change in economic policy, international as well as domestic. They aimed to reverse what they saw as longstanding U.S. economic decline. By 1995–96, however, they were focusing on re-election and beginning to build their case on economic success! And it was not a bad case: strong economic growth, low inflation, expanded exports, and (in the eyes of many), resurgent American competitiveness. To sustain the case of economic success, however, it was better to claim victory in old trade wars than to wage new ones. It was better, for short-run purposes, to work with Japan to strengthen the dollar against the yen (as James Baker had done for Reagan and Bush in 1988). And last, but not least, the case for new American strength was buttressed by new Japanese weakness, with the collapse of the "bubble economy," plummeting asset values, sluggish growth, and a full-fledged banking crisis.

One reason for the Clinton administration's lessening militancy on Japan trade issues was experience: getting "results" was tougher than initially expected. But another was that, once the state of the U.S. economy became deployable as a political asset, the administration's interest shifted from launching new economic initiatives to claiming credit for success in old ones.

Thus, the "political change" in U.S. international relations seemed less profound, and more cyclical, in 1997 than it did in 1993. National security concerns can no longer be expected to dominate, to the degree that they did in the 1970s and 1980s. But economic concerns have not clearly replaced them. Instead, priorities must be fought out year by year, arena by arena, issue by issue, country by country. And the "political" component in U.S. decisionmaking remains high. Clinton may have won his last election; but Gore has already begun the battle for 2000.

Notes

1. M. Destler, *American Trade Politics*, 3rd ed. (Washington, D.C.: Institute for International Economics and Twentieth Century Fund, 1995), 213–14.
2. Survey of June 5–8, 1990.
3. *The Washington Post*, 14 August 1992.
4. Executive Order 12835, January 25, 1993.
5. For the main political story, see Destler, *American Trade Politics*, 218–28. For a comprehensive treatment, see Frederick Mayer, *Interpreting NAFTA: The*

Science and Art of Political Analysis (New York: Columbia University Press, forthcoming, 1998).

6. This comment was made to the author during one of 38 interviews conducted for his recent study, *The National Economic Council: A Work in Progress* (Washington, D.C.: Institute for International Economics, November 1996). Subsequent unattributed quotations in this essay are drawn from these interviews also.

7. At some long-forgotten time, the Department of State might have been the logical leader, but it had progressively lost primary jurisdiction over most international economic issues from the 1960s onward.

8. The President stressed the need to "focus on specific sectors of the economy. ... to obviously have specific results. We had a semiconductor agreement which gave some hope that this approach could work." At a White House background briefing the same day with "a senior administration official," Bo Cutter, the issue of "targets" dominated the discussion, with at least eight questions focusing specifically on the subject. (White House transcripts are available on the White House website: *http://www.whitehouse.gov.*)

9. Around June 1993, Secretary of Commerce Ron Brown and USTR Mickey Kantor signed a joint letter calling on Japan to deliver and live up to what they characterized as commitments for imports of auto parts made during President Bush's visit. This confirmed Japanese fears concerning how U.S. officials would interpret any import targets or goals.

10. Japan Economic Institute, *JEI Report 26B* (July 16, 1993): 6.

11. "Soul-Searching in Tokyo Over Failed Trade Talks," *Japan Weekly Monitor*, 28 February 1994. Several interviews confirmed this account of the abortive Cutter initiative. For general information on other events surrounding the summit, see *JEI Report 7B* (February 18, 1994).

12. The original, statutory "Super 301," operative in 1989 and 1990, had required USTR Carla Hills to identify "priority foreign *countries*" (emphasis added). Hence the authoritative study of the subject labelled the new version "Clinton's Kinder, Gentler Super 301." (Thomas O. Bayard and Kimberly Ann Elliott, *Reciprocity and Retaliation in U.S. Trade Policy* (Washington, D.C.: Institute for International Economics, 1994), 42.) In practice, the Clinton administration has ignored its own executive order, even though its language was included in the Uruguay Round implementing legislation.

13. Japan, and trade, appear to go unmentioned in Dick Morris's interesting memoir, *Behind the Oval Office: Winning the Presidency in the Nineties* (New York: Random House, 1997).

14. For more on this point, see Destler, "American Trade Politics in the Wake of the Uruguay Round," in *The World Trading System: Challenges Ahead*, ed. Jeffrey J. Schott (Washington, D.C.: Institute for International Economics, December 1996), chap. 6; and *Renewing Fast-Track Legislation* (Washington, D.C.: Institute for International Economics, September 1997), 20–22.

15. Destler, *National Economic Council*, 46–47.

16. "Majority Back Clinton on Japan, JOFC Poll Says: President gains among Democratic NAFTA, GATT Foes," *Journal of Commerce* (September 8, 1995).

17. According to Department of Commerce figures, U.S. exports to Japan rose 20 percent in 1995. And measured as a percentage of overall U.S.-Japan trade (as it ought to be), the bilateral deficit in 1996 was at its lowest level since 1980.

18. For development of this argument, see Destler, "A Government Divided: The Security Complex and the Economic Complex," in *The New Politics of American Foreign Policy*, ed. David A. Deese (New York: St. Martin's Press, 1994), 132–47.

19. For development of *this* argument, see Destler, "Has Conflict Passed Its Prime: Japanese and American Approaches to Trade and Economic Policy," *in Maryland-Tsukuba Papers in U.S.-Japan Relations* (College Park, Maryland: Center for International and Security Studies at Maryland, March 1997).

20. For one detailed study concluding that the Bush administration did better, see Leonard J. Schoppa, *Bargaining With Japan: What American Pressure Can and Cannot Do* (New York: Columbia University Press, 1997).

Chapter 4

Japan's Political Changes and Their Impact on U.S.-Japan Relations

Tomohito Shinoda[*]

During the last several years, the Japanese political scene witnessed a series of drastic changes, including the end of the 38-year-long reign of the Liberal Democratic Party (LDP), the establishment of the LDP-Socialist coalition government, and the formation of the current minority government led by LDP President Ryutaro Hashimoto. These changes have not only provided a new political environment surrounding the Japanese government, but have also had impacts on some aspects of Japan's relations with the United States.

Even before Japan's political reorganization took place, bilateral relations had begun to show signs of a shift. Bill Clinton, who entered the White House in January 1993, had, during his presidential election campaign, been critical of President George Bush's foreign policy attitude and promised to bring changes to American politics. Thus, philosophies as well as personnel changed in the U.S. government.

While the security ties with Japan remained important in the eyes of the U.S. government, trade and economic concerns had a higher priority in the new Democratic administration. Clinton formed a new decision-making organ in the White House, the National Economic Council (NEC).

He repeatedly announced that economic issues with Japan would be dealt with separately from security relations. In an April 1993 meeting, Clinton told Prime Minister Kiichi Miyazawa that the U.S.-Japan partnership established during the Cold War era was out of date; and, in addition, the U.S. government would take the kind of action in the area of economic relations with Japan which the previous administrations had been hesitant to take in fear of causing deterioration in the bilateral security ties.

The Clinton administration pictured bilateral relations as a "three-legged stool." The "legs" represented security, political and economic aspects of the relations, and the economic leg, the American officials believed, needed to be repaired. A stronger emphasis was put on the so-called "result-oriented" approach. These officials believed that all past trade agreements with Japan, without specific targets, had proved ineffective in bringing about concrete results, namely, notable increases in U.S. exports to Japan. On the other hand, Japanese officials, who had experience with numerical targets in the Semiconductor Trade Agreement, were unwilling to accept the U.S. demand for results. This difference in attitude toward numerical targets became a central issue in the U.S.-Japan economic relations between 1993 to 1995.

The difference first surfaced when the two governments were preparing a joint statement on the United States-Japan Framework for a New Economic Partnership, which was to be released at the G-7 economic summit meeting in Tokyo in July 1993. U.S. negotiators argued for the inclusion of a numerical target for reducing Japan's trade surplus. Japanese officials adamantly resisted such a target.

When the negotiations were about to break down, Prime Minister Miyazawa showed leadership, believing that a break-up would inevitably lead to deterioration of the bilateral relations. He struck a compromise with President Clinton. Miyazawa, a lame-duck prime minister, who had been forced to call an election due to domestic political pressure, believed and told Clinton that he must reach a compromise because his successor, whoever that might be, would not be able to restore impaired bilateral relations.[1] Japan agreed to try to achieve a strong and sustained domestic demand-led growth, a "highly significant decrease" in its current account surplus, and a "significant increase" in its imports, but without any specific numbers.

This compromise illustrated, again, three traditional characteristics of U.S.-Japan economic negotiations.[2] First, Japanese officials yield in the end to American requests in the name of good bilateral relations even though they may view them as unreasonable. Second, a summit meeting between the top leaders of the two governments marks the final stage of a negotiation, and a dramatic compromise is usually announced. Third, compromises often have ambiguous or kaleidoscopic expressions so that each party can interpret them as they like. A compromise is reached, often with the potential for problems to resurface in the future.

The Hosokawa Cabinet

In June 1993, the lower house passed a no-confidence resolution against the Miyazawa Cabinet, effectively putting an end to the LDP's 38-year reign after the July general election. This was followed by the establishment of a non-LDP coalition government in August. The new prime minister, Morihiro Hosokawa, had to tackle difficult political issues, including the Framework Talks with the United States, the conclusion of the General Agreement on Tariffs and Trade (GATT) Uruguay Round and political reform at home, while leading a coalition of eight political groups with a wide range of conflicting political ideas.

In order to maintain the vulnerable coalition, Hosokawa introduced a new decisionmaking mechanism outside of the cabinet, the Council of Representatives of the Coalition Parties, or *Yoto Daihyosha Kaigi*. The Council was composed of the secretary-generals (second in command), of each party, who would meet and discuss major political issues. In his writings before becoming the prime minister, Hosokawa had repeatedly warned that the rigidity of the Japanese bureaucracy caused problems in Japanese society. One example of this is the so-called "vertical administration" or sectionalism within the government. Under the long LDP reign, policy tribe or *zoku* members formed sub-governments based in the party's policy committees (*bukai*) in each specific policy area. These sub-governments often served as serious obstacles against government policies. By introducing a new mechanism, the Hosokawa government would be able to centralize its decisionmaking power and minimize the problem of sectionalism.

This was not the only reason why the new government introduced the new decisionmaking system. Hosokawa, in an interview with the author, confided about the difficult situation in which he found himself. "Under the coalition government with eight different political parties, the centralization of policymaking was the only choice. It was impossible to have issue-specific committees."[3]

As Hosokawa organized his new government, the Clinton administration welcomed the newly established non-LDP government. Clinton, who himself took office with a claim that he would bring about changes in American politics, had high expectations for changes in Japan. Many American officials, who were fed up with the rigidity of the Japanese government's behavior, hoped to see a new kind of Japanese political leadership which would result in a new U.S.-Japan partnership.

Prime Minister Hosokawa personally placed the highest priority on the conclusion of the GATT Uruguay Round. As he put it: "Japan is in the world system, and I thought that we must show leadership by contributing to the successful conclusion of the Uruguay Round."[4] In order to contribute to the success of the multilateral trade agreement, Japan needed to open up its rice market regardless of the strong pressures from the politically powerful agricultural interest groups and politicians who represented rural areas.

Consensus for opening the rice market had been building up under the Miyazawa administration. Japan, as the second largest economy and export superpower, would not be able to sustain its status were it held responsible for ruining the Uruguay Round. Years of foreign pressure, especially from the United States, had created a mood favorable to the internationalization of Japan's agricultural market. But the political leaders were hesitant to make the final decision—they did not want to invite the wrath of farmers on their administration. Hosokawa, who happened to take office during the final round of the agricultural negotiations, had to make and announce a politically risky decision.

After an agreement was reached between Europe and the United States, Hosokawa announced that his government was ready to accept a compromise on the issue of opening its rice market. Strong opposition, as expected, came from the agricultural interests and LDP politicians who took advantage of being in the opposition to blame the Hosokawa government for damaging Japan's agricultural industry. To make matters worse Hosokawa was faced with a rebellion that erupted within his fragile eight-party coalition government. The Social Democratic Party, the largest among the eight parties, many of whose members were elected from rural agricultural areas, threatened to leave the coalition.

Hosokawa, however, did not yield, knowing that the public was backing him. Every national poll taken in the preceding few months had shown that most Japanese agreed that the time had come to import at least some rice. "It is a role of a leader to present a specific goal. If the goal was right,

I believed, the people would support me,"[5] said Hosokawa, expressing his feeling during that time. The Social Democratic Party (SDP) held a 12-hour meeting to dramatize its opposition. In the end, the party decided that breaking with the popular prime minister and bearing the blame for the collapse of the world trade system would be much more dangerous politically than protecting rice farmers. Hosokawa made a pre-dawn announcement on December 14 that Japan must accept rice imports "for our sake and the world's sake." This announcement received a warm welcome not only from the Japanese public and media but also from the United States.

After this announcement, political and public interest in Japan swiftly shifted to the political reform issue which had been at the center of Japan's political revolution. Meanwhile, however, the Japanese government continued negotiations with its U.S. counterpart as part of the economic Framework Talks. The talks during this stage were primarily focused on Japan's macroeconomic policies. Japan was asked to present an "economic stimulus" package in order to increase its imports. The Hosokawa government thought that it was possible to introduce a large-scale tax cut which the U.S. government requested if, and only if, an increase in the consumption tax would follow in a few years to make up for the income shortage that would result. Without a future tax increase, the powerful Ministry of Finance would never agree to a tax cut.

Prime Minister Hosokawa faced a dilemma. The time for a political debate, where opponents could vent their fury about a tax increase was needed. But if a tax increase was announced, Hosokawa would fall from the political tightrope he was walking at that time. He was trying to achieve political reform which would introduce a new single-seat electoral system for the lower house. He decided to keep the tax issue on the back burner until the political reform bills passed in the Diet.

The Diet session lasted longer than Hosokawa expected. A rebellion of leftist socialist party members in the upper house effectively killed the coalition's reform bills. Hosokawa called for a meeting with LDP President Yohei Kono, and accepted virtually all the LDP's demands in order to reach an agreement. Hosokawa's compromise made possible the passage of the political reform bills. But when they passed both the lower and upper houses, it was already January 29, 1994, less than two weeks before his scheduled meeting with President Clinton where he planned to present an economic stimulus package, including that future tax increase.

A week before the passage of the bills, U.S. Treasury Secretary Lloyd

Bentsen visited Hosokawa, pressing for "concrete results" in the Framework Trade Talks and proclaiming that "no agreement is better than a weak agreement." Although the time given to Hosokawa was very limited, with American pressure, he had to introduce a new tax package before his visit to Washington. While U.S. Trade Representative Mickey Kantor was visiting Japan to place additional pressure on the talks, Hosokawa announced a tax package in the early morning of February 3. This announcement met with strong criticism from the media and the opposition LDP as well as some coalition parties, including the Social Democratic Party, Sakigake, and the Democratic Socialist Party. The public was disappointed to see Hosokawa acting like a servant of the very bureaucrats whose clout he pledged to curb.[6] Without public support, Hosokawa was forced into a retreat on the tax plan the very next day.

The Hosokawa government quickly came up with a $140 billion package of temporary tax cuts and public works programs to lift the economy out of the two-year recession. Without the assurance of a future tax increase, it was as much as the Finance Ministry could offer to the prime minister. This package, however, did not satisfy the U.S. government. Treasury Secretary Bentsen called it "modest" and doubted that it would be adequate to spur strong domestic demand in Japan. The result was the collapse of the bilateral talks at the Clinton-Hosokawa summit meeting on February 11. The Clinton administration decided to cut off trade talks "for a period of reflection."

American officials came to believe the arguments of the so-called "revisionists" who claimed that Japan did not have the same market mechanism as in the United States, and that Japanese bureaucrats were blocking American access to Japan's market which would bring benefits to its consumers. At a press conference, a frustrated White House economic aid, Bowman Cutter, who led an American negotiating team in the Framework Talks, described Japanese negotiators as "the mandarins of the government of Japan." Hosokawa betrayed the American expectation that he would make a political decision curbing bureaucratic influence.

Seven weeks later, Hosokawa announced a package of voluntary market opening measures, hoping that the United States would agree to reopen the talks. American officials, however, dismissed the proposal as not going far enough to justify resuming trade talks. This action as well as American belief in the revisionists' claims hardened the attitude of Japanese negotiators. More and more Japanese officials argued that they should deny such claims and show their belief in free trade and market mechanisms by refusing American demands for numerical targets which would lead to managed trade.

The public support for Hosokawa eroded in the wake of these events, including his failure to introduce a new tax and the collapse of the U.S.-Japan talks. Hosokawa resigned amidst allegations of personal financial impropriety, without seeing the reopening of the Framework Talks.

Under the Hosokawa administration, some traditional patterns of U.S.-Japan negotiations were not followed. In the Framework Talks, finance ministry officials successfully convinced the prime minister that it would be better to break off the trade talks than yield to unreasonable American demands. At a press conference after the summit meeting, Hosokawa said that the approach the U.S. demanded would "lead to managed trade." Both Clinton and Hosokawa refused to compromise on an ambiguous agreement. Clinton said, "We could have disguised our differences with cosmetic agreements," but, he added, "[I]t is better to have reached no agreement than to have reached an empty agreement." Hosokawa also said that two governments sometimes had to disagree in a "relationship between grown-ups as we two are."

The most notable characteristic of Hosokawa's leadership, however, was the centralization of the decisionmaking process. In the opening of Japan's rice market, the prime minister made a decision behind the closed doors of the Council of Representatives of the Coalition Parties without disclosing the negotiation process with the United States to the public. Hosokawa announced his acceptance of the GATT proposal. The unprecedented high public support successfully contained political opposition and enabled him to achieve this goal. The same policy process, however, turned out be inappropriate for a highly unpopular proposal to raise a tax rate. The public argued that the tax decision was made in an undemocratic process in which a very limited number of policy makers were involved. Hosokawa's credibility and leadership capability were questioned, leading to his resignation.

The Murayama Cabinet

The United States and Japan agreed to reopen the Framework Trade Talks during the short reign of Prime Minister Tsutomu Hata. The Social Democratic Party rejected the centralized control of decisionmaking in the coalition government and broke away from the coalition, leaving the new government in a vulnerable, minority status. The Hata cabinet lasted only two months without achieving any progress in the bilateral trade talks. Since the Clinton administration saw Hata and his predecessor, Hosokawa, as political reformers who could open Japan's markets by forcing their will on the bureaucrats, Hata's resignation disappointed and frustrated American negotiators in the trade talks.

A new coalition was formed by the LDP, the Social Democratic Party and Sakigake to elect Tomiichi Murayama as the national leader. This news caught many Japanese as well as Americans by surprise. The Clinton administration now saw a glimmer of hope in the bilateral trade talks under the political leadership of the new, inexperienced Socialist prime minister. American officials did not even know if Japan's new leader would be able to depart from the traditional Socialist stance against the will of many other Socialist members to support the U.S.-Japan alliance and Japan's Self-Defense Forces (SDFJ).

Murayama was eager to remove such American anxiety. An opportunity to do so came within his first ten days in power when he attended the G-7 economic summit in Naples. In his memoirs, Murayama confesses that he was very nervous about whether or not he could reach a basic understanding with President Clinton. At the summit meeting with the American leader, Murayama opened the conversation with the statement that he was committed to maintaining Japan's established foreign policy line and firmly supported the bilateral security ties. Further, he was committed to promoting the democratic political process. Clinton expressed his satisfaction with Murayama's statements.[7] At a press conference Murayama and Clinton reaffirmed the need to proceed with the Framework Trade Talks. Murayama, thus, successfully completed his first major international mission.

Murayama's determination to support the U.S.-Japan security alliance and the SDFJ was firm. Within two weeks of the Naples summit, the Socialist prime minister officially declared in the Diet that the Self-Defense Forces were constitutional. There was a strong concern that Murayama's policy shift would split the Social Democratic Party into two fringe parties and jeopardize the coalition government. The real test came in September 1994 when the Socialists held a national convention. Heated debates ensued, but in the end the party approved the policy shift. Murayama described this process to the author as follows:

> The prime minister, who is supreme commander of the Self-Defense Forces, cannot maintain his office and coalition government while denying the SDFJ. I decided to accept the legality of the SDFJ as prime minister

without consulting the Social Democratic Party. This turned out right. The party chose to approve my policy, recognizing that I was willing to resign if they did not do so.[8]

This "historical policy shift" of the Social Democratic Party in effect put an end to the 1955 system, the political framework under which the LDP, as the government, and the Socialists, as the main opposition party, were ideologically split.

As the biggest policy gap between the Social Democratic Party and the LDP was thus filled, Murayama, who had opposed the undemocratic decisionmaking process under the Hosokawa and Hata governments, introduced a new process to deal with policy differences within the coalition. He formed issue-specific project teams for major policy issues where the three government parties could exchange their views and find agreeable solutions. Murayama said to the author in an interview, "Clearly, policy differences existed among the three parties. In many cases, we did not reach an agreement. But through serious discussions, I believed, we could develop mutual understanding and trust."[9]

It is worth noting that though nearly 20 project teams were formed under the Murayama Cabinet, none was formed to discuss the National Defense Program Outline (approved by the cabinet in November 1995). Murayama knew that the security policy gaps among members of parliament in the coalition parties were still too irreconcilable to permit formulation of concrete defense policies, and intentionally avoided creating an inter-party project team on this issue.

Besides these project teams, three-party policy coordination committees, sub-divided like the LDP's issue-specific policy sub-committees, or *bukai*, were formed to discuss policy matters. In order to avoid the LDP's dominance in policymaking, the representation of the LDP, the Social Democratic Party and Sakigake was set at the ratio of 3:2:1 in proportion to the numbers of Dietmen affiliated with each party. For foreign ministry officials, as well as other bureaucrats, it became a considerably more time- and energy-consuming process to build consensus within the coalition government than under the LDP government.[10]

At any rate, the old LDP *zoku* members regained their places. In the budget-making process in the summer of 1994, immediately after the LDP returned to power as part of the government coalition, *zoku* members started exerting their political influence. Their resurgence may serve as a serious obstacle to future government policies as they did under the long LDP reign.

On the trade front, experienced LDP politicians came forward. Since the Hosokawa government had failed to deliver a macroeconomic proposal, the emphasis of the Framework Trade Talks shifted to microeconomic issues, such as autos and auto parts. Frustrated U.S. negotiators set September 30, 1994, as the deadline to initiate action against Japan under the Super 301 provision of the U.S. trade law. Under the threat of American punitive action, Ministry of International Trade and Industry (MITI) Minister Ryutaro Hashimoto and Foreign Minister Yohei Kono—both LDP members—reached compromises with their American counterparts in last-minute, all-night negotiations on September 30 and October 1.

Agreements were concluded on Japanese government procurement of medical and telecommunications equipment and action on Japan's insurance market. The more experienced Japanese negotiators seized the moral high ground in public relations during the negotiations by portraying the U.S. position as an attempt to manage trade. They successfully reached agreements with U.S. negotiators without guaranteeing any specific numerical targets.

No agreement, however, was reached on the pending issues in the critical sector of autos and auto parts. This prompted President Clinton to order initiation of a section 301 investigation focusing on the aftermarket for auto parts. Negotiations on autos and auto parts were restarted and became central in the U.S.-Japan economic relations for more than half a year.

Frustrated over the unsettled auto issues, American trade officials announced on May 16, 1995, that they would take an aggressive stance against Japan. They threatened sanctions in the form of 100 percent punitive tariffs on Japanese luxury cars worth $6 billion unless an agreement was reached by June 28. Even under this intensified threat, Japanese negotiators, led by MITI Minister Hashimoto, refused to include numerical targets in the text of the agreement. As the U.S. side refused to accept an agreement without them, the negotiation remained deadlocked.

The Japanese negotiators maintained strong unity among the ministries involved throughout the auto negotiations. The Foreign Ministry had traditionally taken a "security-first" attitude, while MITI tended to play the protector of domestic industries. However, a change in this traditional pattern was evident. A foreign ministry official admitted that his ministry was turning "MITI-like."[11] As the Clinton administration decoupled trade and security matters, so did the Japanese government. The Japanese officials now believed that U.S.-Japan security cooperation, such as toward

China and the Korean Peninsula, would not be significantly affected by bilateral trade disputes.[12]

The Japanese officials countered with offensive actions. Two days after the sanction announcement, they filed a petition against the American action with the newly created World Trade Organization (WTO). Japan, in effect, brought the issue onto the international forum. On May 21, MITI Minister Hashimoto lobbied European representatives at an Organization for Economic Cooperation and Development (OECD) meeting in Paris to gain their understanding for the Japanese petition before the WTO. At the OECD meeting, all 24 countries, except the United States, agreed to include a clause barring any unilateral actions which were illegal under WTO rules.[13]

Asian countries also were critical of the American unilateral action. They hoped to see Japan as an Asian representative who would courageously defy unreasonable American pressure. If Japan accepted the American demand, they believed that they would become future victims.[14] International opinion fully supported Japan on this issue, leaving the United States out in the cold.

A long series of negotiations were conducted in Geneva between June 22 and 26 in order to avoid a trade war which would be triggered by the threatened American sanctions. A few hours before the deadline, the Japanese and American negotiators finally reached a compromise. In a joint statement, the American government included its own estimate of an increase in the imports of American autos and auto parts. In the same statement, however, it was clearly stated that the Japanese government had nothing to do with these numbers. Japan successfully denied the validity and relevance of any numerical targets.

Under the Murayama administration, the U.S.-Japan ties remained Japan's most import foreign relationship. Murayama made a critical decision for his party to show good will toward the United States and to maintain his coalition government. There is, however, no evidence that the prime minister played a major role in the auto negotiations. MITI Minister Hashimoto was the main actor who adamantly and successfully refused to conclude any ambiguous agreement. His style of hard negotiation brought the talks to the brink of breaking-down. But neither Hashimoto nor the Foreign Ministry was willing to yield to the United States demands for security reasons.

The Hashimoto Cabinet

The Murayama Cabinet faced another difficult problem in U.S.-Japan relations after the abduction and rape of a 12-year-old Japanese girl by three U.S. servicemen on Okinawa in September 1995. This incident triggered the rage of the long-frustrated Okinawans who had suffered from the overpresence of American troops on their small islands. Their prefecture hosts 75 percent of U.S. bases in Japan on 0.6 percent of Japan's land, and the rape incident was just one of more than 4,500 crimes that had been committed by American servicemen in Okinawa since 1972. In November, Murayama and U.S. Defense Secretary William Perry agreed to set up a joint Japanese-U.S. commission to explore ways to reduce the burden on Okinawa. Two months later, however, the 71-year-old prime minister exhausted himself in this hard post and resigned without seeing any concrete results from the work of this commission.

LDP President and MITI Minister Ryutaro Hashimoto was endorsed by the same coalition to succeed Murayama. The highest priority in the foreign policy area for the new prime minister was promotion of relations with the United States. Hashimoto actively sought a way to resolve the Okinawa problem. The Prime Minister's Office, especially Hashimoto himself, and Cabinet Secretary Seiroku Kajiyama, initiated action to bring about a meeting with President Clinton—rather an unusual action because such meetings are usually initiated and arranged by the Foreign Ministry.

When Hashimoto met with Clinton in Santa Monica, California, in February 1996, he brought up the possibility of the return of the Futenma Marine Corps Air Station. A foreign ministry official commented that the timing was premature for the prime minister to refer to the return of Futenma.[15] After the meeting, however, Futenma became the crux of the Okinawa base issue. The U.S. government in the end agreed to return the air station if the U.S. military could maintain the same level of functionality through consolidation of its facilities. The Japanese government would have to bear the costs associated with the consolidation. American officials were not certain whether Japan, with a huge fiscal deficit, was willing to pay such costs.

Hashimoto showed leadership over this issue, fully taking advantage of his influence over the powerful Finance Ministry. In the presence of U.S. Ambassador Walter Mondale, as well as Foreign Minister Yukihiko

Ikeda and Director of Defense Agency Hideo Usui, the prime minister made a phone call to the budget bureau's director-general to order him to prepare a budget for the consolidation, estimated at about one trillion yen.[16] On April 15, just before President Clinton's state visit to Japan, the U.S. government agreed to give back about 20 percent of the land it occupied on Okinawa, including the Futenma Marine Corps Air Station.

The return of the Futenma air station was decided under the strong leadership of the prime minister. Even the austerity-minded Finance Ministry, which is usually unwilling to approve new expenditures without offsetting revenue, could not refuse Hashimoto's request for the consolidation funds. Hashimoto himself set the stage for the meeting with Clinton, which American officials called "the most important [U.S.-Japan] summit meeting since the end of the Cold War."[17]

Conclusion

In the early 1990s, both the United States and Japan experienced important changes in domestic politics that significantly impacted bilateral relations. Changes first came to the American side. When Bill Clinton's transition team entered the White House at the end of 1992, the president-elect announced that their efforts for reelection in four years had just started. Priority issues in the government's agenda shifted to the domestic economy from foreign policy issues.

During his first administration, Clinton and his government sought achievements and progress in, among other policy areas, trade relations with Japan for the benefit of the American economy. American officials believed that they needed specific targets to increase U.S. exports to Japan.

When initiating the U.S.-Japan Framework Trade Talks, the Clinton administration made Japan promise a "highly significant decrease" in the current account surplus. Although the wording in this initial agreement was ambiguous, the American officials were hopeful of reaching a more concrete agreement with Japan's new coalition government. In the eyes of American officials, opening Japan's markets would benefit Japanese consumers. With strong public opinion pressing for reforms in Japan, they believed political reformers, especially Prime Minister Morihiro Hosokawa, would place priority on the interests of consumers over those of industries and could force their will on the bureaucrats.

Although Hosokawa partly met this American expectation by opening Japan's rice market, he failed to introduce an economic stimulus package which the U.S. government had demanded during the Framework Trade Talks. The powerful Finance Ministry convinced the prime minister not to make any commitments in the macroeconomic field without a tax increase. At a summit meeting with Clinton, Hosokawa chose to allow the talks to collapse, instead of reaching a compromise on numerical targets. Similarly, under the Murayama administration, MITI Minister Hashimoto flatly rejected any numerical targets in the auto negotiations.

These cases show that the U.S.-Japan trade negotiations under the coalition governments moved away from traditional patterns. Summit meetings between the two national leaders did not serve as the final stage of a negotiation that had already been wrapped up as such meetings had in the past. Japan did not hesitate to break off the talks or to refuse ambiguous compromises as they once had. Although the security ties remained important for the national leaders, as seen in Murayama's "historical policy shift" and Hashimoto's handling of the Okinawa problem, the Japanese officials, as well as their American counterparts, dealt with trade issues separately from security issues.

Several factors contributed to these changes in Japan's attitude. The first factor was related to the American attitude. Compared with their previous administrations, Clinton and his government were more inward-looking. After the Cold War, there was no longer a direct security threat to the United States. This allowed President Clinton to shift his attention to the domestic economy as he promised to do in his election campaign. The U.S. government began taking whatever measures necessary to protect and promote domestic interests without any firm and discernible principles. Japan, on the other hand, no longer hesitated to point out that some American action was internationally unacceptable.[18]

The newly established international forum was a probable second factor. The World Trade Organization was becoming central to building international trade rules and standards and for settling trade disputes. European and Asian nations would not allow American unilateral action or bilateral agreements between the United States and Japan which were illegal under WTO rules. Backed by international support, Japan could refuse America's unreasonable demands, such as the setting of numerical targets in auto trade.

The third factor probably was related to the emerging regionalism in Asia after the breakdown of the Cold War framework. Japan was seen as a leader in economic fields by some Asian nations. They would like to see their leader able and willing to refuse unreasonable demands made by the United States. If Japan accepted such demands, Asian nations were afraid they would be the next American target. By yielding to U.S. pressure, Japan would have lost its credibility as an Asian leader. Japan, therefore, needed to show its strength vis-à-vis the U.S. government in order to maintain the trust of Asian nations.

Finally, Japanese government officials were more confident of the openness of their own markets. After a series of trade agreements and substantial deregulation, they believed that Japan's markets were fairly open. They were willing to correct market distortions, if necessary, but unwilling to bend on unreasonable demands. In the Framework Trade Talks, Japan successfully asserted that numerical targets would lead to managed trade and that Japan was a country that stood for free trade.

The end of the Cold War brought changes in Japanese politics and its style in bilateral negotiations with the United States. These changes will probably prove enduring because the international and domestic factors, described above, seem long-lasting. Japanese government officials are working to redefine Japan's economic and political relationships as well as security ties with the United States in order to accommodate the post-Cold War phenomenon.

Notes

* This paper was written in cooperation with Haruhiro Fukui who provided information based on his interviews with Japanese government officials. Any errors and mistakes, however, must be charged to the author.

1. Miyazawa Kiichi, *Shin Goken Sengen* [New Declaration for Protecting the Constitution], (Tokyo: Asahi Shimbun-sha, 1995), 158.
2. For the characteristics of the negotiations between the two countries, see Hosoya Chihiro, ed., *Nichibeiou no Keizai Masatsu wo meguru Seiji Katei* [Political Process of Economic Friction in Japan, the United States and Europe], (Tokyo: National Institute for Research Advancement, 1988), 28–31.
3. Morihiro Hosokawa, interview by author, November 15, 1996.
4. *Ibid*. Hosokawa told the author that, compared to the conclusion of the Uruguay Round, his push for political reform, which is generally seen as his biggest political achievement, was merely a "side job." The main reason why Hosokawa's Japan New Party did not merge with another new conservative party, Sakigake, as originally planned, was the rice issue. Masayoshi Takemura,

Sakigake's leader from the rice-rich prefecture of Shiga, refused to include in their joint policy platform a commitment to open the rice market which would have assured the success of the Uruguay Round.

5. *Ibid.*

6. Michiyo Nakamoto, "Hosokawa plan has pleased few and made many unhappy," *Financial Times*, 4 February 1994. See also Paul Blustein, "Japanese Leader Forced to Retreat on Taxes," *The Washington Post*, 5 February 1994.

7. Murayama Tomiichi, *Watashi no Rirekisho* [My Personal History], *Nihon Keizai Shinbun*, no. 26 (August 1996).

8. Tomiichi Murayama, interview by author, September 13, 1996.

9. *Ibid.*

10. Foreign Ministry officials, interview by Haruhiro Fukui, July 4, 1996. Also, a MITI official, interview by Haruhiro Fukui, July 1, 1996.

11. A foreign ministry official, interview by Haruhiro Fukui, July 4, 1996.

12. A MITI official, interview by Haruhiro Fukui, July 5, 1996.

13. A MITI official, speech on November 2, 1995.

14. *Ibid.*

15. *Asahi Shimbun* (Tokyo), 17 June 1996. It is believed that Hashimoto gained influence over the ministry when he was the finance minister. He resigned as minister taking full responsibility for financial scandals without sacrificing any bureaucrats in 1991.

16. *Ibid.*

17. Kevin Sullivan and Mary Jordan, "U.S. to Trim 11 Bases on Okinawa," *Washington Post*, 16 April 1996.

18. A foreign ministry official, interview by Haruhiro Fukui, July 1, 1996.

Chapter 5

Economic Development in China and her Relations with Japan and the U.S.

Akinori Marumo
Chung-Hsun Yu
Hiroshi Ouchi
Yasuko Ikemoto

Recently, the influence of China in the world's economies has been rapidly increasing due to her growth under the policy of "openness and reform." Particularly, China's economic relations with both Japan and the U.S. have become very close, so much so that both these countries seem to be paying more attention to China than to each other.

In this essay, we will try to assess the future potentiality of the Chinese economy, analyze the developments of economic relations between China and Japan/U.S. and consider future prospects—possible conflicts of interest and possible fields where Japan and the U.S. share a common interest.

The first section briefly analyzes the past performance of the Chinese economy and points out certain issues that must be solved in order for the current rapid economic growth to continue in the future. The second section addresses the issue of future development models such as the priority in infrastructure investments. The third section analyzes trade and investment flows between China, on the one hand, and Japan and the U.S., on the other, with particular emphasis on the trade balances and the role of foreign direct investment (FDI) in the economic growth of China. The fourth section points out certain issues related to Hong Kong and Taiwan. The final section deals with ethnic Chinese economies.

Potentiality of the Chinese Economy

Rapid Growth of the Economy and Contributing Factors

Since 1978, when economic reform was implemented, the Chinese economy has been growing rapidly, her real growth rate exceeding 9% per year. As a result, the status of China in the world economy has been enhanced remarkably in the past 18 years or so. According to the International Monetary Fund (IMF), her share in the world total exports rose to 3.0% in 1995, while, according to the estimates of the Economic Planning Agency (EPA), her share in world GDP (gross domestic product) reached 2.5% that same year. The inflow of foreign direct investment into China amounted to $38 billion, accounting for 11% of all FDI in the world.

Such a rapid emergence of the Chinese economy has naturally attracted attention throughout the world, particularly among the developed countries whose concerns about a possible threat from China have been expressed in recent years. In the early 1990s, several international organizations published successive long-term projections of the Chinese economy. All of them estimated that China will be an economic superpower in the early twenty-first century. These estimates adopted purchasing power parity (PPP) based GDP in discussing the future of the Chinese economy. However, while PPP-based GDP is suited to measuring the relative levels of per capita income or consumption, it is not suited to measuring the scale of the economy.

By analyzing the economic performance of China over the past 18 years, we can identify the most important factors responsible for such continuous high growth as follows.

(1) *High savings rate supported by an increase in income level*: For example, the national savings rate as a percentage of GDP increased from 35% in 1980 to 44% in 1994. Agricultural reform and promotion of rural enterprises in the initial phase of the

economic reform elevated the income levels of the rural areas. In the first step of economic reform, the Chinese government emphasized improving the income of farming areas, which accounted for 80% of the total population, increasing the purchase prices of farm products, and introducing a contract system to enhance the incentive to work among farmers. Moreover, the encouragement of rural enterprises related to the secondary and tertiary industries brought about rapid improvement in the income levels of the farm-village populations.

The increased savings were absorbed by the successive establishment of financial organizations since the end of the 1970s (e.g., the Agricultural Bank, the Industrial Bank, and so forth).

(2) *Vigorous investment activity*: Vigorous investment activity, supported by a high savings rate and, later, inflows of foreign capital, together with an increase in the efficiency of investment, contributed greatly to the rapid growth of the economy. The shares of gross domestic fixed investment increased from 29% of the GDP in 1980 to 39% in 1994.

(3) *Improvement in productivity*: In addition to the rapid increase in capital stock due to the high investment ratio and the abundant supply of labor, increases in productivity have been a very important factor in the growth of the Chinese economy. According to the report of the Economic Research Institute of the EPA, about half of the 10% annual growth rate can be attributed to the increase in total factor productivity. Many factors contributed to this productivity increase: imported technology associated with the inflow of FDI, the improved educational level of workers, the enhanced incentive to work due to the introduction of market mechanisms, etc.

Future Prospects

In March 1996, the Chinese government announced "the 9th five-year plan and long-term objectives of development to 2010." According to this document, it was pointed out that by the year 2000 real GNP (gross national product) per capita should increase to four times that of 1980, and that, by 2010 the GNP per capita would double. Achievement of these targets was said to be indispensable in maintaining the stability of the economy and society in China. Whether or not the Chinese economy can continue its rapid pace of economic growth as recorded in the past two decades has been discussed by many observers. It is beyond our task to make any elaborate projections of the Chinese economy, and we intend to assess, rather qualitatively, the issues and problems China may encounter in achieving and maintaining a similar rapid growth of the economy in the decades to come.

Lagging development of inland areas

How to develop the inland areas where economic development is far behind that of the coastal regions is a big problem. Recently, an exodus of large numbers of people from inland areas to prosperous coastal regions has become an important social problem.

It is desirable that the inland areas also develop rapidly, centering on small- and medium-sized cities so that they can absorb underutilized manpower in those areas. However, it appears to be very difficult to achieve such a balanced growth, because foreign direct investment has been concentrated in the coastal regions thus creating acute infrastructure shortages in the inland areas.

Reforming state-owned enterprises

Although the shares of state-owned enterprises (SOEs) in the total economic activities have been gradually reduced, in terms of the number of employees and the number of firms, the state-owned enterprises still account for a large share even today. In 1995, two-thirds of the workers in the manufacturing industry were employed by state-owned enterprises. Moreover, one-third of the SOEs are suffering losses. This is not only a heady burden on government finance but also a serious problem hindering the improvement of international competitiveness of the Chinese industries. Efforts to reform the SOEs have been made since the middle of the 1980s. However, because many SOEs take the form of small communities, including various social functions, the government has not been able to implement sweeping measures lest they result in mass unemployment.

Bottlenecks: infrastructure, food and energy

Provisions for transportation and communication infrastructures have not caught up with the pace of economic growth and this deficiency is a serious obstacle especially in the inland areas. Currently, because of the huge capital required to furnish infrastructure needs, the government is trying to utilize private sector activities for improving infrastructures.

Another important issue to be faced is a possible shortage in the domestic food supply since arable land is limited. Meanwhile, the demand for food and grains is expected to increase due to the population growth and the improvement of living standards of the Chinese. The problem may be solved by enhancing the yield per acre through technological progress.

Another possible bottleneck is the shortage in domestic supply of energy, particularly petroleum. China was once a large net exporter of petroleum, but has become a net importer in recent years. A potential supply of coal is, and will be, abundant in the foreseeable future. However, the lack of transportation facilities, especially railroads, is a big problem. Therefore, improving the transportation infrastructure and enhancing the efficiency of energy use are indispensable measures to be undertaken.

China's Economic Development Model

Supply and Demand of Food and Energy

China began to change its development strategy from placing emphasis on the coastal areas to placing it on the inland areas. This is the beginning of the era of Western development in China, similar to the one in the United States. Economic factors are shifting from the east to the west in China. A potentially very large economic superpower like China cannot follow the type of production strategy of placing emphasis on overseas markets that is common among the Newly Industrialized Economies (NIEs). It was only a question of time before China shifted to a domestic demand-oriented type of production, and the strategy has just begun. In the past, the largest U.S. trade deficit was with Japan, but it has been observed that the trade deficit with China might become the largest in the near future. China has a large foreign currency reserve. On December 1, 1996, China shifted to an Article 8 nation in the IMF. Therefore, even the largest economic superpower, the United States, cannot absorb much of China's production. China should change her NIEs-type production strategy from placing emphasis on overseas markets to emphasis on domestic markets. With this strategic change, not only the differences between the economic levels of the coastal areas and the inland areas can be improved, but also development of agriculture and domestic resources can be advanced. Lester R. Brown pessimistically argues that China cannot but help importing a great deal of food from abroad.[1] However, it is a popular view that China can, to a great extent, solve this problem by developing its own potentiality and, therefore, Brown's estimate is too extreme. In actuality, China managed to produce five hundred million tons of food in 1996 which was the planned figure for the year 2000.

Priority of Infrastructure Investment

The overheating of production and inflation have been overcome and China is now succeeding in "softlanding" its development. As a result, an explosive development like in the past may not appear again. Hereafter, investments in the real assets and stock will be increased in the inland areas instead of in the coastal areas.

Special priority will be placed on the primary industry of agriculture and natural resources development. Particularly, the development of the Chang-jiang (Yangtze River) area is very important and the development of communication and transportation for the area is urgent. For the time being, emphasis is being put on Shanghai's Pudong development project and Chang-jiang's Sanxia-dam development project. However, the question still remains for China to answer: which development strategy is more important for the future, railways or automobiles? At the present time, Chinese political leaders seem to have chosen the latter. However, the former may prove to be more important since railways can transport more goods and people more efficiently. A railway system does not need highways or gasoline. In addition, China is abundant in coal while oil is imported from abroad.

Socialist Market Economy

Socialism and a market economy can supplement each other. If socialism from above and a market economy from below develop well, supplementing each other, it is advantageous for both. Even in Japan, we cannot let the market forces go at it alone completely excluding economic intervention by the administration. This is especially true for the socially weak.

On the other hand, we cannot deny a possibility for both to contradict each other. If China develops a free market economy, the socialist economy would be destroyed. How to solve this contradiction is in the hands of the political leaders. There is no overall cure and China will also have to learn by trial and error, which will not be an easy task.

The national enterprise system is an especially difficult situation to resolve. China is now trying to proceed with her reforms in two directions: the first direction is that ownership be reserved in the hands of the government, but that management be privatized. The second is that enterprises be transformed into stock companies. In this case, in order to reserve ownership, the government need not control 100% of a company's total stock. By keeping at least half, the government may retain ownership of an enterprise.

At the same time, the system in which the enterprise has responsibility for its retired workers should also be abolished and transformed into a system in which the government has the responsibility for social security instead. For that purpose, it is necessary for the government to acquire additional revenues. It is especially important to secure tax revenues, to raise the people's consciousness for paying these taxes and to revolutionize the law-abiding consciousness of all citizens.

China's Economic Relations with Japan and the U.S.

Trade and Investment Flows

1980s: Imports from China rose faster than exports

Chinese market remained small

During the 1980s, in spite of China's rapid economic growth with it's "open door" policies, imports from both Japan and the U.S. increased only modestly.

Japan's exports (in terms of U.S. dollars) to China increased by only 14% between 1980 and 1990. As a result, China's share in total Japanese exports declined from 4.1% in 1980 to 2.1% in 1990 (see table 5-1).

Table 5-1
Japan's Trade with China

	1980	1990	1995	90/80	95/90
Value ($ million)					
Export	5,368	6,130	21,931	1.14	3.57
Import	4,323	12,054	35,922	2.79	2.98
Balance	1,045	-5,724	-13,991	--	--
Percent of Total Japanese Trade					
Export	4.1	2.1	6.1		
Import	3.1	5.1	14.9		
Composition of Export (%)					
Total	100.0	100.0	100.0		
Textile Products	8.8	9.9	10.8		
Chemicals	10.7	12.2	9.3		
Iron & Steel	27.0	17.3	10.7		
Machinery	42.3	46.2	55.8		
Composition of Import (%)					
Total	100.0	100.0	100.0		
Food and Beverages	10.9	16.1	13.1		
Raw Materials	11.6	9.0	3.8		
Mineral Fuels	55.0	24.2	5.8		
Textile Products	12.3	26.5	34.4		
Iron & Steel	0.8	2.9	6.1		
Machinery	0.1	4.3	14.4		

Source: Ministry of Finance, *Foreign Trade Statistics* (Tokyo, various years).

However, there were significant fluctuations during those years. Japanese exports rose rapidly during the first half of the decade, rising from $5.3 billion in 1980 to $9.9 billion in 1986, then declining to $6.1 billion in 1990. This was mostly due to drastic changes in the economic policy stance of the Chinese government. Immediately after economic reform, the Chinese government ordered vast amounts of machinery and equipment to be imported mostly from Japan, in order to set up modern plants. A few years afterwards, however, it was realized that prospective import bills would far exceed the capability of the country. Therefore, the Chinese government began to cancel large portions of its import orders, especially those with Japan. In spite of such a drastic measure, China's trade deficit increased from $1.3 billion in 1980 to $12.0 billion in 1985.

Although the performance of U.S. exports during the 1980s was a little better than that of Japan, an increase of 65% between 1982 and 1990, China's share in total U.S. exports remained at a very low 1.2–1.3% (see table 5-2).

Table 5-2
U.S Trade with China

	1982	1990	1995	90/82	95/90
Value ($ million)					
Export	2,912	4,806	11,754	1.65	2.25
Import	2,284	15,237	45,563	6.67	2.29
Percent of Total					
U.S. Trade					
Export	1.31	1.2	2.0		
Import	0.9	3.1	6.1		

Source: U.S. Department of Commerce, *Statistical Reports* (various years).

It is well known that during the 1980s, China's economy continued to grow rapidly. It's real GDP rising 2.4 times. In addition, the value of imports in terms of the U.S. dollar more than doubled. Consequently, as illustrated in table 5-3, during the 1982–1990 period the shares of both Japan and the U.S. in total imports from China declined sharply from 20% to 14% and 22% to 11%, respectively. In the meantime, the shares of Western Europe and Hong Kong rose .

Marked increase in imports from China

On the other hand, imports from China to both Japan and the U.S. increased markedly during the 1980s.

In the case of Japan, imports from China tripled from $4.3 billion in 1980

68　　　　　　　Redefining the Partnership

to $12.1 billion in 1990. U.S. imports from China rose even more vigorously, rising from $2.2 billion in 1982 to $15.2 billion in 1990, almost a seven-fold increase. Reflecting such big rises in imports, both countries' trade balances with China turned from one of surplus to one with a substantial deficit during this period (see tables 5-1 and 5-2).

Table 5-3
Trade with China: Regional Composition
(% of total)

	Japan	U.S.	Hong Kong	West Europe*	Korea/ Taiwan	ASEAN**
Export						
1982	21.5	7.9	23.2	8.8	n.a.	2.8
1985	22.3	8.5	26.1	8.5	n.a.	2.7
1990	14.8	8.6	43.8	6.9	n.a.	2.9
1995	19.1	16.6	24.2	8.3	6.6	3.7
Import						
1982	20.2	22.3	6.8	9.2	n.a.	4.1
1985	35.9	12.3	11.3	11.4	n.a.	2.1
1990	14.4	10.7	27.3	13.4	n.a.	4.1
1995	22.5	12.5	6.7	12.2	21.9	4.6

Notes: *Germany, the U.K., France and Italy
　　　　**Thailand, Malaysia, the Philippines and Indonesia

Source: Economic Planning Agency, "Data on Foreign Countries," (Tokyo, 1997).

1990s: China looms as a big market

Fastest growing market

Since the beginning of the 1990s, exports to China from both Japan and the U.S. have been increasing vigorously. Japan's exports to China increased more than 3.5 times in the first half of the 1990s, raising China's share of total exports to 6.1% in 1995, compared with only 2.1% at the beginning of the decade. Also, U.S. exports to China more than doubled in the same period, resulting in a share increase from 1.2% to 2.0%.

As a result, Japan's share of total Chinese imports rose sharply, exceeding that of the early 1980s. The corresponding shares of the U.S. also expanded, but to a rather modest extent, the shares remaining much lower than in the early 1980s (see table 5-3).

For both Japan and the U.S., China was the fastest growing export market during the period 1990–1995.

Changes in commodity structure of exports

During the period under review, we can observe significant changes in the commodity composition of exports to China from both Japan and the U.S. Concerning Japanese exports to China, we can point out three major changes (see table 5-1).

(1) Relative importance of iron and steel products diminished sharply from more than one-quarter to one-tenth during the 15-year period of 1980–1995. This reflects the rapid change in the relative competitive position of the two countries. (On the import side, the share of iron and steel products rose from almost zero to 6% during the same period.)

(2) Exports of machinery increased rapidly and now account for more than half of the total exports to China.

(3) It is quite noteworthy that the share of textile products rose gradually to almost 11% in 1995, in spite of the diminishing competitiveness of the Japanese textile industry in world markets. This seeming paradox reflects the increasing importance of "process diversification," where Japan exports yarns and fabrics to be further processed in China and then shipped again to other countries, including Japan.

On the other hand, changes in the commodity structure of U.S. exports to China were rather limited compared with the case of Japan (see table 5-4).

(1) The share of machinery rose, accounting for 55% in 1994.

(2) With "machinery," the importance of aircraft and telecommunications equipment rose significantly.

(3) The share of fertilizers almost tripled, perhaps reflecting urgent needs in China to enhance yield per acre of staple foods.

(4) Though not shown in the table, according to Chinese statistics, imports of textile products have increased rapidly in recent years: from less than $600 million in 1992 to more than $1.3 billion in

1995. (This seems to reflect a situation similar to the one mentioned above concerning Japanese exports of textiles to China.)

Table 5-4
Commodity Composition of U.S. Trade with China
(percent of total)

SITC		Export		Import	
		1987	1994	1987	1994
0+1	Food and Beverages	7.9	3.0	4.4	1.4
2	Raw Materials	12.8	12.4	2.4	0.6
3	Mineral Fuels	0.3	0.7	7.6	0.9
5	Chemicals	21.5	16.2	3.1	1.9
	Fertilizers	3.7	10.2	--	--
6	Mfrs. (classified by materials)	7.6	4.4	14.2	8.1
7	Machinery	42.4	55.1	7.5	23.4
	Aircraft	13.9	20.6	--	--
	Telecom. Equipment	2.4	6.1	1.2	2.4
	Industrial Machinery	3.1	3.5	2.1	*3.5
	Motor Cars	--	1.9	--	--
8	Miscellaneous Mfrs.	6.9	6.5	59.2	62.4
	Toys, etc.			11.4	14.3
	Footwear			2.3	13.6
	Men's and Women's Coats			16.3	7.8
	Other Apparel			11.5	7.5
	Bags, Suitcases, etc.			4.7	4.0

Note: *Radios

Source: U.S. Department of Commerce, *Statistical Reports* (various years).

Vigorous increase in imports of manufactures

Imports from China continued to rise rapidly in the first half of the 1990s: nearly 3 times for Japan and more than 2 times in the case of the U.S. Particularly, imports of manufactured goods increased sharply. While total Japanese imports from China tripled between 1990 and 1995, imports of textile products quadrupled, iron and steel products rose six-fold, and machinery ten-fold, though from a very low level. On the other hand, the shares of primary commodities were drastically reduced as table 5-1 shows. In the case of the U.S., the bulk (90%) of imports from China in 1990 was already accounted for by manufactured goods. In 1994, practically all (97%) of the imports were manufactures, and more than 60% was accounted for by miscellaneous manufactures; i.e., SITC Group 8, comprised mainly of apparel, footwear, traveling goods, toys, etc. (see table 5-4).

As a consequence of such a rapid increase in imports, trade deficits with China increased further during the first half of the 1990s. For Japan, the size of the deficit increased to $14 billion in 1995, and for the U.S. the deficit amounted to $33.8 billion, the second largest deficit after that with Japan of $59.1 billion (see table 5-5).

Table 5-5
China's Trade Balance
(U.S.$ billions)

U.S.-China Trade (1995)			
Statistics of:	U.S. → China	China → U.S.	Balance
U.S.	11.8	45.5	33.8
China	16.2	24.7	8.7
Japan-China Trade (1995)			
Statistics of:	Japan → China	China → Japan	Balance
Japan	21.9	35.9	14.0
China	29.0	28.5	0.5

Source: U.S. Statistics: U.S. Department of Commerce, Customs Statistics (1995); Japanese Statistics: Ministry of Finance of Japan, Customs Statistics (1995); Chinese Statistics: Government of China, Customs Statistics (1995).

Rapid increase in FDI to China

Foreign direct investment to China from both Japan and the U.S. is still rather limited in its absolute amount, accounting for only 1.7% and 0.3%, respectively, of the total values of FDI outstanding in 1994 of Japan and the U.S. However, FDI from both countries has been increasing rapidly in recent years. The stock of Japan's FDI in China increased 3.5 times to $8.9 billion between 1989 and 1994, compared with the 83% increase in total Japanese FDI.[2] Likewise, U.S. FDI outstanding in China rose 4.7 times between 1991 and 1995, much faster than the increase of 53% in total U.S. FDI.[3]

In addition, FDI into China has been playing a very significant role in the modernization and rapid growth of the Chinese economy, especially in the coastal regions. In 1995, for instance, the share of industrial output of foreign-owned firms, including subsidiaries of foreign companies and joint ventures, amounted to 14.5%, compared with only 4.9% in 1991.[4] The cumulative total value of FDI realized into China for the period 1979–1995 amounted to $135 billion, an equivalent of 1.9% of GDP in 1995.[5]

The bulk of FDI into mainland China comes from Hong Kong (about 60%) and Taiwan (8.5%). The U.S. and Japan each account for about 8% of the total. However, if we take into consideration the fact that a substantial portion of the FDI from Hong Kong is accounted for by the return of funds which originated in mainland China, the relative importance of Japan and the U.S. seems to be much larger than these figures indicate.

Japanese FDI in China

After the Plaza Accords in 1985, many Japanese companies, especially manufacturers, began to invest and set up subsidiaries in East Asia and China in order to cope with the rapid appreciation of the yen. The rapidly growing market in this region was also an important factor in this development.

There are two patterns of Japanese direct investment in this region. One is manufacturing goods cheaply and exporting them to Japan and other advanced countries. Another is manufacturing goods in East Asia and selling them in the domestic markets. The electric industries, for instance, are drastically shifting from the first to the second pattern.

As of 1991, of all the Japanese overseas subsidiary companies, those which were established in East Asia accounted for nearly 20% on a value-added basis, and a little over 40% in terms of employment.[6]

For Japanese investment in East Asia, China has become the most attractive country in recent years. Investment by Japanese companies has been widely spreading from electric and electronics to auto and machine parts. The number of Japanese subsidiaries and employees has been growing very rapidly, as shown in table 5-6.

Table 5-6
Japanese Foreign Direct Investment in East Asia

	Amount of FDI (U.S.$ billion)				No. of Subsidiaries		No. of Employees (1,000)	
	1988	1990	1992	1994	1988	1994	1988	1994
China	3.2	3.5	11.2	33.8	159	1,055	29	153
Taiwan	1.0	2.3	1.5	1.6	633	789	172	131
Korea	0.9	0.7	0.6	1.3	372	390	179	191
Hong Kong	0.3	0.3	0.3	0.3	660	1,000	38	91
Singapore	3.7	5.6	6.7	5.5	579	941	67	89
Thailand	1.1	2.4	2.1	2.2	512	900	110	258
Indonesia	0.6	1.1	1.8	4.0	222	431	61	150
Malaysia	0.7	2.3	5.2	5.1	356	681	70	180
Philippines	0.9	0.5	0.2	1.7	142	226	36	82
Vietnam	--	--	0.7	1.4	1	22	(*60)	1

Note: *60 persons

Source: *Nihon Kigyo no Asia Shinshutsu Map* (Tokyo: Toyo Keizai Shimposha, 1995).

In what areas and how well have Japanese companies been investing in China? Among the electric industries, Sanyo Electric Corporation has been most successful in handling its subsidiaries in China. It owns thirteen factories, including 100% investment and joint ventures, and is producing 600,000 sets of color TVs and 1,600,000 tape recorders annually. China will be pivotal for the company in manufacturing audio-visual goods. It also plans to establish a factory to produce large-sized refrigerators in Daren. Matsushita Electric Corporation has also been very aggressive in setting up subsidiaries in China, already having nineteen factories in its possession. Sanyo, Matsushita and others are exporting their products to Japan and the world market, but also intend, because of growing demand, to develop a domestic market in China.

The machine parts industries are also very active in China. Mitsumi Electric Corporation, a well-known producer of switches, FDD and CD-ROM drives for computers recently transferred its subsidiaries from Malaysia and the Philippines to China. Good quality of labor was the major reason. Mabuchi Motor Corporation has shifted its production to China and has established five factories in the Canton area. Mabuchi has a 50% share of the world market in small-sized motors.

The automobile market in China already exceeded 1,200,000 cars in 1993, and it is expected that the size of the market will surpass three million cars in the year 2000. Although there are some limiting factors, such as under-developed roads, high cost of gasoline and environmental problems, the emerging middle-income population will rapidly accelerate the demand for cars. European, American, Japanese and Korean automobile manufacturers are eagerly observing the great opportunities in China and gradually expanding subsidiaries there. Honda has been successful in producing motorcycles in China, and is now planning to move into production of four-wheeled "Asia Cars" in the near future. Toyota, which tends to be careful in making new investments, also declared its intention to produce cars in China. However, there exist some uncertainties in this industry because of interventions by the Chinese government.

Trade Problems with China and Policy Issues

Future trade prospects with China

As described above, China is becoming a large and important market for both Japan and the U.S. It is the 6th largest export market for Japan, accounting for 6% of total exports. For the U.S., it is still the 13th largest market, but the fastest growing one. On the other hand, imports from China have been increasing even faster than exports, resulting in sizable trade deficits for the two countries.

It is expected that such trends will continue at least into the coming decade or so. Exports of manufactured goods to China will continue to increase rapidly, because the Chinese economy is expected to grow rapidly at least in the near future and the market for manufactured goods will expand accordingly. In the case of the U.S., exports of certain primary commodities, wheat, for instance, may also increase considerably, reflecting a growing shortage of domestically produced grains in China.

Considering the vigorous expansion of Chinese industries, together with the help of foreign direct investment into China, imports of manufactured foods from China to these two countries are also expected to increase rapidly. Not only will the volume of imports rise, but increasingly more sophisticated products will be imported due to China's progress in industrialization.

It is very likely that trade deficits with China will remain large both for Japan and the U.S., especially if we take into account the protected nature of the current Chinese market. For Japan, the current and prospective size of the deficits will not cause any problems, as long as Japan's overall current account remains a surplus. However, for the U.S., whose current account has been and will remain as a large deficit, the matter seems to be quite serious. Of course, theoretically, bilateral trade balances should not be considered a problem. However, in reality, as the records of Japan-U.S. trade frictions clearly show, a large trade deficit with a particular country tends to be politicized.

Growing trade deficit with China

In the past several years, as mentioned earlier, the U.S. deficit with China has grown rapidly. At the same time, her deficit with Japan has been reduced substantially, mostly due to the appreciation of the yen against the dollar. As a result, in 1996, the U.S. trade deficit with Japan was reduced to $48 billion (27% below that of two years before), her deficit with China rose to $40 billion (a 34% increase over the two proceeding years).

This deficit problem, together with the lack-luster performance of the Japanese economy since the beginning of the 1990s, has contributed to the mitigation of U.S.-Japan economic frictions these past few years.

If such a trend continues, it is very likely that the U.S. will become increasingly concerned with the trade deficit with China. Therefore, there will be enhanced U.S. demand for China to open up her market in general, and to improve the working conditions of Chinese workers, e.g., the elimination of sweat-shop practices in Chinese factories.

Although, according to U.S. trade statistics, the U.S. trade deficit with China is very large, it is much smaller based on the Chinese statistics. As shown in table 5-5, the U.S. deficit with China in 1995 amounted to $33.8 billion according to the former, but it was only $8.6 billion according to the latter. It is very difficult to explain such a huge discrepancy. It is sometimes pointed out that the trade through Hong Kong could be a major factor. Similar discrepancies, though on a much smaller scale, can be observed in the trade imbalance between Japan and China, as seen in the lower panel of the table.

However, aside from absolute numbers, there is no denying that the trade balance between the U.S. and China has been moving rapidly in favor of China. Even according to the Chinese statistics, China's trade surplus with the U.S. increased from $1.3 billion in 1990 to $8.6 billion in 1995.

Hong Kong/Taiwan Issues

Needless to say, Hong Kong's reversion to China is very favorable to the Chinese economy. Otherwise, why has China been so eager for this reversion? The reason might not be simply a political slogan to regain the territory.

However, in order to allow Hong Kong full play of its vitality, the reversion should also be favorable to Hong Kong itself. It is necessary for China not to damage this vitality. China will have to adopt the policy of separating politics from the economy and attach importance to Hong Kong's free economy.

However, even if the top Chinese political leaders truly understand the importance of the policy, we are afraid of the possibility that the rigid method of economic administration, human connections in a bad sense, corruption, and so on, might continue to be conducted by the middle and lower strata of Chinese government officials; especially those who have some responsibility for matters related to Hong Kong in both Hong Kong and mainland China. Also, including politics, if China should force policies on Hong Kong that are too rigid, Hong Kong will not be able to develop its economy well. It has been reported that the news media agencies in Hong Kong are self-regulating and we are afraid of the negative influence they might have on economic development, as Hong Kong is famous for its unrestricted reporting.

Nevertheless, as a whole, China should settle the Hong Kong issue in order to resolve the Taiwan issue as well and then we could have an optimistic view about Hong Kong's future. The political democracy is currently better than that which supposedly existed under British rule. The political situation will improve gradually. The outflow of human resources may continue for several years after the reversion of Hong Kong, but there are still many who have left their families abroad and have returned to Hong Kong to work. There are many young mainland Chinese students who have studied abroad and after graduation want to then work abroad, including Hong Kong. Therefore, concern about the human resources outflow is not necessary.

Rather, the competition between Hong Kong and Shanghai might become serious as a result of the Chinese economic development. However, there is a view that both will develop well by supplementing each other. At one time, Shanghai used to be largest international city in Asia, only to be surpassed by Tokyo, Japan. However, in the near future, Shanghai may once again become the largest international city in Asia.

After Hong Kong's reversion, China might agree with the Hong Kongese living in mainland China to organize a ninth opposition party like the Taiwan National Union in China. This might lead to a more rapid development of democracy in China,

As for the Taiwan issue, it is favorable for Taiwan to strengthen economic ties with mainland China. The reason is that there are many business opportunities of which the Taiwanese may easily take advantage because they can understand the Chinese language and culture. However, in terms of political, military and other aspects, opposition between Taiwan and mainland China will interfere with the strengthening of these economic ties. This depends on the future policies of both sides and there is no way for us, at this time, to tell whether or not both sides will follow a policy of keeping politics and economics separate.

Japan, the U.S. and the Ethnic Chinese Economic Cooperative Body

Development Prospects for the Ethnic Chinese Economies

It might not be so far into the future that we see the size of the ethnic Chinese economies reach the largest scale in the world economy. Here, "the ethnic Chinese economies" mean the economies of mainland China, Hong Kong, Macau, Taiwan, and the ethnic Chinese overseas, including those in Singapore. The ethnic Chinese overseas are those Chinese and their descendants who live in other, mostly Western, countries.

According to the World Bank's estimate, based upon the purchasing power parity, the GDP of three of the ethnic Chinese areas (mainland China, Hong Kong and Taiwan) will surpass that of the United States by the year 2002. According to the estimate by OECD (Organization for Economic Cooperation and Development), which will be published in the near future, and also based on the purchasing power parity, the economic scale of mainland China will be more than that of the United States by 2020. The estimate by the Ministry of International Trade and Industry in Singapore, also PPP-based, is shown in table 5-7.

Table 5-7
Economic Scale and Per-Capita GDP
of each Country and Area in 2020 and 2050
(based on the purchasing power parity as of 1993)

Economic Scale ($trillion)			Per-capita GDP ($1,000)			
Country or area	2020	2050	Country or area	2020	Country or area	2050
China	20.2	56.8	Hong Kong	65	Hong Kong	142
U.S.A.	13.4	28.2	Singapore	61	Taiwan	129
India	5.4	27.0	Taiwan	55	Singapore	127
Japan	4.8	9.3	U.S.A.	42	Korea	87
Indonesia	3.2	8.6	Japan	38	U.S.A.	81
Thailand	2.0	5.2	Korea	38	Japan	78
Korea	2.0	4.9	Thailand	28	Thailand	63
Taiwan	1.4	3.3	Malaysia	28	Malaysia	62
Malaysia	0.8	2.4	China	14	China	35
Hong Kong	0.4	0.7	Indonesia	12	Indonesia	29
Singapore	0.2	0.5	India	4	India	16

Source: A forecast by the Ministry of International Trade and Industry in Singapore (Reproduced from *Rianho Zaobao* [in Chinese] (Singapore), 19 December 1996 by Yu).

As a result, the so-called "China century" and "the ethnic Chinese century" will come. However, this only concerns the size of the total economic scale. Whether or not their century will come, even in politics, culture, military affairs and so on, is another thing.

In order to reach the real "China century," in terms of the economy, the ethnic Chinese economies will have to arrive at the top economic level in the world in per-capita GDP. According to the above mentioned Singaporean government's forecast, it is only a matter of time before some ethnic Chinese economies such as Hong Kong, Taiwan and Singapore reach the top level in the world, far surpassing the per-capita GDP of the United States and Japan.

However, it seems very difficult and unlikely that mainland China will reach the top level in the first half of the twenty-first century. It might take until the end of the twenty-first century or even into the twenty-second century. If it is so far in the future—in terms of the food question, resources question, particularly the energy question, natural environment question, population question, international relations and so on, and furthermore the very large question of whether or not the Chinese people can develop their production power infinitely—then it is not clear whether China can reach the top per-capita economic level in the world or not.

The Ethnic Chinese Economic Network and the Ethnic Chinese Economic Cooperative Body

One reason why the ethnic Chinese economic development is so remarkable is that their personal network is very strong. Japan is also a society in which human connections are very strong, but in the case of ethnic Chinese societies, it is especially so. Therefore, some call the ethnic Chinese economies "Connection Capitalism" or "Network Capitalism."

The ethnic Chinese economic network can be divided into two kinds. One is the traditional relations of three ties: blood ties (the same family), territorial ties (persons from the same area speaking the same dialect), and professional ties (persons engaging in the same trade). As a result, there are three kinds of groups based on these three ties, which are called *Bang* in Chinese. The same territorial groups based on the same dialect are the most important ones, because members of the same family speak the same dialect and those who speak the same dialect are engaged in the same trade. There are five main dialect groups: Cantonese, Fukkenese, Teochew, Hakka, and Hailam. In Japan, the Hakka group is regarded as the most important one. However, in actuality this is not the case, because the term Hakka means guests and they are not the mainstream of the ethnic Chinese, including those in mainland China.

The second ethnic Chinese economic network is a new one though based on the above mentioned three-tie relations. However, to enumerate, this network includes ties with:
(1) All ethnic Chinese and Mandarin, the standard language in China. Sometimes even English is used among the ethnic Chinese.
(2) Alumni associations. Especially, those of the schools of overseas Chinese and their descendants are important. Recently, the network of those who had studied in the United States has also become important.
(3) Parents and teachers associations of the schools of overseas Chinese and their descendants.

(4) Statesmen. Ties with influential and successful ethnic and non-ethnic statesmen are taken advantage of. Many of the prime ministers and the presidents in Southeast Asian countries are ethnic Chinese in origin.
(5) The ethnic Chinese economic cooperative body which is often called "Greater China Economic Zone" or "the Ethnic Chinese Economic Zone." There are two kinds of cooperative bodies, one is "the Coordination System of the Chinese Economies" and another is "the World Chinese Entrepreneurs Convention." The former is an organization for mainland China, Hong Kong, Macau and Taiwan. It aims for regional economic integration. The latter is an organization of the ethnic Chinese throughout the entire world. It aims for national or ethnic economic integration. The latter should not be called an economic zone because it has nothing to do with territorial or regional connections.
(6) Databases on the ethnic Chinese firms and entrepreneurs in the world arranged in Singapore. This was initiated at the World Chinese Entrepreneurs Convention; and
(7) Internet using the above mentioned database.

Conclusion

As mentioned earlier, there are a number of difficult problems to be solved in order for China to continue her rapid economic growth in the upcoming decades, including the reform of state-owned enterprises and the development of inland areas. However, we think that a fairly high rate of growth, although somewhat lower than in the past decade, could be realized if the "reform and openness" policies are maintained.

The continuation of the rapid growth of China with her huge population means the emergence of China as one of the largest economic powers in the world, whether measured by the market exchange rate or by PPP. This will inevitably bring about two important issues in the relationship among China, Japan and the U.S.

First, the rapid increase in the trade deficit of the U.S. against China is expected to divert the trade concerns of the U.S. away from Japan, as already seen in such expressions as the "Japan passing." Together with the diminution, and perhaps, the disappearance of the American feeling of the threat of Japan, this may contribute to reducing the tension and conflicts between the two countries.

Apparently, such a development seems to be a welcome thing. However, if this signifies a tendency on the part of the Americans to think lightly of the relationship with Japan, it could be rather dangerous in the long term because this might lead to an undervaluation of the importance of Japan-U.S. relations in both politics and economics.

Second, the rapidly expanding market of China will tend to cause a rivalry between Japan and the U.S. in securing markets for its own industrial products, both in terms of commodity exports and in direct investments in the form of both green investments and joint venture activities.

Certain initial indications of such a conflict can already be observed in the fierce competition between the automobile manufacturers of the two countries in obtaining a permit from the Chinese authorities to establish car manufacturing plants in China.

On the other hand, there seem to be certain issues or spheres in which Japan and the U.S. can act in cooperation to pursue activities beneficial to both nations: asking China to reduce the degree of protection of her market; reducing tariff and non-tariff barriers; etc. Securing intellectual property rights in China, more in line with the standards of developed countries, will also be an issue that the two countries might pursue in cooperation.

Also, demanding the Chinese authorities to improve their legal system, especially on matters concerning economic and commercial activities, will be of mutual benefit to Japan and the U.S. At present, an out-of-date and peculiar legal system or practices, and additionally, frequent and arbitrary manipulation of the system—or non-system—are a major concern for the expansion of business activities in China for firms of Japan, the U.S., and European countries.

Finally, Japan and the U.S. should try not to provoke China by demanding drastic changes in sensitive areas, but should endeavor to cooperate in furthering her economic development and modernization. Through such efforts, they could gain more in the long run by inducing China into becoming an ordinary member of the world community with gradually enhanced human rights and democracy. This will, in turn, contribute to the prosperity of not only Japan and the U.S., but also of the East Asia region and ultimately of the world.

Notes

1. Lester R. Brown, *Who will Feed China* (New York: W.W. Norton & Company, 1995).
2. Ministry of Finance, Japanese government
3. U.S. Department of Commerce, "Survey of Current Business," various issues.
4. Government of China. According to Economic Planning Agency of Japan, "Report on the Future of China and the Economy of APEC," April 1997 (in Japanese).
5. *Ibid.*, 32.
6. "Present Situation and Issues of Direct Investment," *NIRA Policy Research* 9, no. 10 (1966).

Chapter 6

U.S.-Japanese Economic Relations and the Southeast Asia Connection: A Boring Analysis

Charles Chang
David Fernandez
James Riedel

Sex Appeal and the Dismal Science

Many books have been written mainly by political scientists about the troubled state of U.S.-Japanese economic relations. At the heart of the matter is the bilateral trade imbalance between the two countries. Many articles have been written and many hours of testimony have been given before various congressional committees by mainstream economists arguing that the bilateral trade imbalance between the U.S. and Japan is irrelevant. Economists argue that a country's overall trade balance is determined mainly by domestic macroeconomic conditions, and not other countries' trade or industrial policies. Bilateral balances, on the other hand, mainly reflect relative comparative advantages in international trade, though they can be influenced by trade and industrial policies. Bilateral balances are nevertheless irrelevant because they are offsetting—

to the extent that overall trade is balanced, every bilateral deficit is matched by a bilateral surplus; to the extent that overall trade is not balanced, it is macroeconomic factors, not trade or industrial policies, that are at the core of the problem—if indeed the imbalance is a problem. No one to our knowledge has refuted the economic logic of the irrelevance of bilateral trade balances. Nevertheless, books keep getting written about the U.S.-Japan "problem," and the underlying plots keep getting more and more complicated and intriguing. No doubt the most intriguing recent plot is the Southeast Asia connection. The rapid growth of China and the Southeast Asian countries, and Japan's increasing level of trade with and investment in these countries have provided a new context for analyzing the inscrutable ways in which the Japanese have maneuvered to take advantage of hapless American business. As one recent study concludes, "Japan is beginning to regionalize [in East Asia] its developmentalist policies and practices—a strategic move that, if pursued with any success, will further widen the technological gap between Japan and Asia, and exacerbate the existing trade conflict between East and West."[1] Another study warns,

> Japanese investments in East Asia can be seen as expanding an already intense three-front contest—as import competition now emanates from both Japan and East Asia—with products feeding expanded Japanese investments in U.S. manufacturing and distribution, all integrated and coordinated by the same Japanese multinationals.[2]

In terms of sex appeal and the potential to sell books, the stale logic of economics is no match for tales of nefarious plots and strategic moves on the world stage, no matter how valid it is. It is, nevertheless, the job of the economist to take the fun out of life, to keep reminding people that there is no free lunch, and that, no matter how boring, simple explanations are always to be preferred to more complicated ones, a principle that has stood the test of time since at least the fourteenth century when William of Occum enunciated it.[3] That is our job here, to provide a simple explanation to U.S.-Japanese economic relations and the Southeast Asian Connection.

Some Boring Facts of Life

Fact of Life Number One

Because Japan is scarce in natural resources, it must import them, which it can only do by producing and exporting manufactures. Inevitably, therefore, Japan runs bilateral trade deficits with natural resource exporting countries and bilateral trade surpluses with other countries, such as the United States and the resource poor East Asian countries, which provide markets for its manufactures.

This fact is no great revelation; everybody knows it. Nevertheless, every diatribe about the problem of unbalanced trade between the United States and Japan implicitly, if not explicitly, ignores this fact of life. As an indication of just how dependent Japan is on imported natural resources, we present table 6-1, which gives the share of imports in apparent consumption of some key raw materials in Japan and the United States.

Table 6-1
The Share of Imports in Apparent Consumption of
Key Raw Materials in Japan and the United States
(percentages)

Raw Material	Japan	United States
Coal	86.7	3.8
Oil	99.6	36.8
Natural Gas	94.8	4.1
Iron Ore	99.8	28.7
Copper	97.4	24.4

Source: Edward J. Lincoln, *Japan's Unequal Trade* (Washington, D.C.: Brookings Institution, 1990).

It is obvious that if Japan could not export manufactures, it could not import key raw materials, and if it could not import key raw materials, it could not be an industrial nation. Where should Japan export its manufactured products? Answer: where the market is. In other words, Japan should sell its products to those countries which have the purchasing power to buy them and whose markets are open to trade. As table 6-2 shows, that roughly explains the geographic destination of Japanese exports. The United States accounts for about 20% of world income and a somewhat larger share (about 27%) of Japanese exports.

Table 6-2
The Destination of Japanese Exports
and Relative Market Size

Country or Region	Share in World Income	Share in Japanese Exports
United States	19.2	27.5
Other Developed Countries	26.2	20.1
Developing Asia	22.5	43.6
Other Regions	32.1	8.6

Source: Isaiah Frank, "US Economic Policy toward the Asia-Pacific Region," mimeo, 1997; IMF Direction of Trade Statistics, 1997.

There are, of course, factors other than market size that determine the geographic pattern of trade, such as market openness and relative strength of comparative advantage. Clearly these factors should be taken into account before resort is taken to nefarious plots and strategic maneuvering. The conventional procedure for analyzing the "normality" of trade patterns is to apply a gravity model and then to introduce a dummy variable into the model to test for special significance of a particular country, such as the United States, or group of countries, such as the East Asian developing countries.

We estimate separate gravity equations for the U.S. and Japan to test for structural trade patterns in Japanese and U.S. trade. The specifications are as follows:

$$\log(T_{ius}) = \alpha + \beta_1 \log(Y_i) + \beta_2 \log(YPC_i) + \beta_3 (DNR_i) + \beta_4 \log(D_i) + \delta_1(EA) + \delta_2(JPN) + \mu_i$$

$$\log(T_{ijpn}) = \gamma + \tau_1 \log(Y_i) + \tau_2 \log(YPC_i) + \tau_3 (DNR)_i + \tau_4 \log(D_i) + \phi_1(EA) + \phi_2(US) + \nu_i$$

where T_{ius} and T_{ijpn} are U.S. and Japanese exports to country i; Y_i and YPC_i are GNP (gross national product) and GNP per capita of country i; DNR_i is a dummy variable for natural resource exporters; D_i is the distance from Tokyo (Washington, D.C.) to the capital of country i; and u_i is the random disturbance term. The baseline model therefore attempts to explain the geographic pattern of trade, accounting for market size (GNP), comparative advantage (income per capita and resource endowment) and distance between trading partners. To this set of explanatory variables, we introduce dummy variables for East Asia (EA) and the United States and Japan to test for regional and bilateral biases in Japanese and U.S. trade patterns.

Following standard practice, our gravity equations are log-linear in functional form and consider no non-linearity in any of the explanatory variables. We apply the model on a cross section of 114 countries using period averages over the 1990–95 period. Data on Japanese and U.S. bilateral exports, imports and trade are taken from the International Monetary Fund's (IMF) Directory of Trade Statistics; GNP and GNP per capita are from the World Bank's World Development Indicators (WDI); and distances between capitals are measured in kilometers, provided by Xerox Palo Alto Research Center (PARC). For the dummies, DNR takes the value of one for countries whose non-food primary exports exceed 25% of total exports (WDI), and the East Asia, U.S. and Japan dummies equal one for the specified countries,[4] zero otherwise.

The literature using gravity equations has generally reached the following unsurprising conclusions: countries tend to trade more with partners who are larger, richer, and closer. Thus, Y_i and YPC_i are expected to have positive coefficients, and distance is expected to have a negative sign. We also expect the primary exporter dummy to carry a positive sign. The reasoning is simple: relative to others, resource-rich exporters supply more primary inputs to the world and hence enjoy surpluses on the balance of primary goods. Against this, partner countries must run surpluses in manufactured goods either to balance or alleviate the deficits they suffer on primary commodities. The scenario intuitively implies incentives for both sides to export more to the other, thereby expanding bilateral trade. After controlling for these structural factors, it is unclear whether a bias would remain toward East Asia, and of no less importance, whether Japanese trade is particularly directed toward the United States. It is the warning of some critics that America is standing by—indeed, losing out—as Japan increasingly targets Asia in their "strategic" trade policies. The same warnings, of course, are often made of Japan's designs on the U.S. market itself. The coefficients on the regional and country dummies will allow the

U.S. to verify empirically whether such regional and bilateral biases exist in Japan's trade flows.

The results are presented in table 6-3. High R-squared values in all specifications show that the model fits the data rather well. As seen in the basic specification, of the variations observed in U.S. (Japanese) trade with the 114 countries in our cross section, some 79% (74%) is accounted for by the gravity and resource variables alone. Introducing the dummies for East Asia, the United States and Japan improved the model's fit, but

Table 6-3
Gravity Model Estimates of Bilateral Trade, 1990–1995

	United States		Japan	
Constant	4.83**	7.97**	5.74**	-1.88
	(2.99)	(6.08)	(2.71)	(-0.60)
ln (Y_i)	0.89**	0.81**	0.81**	0.75**
	(23.36)	(22.02)	(18.08)	(15.87)
ln (YPC_i)	0.01	0.01	0.18**	0.22
	(0.13)	(0.27)	(2.81)	(3.47)
ln (D_i)	-0.74**	-1.03**	-0.98**	-0.14
	(-4.63)	(-7.80)	(-4.72)	(-0.43)
DNR	0.25**	0.35**	0.64**	0.22
	(2.44)	(3.41)	(4.13)	(1.22)
JPN		1.09**		
		(4.93)		
US				1.22**
				(4.84)
EASIA		2.03**		2.32**
		(8.55)		(5.48)
R^2	0.79	0.84	0.75	0.79
adj. R^2	0.79	0.83	0.74	0.78

Notes: ** Significant at the 5% confidence level.

T-statistics appear in parenthesis and are based on standard errors calculated with White's correction for heteroskedasticity.

not by a large margin (the adjusted R^2 increases from 0.79 to 0.84 in the U.S. model, and from 0.74 to 0.78 in the Japan model). In general, estimators on the explanatory variables turned out as expected. Most gravity variables are highly significant while all carry the expected signs. Strong evidence suggests that the United States trades more with larger countries and countries of closer geographic proximity. We also see that the United States trades more with natural resource exporters, but not necessarily with high income per-capita countries. Similarly, Japanese trade patterns are largely explained by the same set of gravity variables, with the country size and per capita income variables both highly significant.

As for the warnings that Japan's trade policies target certain key regions of the world, there is indeed evidence showing a bias in Japanese trade toward East Asia and the United States—even after accounting for geographic proximity and other structural factors.[5] However, the gravity model yields two results that undermine any thesis that Japan is strategically targeting its trade. First, the model reveals that the United States shows a similar positive bias towards both East Asia and Japan. So, if the regional and bilateral biases we observed in Japanese trade patterns suggest the presence of strategic Japanese trade policies, then the same could be said about American trade policies towards the same targets. Indeed, we can say with much empirical confidence that the United States has not been standing idly by, but has instead expanded trade more with East Asia and Japan than with other trading partners. Second, the size of the regional biases are small. Taking into account all other factors, Japan is found to trade more (higher than average, that is) with East Asian countries by $10.2 million and more with the United States by $3.4 million over the 1990s. Considering that Japan's trade with Thailand in 1995 alone was $29.8 billion, these biases seem of little significance. Even in the unlikely event that these biases are wholly induced by Japan's calculated policies, their magnitude certainly do not deserve the ominous portends often assigned to them.

It seems clear from this analysis that Japanese and U.S. trade patterns in the 1990s are quite similar and can largely be explained by simple structural factors of natural design. Factors important in explaining the remaining variations—be they calculated policies or other non-policy determinants—necessarily take a minor role in explaining currently observed trade patterns. As for the critics' warnings, although the empirical evidence indeed suggests the presence of biases in Japanese trade with Asia and the United States, the same biases are observed in U.S. trade patterns as well.

At the end of the day, we see that natural resource endowments and other determinants of comparative advantage dictate that it is "natural" for the United States to run a trade deficit with Japan. The bilateral trade imbalance between the United States and Japan is therefore best understood as a structural phenomenon, reflecting the relative comparative advantages of the two countries. This boring, though important hypothesis is empirically supported by the results of our gravity model which show that most of the bilateral trade patterns of the United States and Japan can be explained by standard economic variables. As for the overall trade balances of the two countries, those are macroeconomic issues to which we return later.

Fact of Life Number Two

China and most of the other Southeast Asian developing countries are natural resource poor, densely populated and vastly endowed with human resources. For such countries the only proven path to prosperity is export-oriented industrialization, specializing in labor-intensive manufactured goods. This strategy involves combining imported machinery and industrial materials with domestic low-wage labor, and exporting output to major markets for manufactured products. A bilateral deficit with Japan (a principal source of machinery and equipment) and bilateral surplus with the U.S. (a major market for labor-intensive manufactures) are an inevitable consequence of this successful industrialization strategy.

In the vast literature on economic development over the past 100 years there is no empirical regularity that is more robust and universal across time and across countries than the positive relation between openness to trade and economic growth. This fact was not always known or appreciated, and indeed most developing countries commenced their industrialization by closing their economies to international trade. The import-substitution strategy of industrialization, which virtually every developing country (except Hong Kong) adopted at the outset of industrialization, was based on two false premises. One was the premise that export-oriented industrialization was bound to fail because developing countries would find no market for their products in the developed countries. The other false premise was that developing countries, by closing their economies and protecting domestic industry, would be able to capture economies of scale and economies of time (learning by doing), which would eventually make them competitive in industries in which they initially lacked comparative advantage. Both of these premises were proved false by the cumulative experience of developing countries over the past four decades. The experiences of Hong Kong, Singapore, Taiwan and South Korea, which were the first countries to abandon the conventional wisdom of the day and adopt the export-oriented industrialization strategy, were a powerful demonstration of the fallacy of the premise of export pessimism. In spite of the evidence, however, export pessimism persisted in the form of the "fallacy of composition" argument, which held that the success of the first-comers to export-oriented industrialization (the four "Tigers") could not be replicated by late-comers on the grounds that the first-comers had saturated the market for labor-intensive manufactures in developed countries. However, this last stand of export pessimism was thoroughly demolished when, following the success of the Asian Tigers, a succession of other developing countries, including China and most of the Southeast Asian countries, adopted and succeeded with the export-oriented industrialization strategy in the 1980s.

The second premise—that scale economies and learning by doing would allow developing countries to revoke the law of comparative advantage and instead put their scarce investible resources into capital-intensive, high-technology industry—was proved equally false and disastrously costly for developing countries. Certainly the import-substitution strategy did create large industrial bases in the larger continental developing countries (like China, India, Brazil and Turkey), but in every case it carried an enormous cost in terms of economic inefficiency and often brought with it macroeconomic instability.

The positive experiences of countries following the export-oriented industrialization strategy, combined with the overwhelmingly negative experiences of countries following the inward-oriented, import-substitution strategy, have impelled many countries to undertake broad-based programs of economic reform since 1985. Indeed, outside of Sub-Saharan Africa, there is nothing short of a revolution in policy reform underway in developing countries, as one country after another has undertaken unilaterally to lowers its barriers to trade and institute market-oriented reforms.

There is nowhere in the world where the revolution in policy reform has advanced further than in East Asia, nor is there any place in the world that has achieved more under the export-oriented industrialization strategy than in East Asia. A natural consequence of this industrialization strategy has been the emergence of structural trade surpluses on the part of the East Asian developing countries vis-à-vis the United States and structural trade deficits vis-à-vis Japan. This pattern emerged in Taiwan and Korea in the 1970s and 1980s, just as it emerged in the 1990s in China and the Southeast Asian countries which later followed the export-oriented industrialization strategy. It is not a trade pattern that is uniquely associated with the recent flood of Japanese investment into the East Asian developing countries; it is instead a normal pattern of trade that follows from a successful industrialization strategy that is based on the principle of comparative advantage.

Fact of Life Number Three

The surge in Japanese foreign direct investment (FDI) in East Asia is not unique—it is matched, indeed exceeded, by a similar surge from the Asian Tigers (Hong Kong, Taiwan, Korea and Singapore). Since the FDI flows from these countries are presumably market determined, with governments in these countries playing no particularly decisive role, the presumption is that Japanese FDI flows are similarly motivated. Put differently, no conspiracy theory is required to explain Japanese flows into East Asia.[6]

In the 1990s, the East Asian countries absorbed about 65% of the total net FDI in developing countries. As table 6-2 shows, about 90% of it went to four countries: China, Indonesia, Malaysia and Thailand. In 1993, China alone accounted for about 40% of net FDI in developing countries.

In order to appreciate the relative importance of these flows to the host countries, it is useful to express them as percentages of GNP. As table 6-4 shows, FDI played no appreciable role in the South Asian countries, with the minor exception of Sri Lanka, where it has risen in the last two years to almost 2% of the GNP. Liberalization in India since 1991 has led to a significant increase in FDI approvals, but the actual amounts invested remain minuscule in relation to Indian GNP.[7]

In the four major recipient countries of East Asia, FDI flows, although large in comparison to the flows to other countries, are relatively small in

Table 6-4
Net Foreign Direct Investment Flows
to Selected Asian Developing Countries
($ millions and as percentage of GNP)

	1970	1980	1990	1991	1992	1993	1994
FDI in U.S.$ millions							
East Asia (6)	261	1204	10675	13584	21187	37602	42693
S. Korea	66	6	788	1180	727	588	809
China	0	0	3487	4366	11156	27515	33787
Indonesia	83	180	1093	1482	1777	2004	2109
Malaysia	94	934	2333	3998	5183	5006	4348
Philippines	-25	-106	530	544	228	763	1000
Thailand	43	190	2444	2014	2116	1726	640
South Asia (4)	69	185	452	447	613	828	1227
Bangladesh	0	0	3	1	4	14	11
India	46	79	162	141	151	273	620
Pakistan	23	63	244	257	335	346	430
Sri Lanka	0	43	43	48	123	195	166
FDI as % of GNP							
East Asia (6)	0.2	0.3	1.2	1.4	2.0	3.3	3.2
S. Korea	0.7	0.0	0.3	0.4	0.2	0.2	0.2
China	0.0	0.0	1.0	1.2	2.7	6.4	6.5
Indonesia	0.9	0.2	1.0	1.2	1.3	1.3	1.3
Malaysia	2.3	4.0	5.7	9.0	9.4	8.3	6.5
Philippines	-0.4	-0.3	1.2	1.2	0.4	1.4	1.5
Thailand	0.6	0.6	2.9	2.1	1.9	1.4	0.5
South Asia (4)	0.1	0.1	0.1	0.1	0.2	0.2	0.3
Bangladesh	0.0	0.0	0.0	0.0	0.0	0.1	0.0
India	0.1	0.0	0.1	0.1	0.1	0.1	0.2
Pakistan	0.2	0.3	0.6	0.6	0.7	0.7	0.8
Sri Lanka	0.0	1.1	0.5	0.5	1.3	1.9	1.4

Source: World Bank, World Debt Tables, 1996.

relation to the recipient countries' economies. Only in Malaysia has FDI, in recent years, risen to a significant proportion of GNP (about 8%) and investment (about 25%). The level of FDI in China in 1993, at almost 7%

of GNP, is also exceptional. Indeed, in relation to the size of the regional economies in which it is located (e.g., Guangdong and Fujian), its role is, of course, far greater. Even at the national level, however, FDI in China, in 1993, accounted for about 15% of gross domestic investment and about 30% of exports.[8]

The source of FDI in East Asia is, as table 6-5 shows, predominantly from within the region itself, Hong Kong and Taiwan together accounting for about 45% of FDI in the major recipient countries. These two sources—which really cannot be separated, since a significant amount of Taiwanese investment is channeled through Hong Kong—account for almost 70% of FDI in China.[9] Behind the East Asian newly industrialized economies (NIEs), Japan ranks as the second largest investor in the region; its investments spread more or less equally between China, Malaysia and Thailand, with Indonesia joining the other Association of Southeast Asian Nations (ASEAN) in terms of importance as a destination for Japanese investment only in the 1990s.

Foreign direct investment can be classified into three broad categories according to its main purpose: (1) to exploit a natural resource abundance, (2) to circumvent trade barriers in order to serve the host-country market, and (3) to take advantage of relatively low labor costs to produce for export. Indonesia and Malaysia, in particular, have attracted FDI of the first variety. China is currently attracting a substantial amount of foreign investment of the second variety, especially from Japan, the United States and Europe. However, even in China, Indonesia and Malaysia, the most rapidly expanding form of direct foreign investment, especially that originating from within the region, is the export-oriented variety.

The surge since the mid-1980s in export-oriented FDI in China and Southeast Asia by firms (mostly small- or medium-sized) from Japan, Taiwan and Hong Kong is explained by several conducive push-and-pull factors. On the push side, the loss of international competitiveness of export-oriented firms in Japan and the newly industrialized countries (NICs) (Korea, Taiwan, Hong Kong and Singapore) due to rising real wages and currency appreciation was especially important. On the pull side, a key inducement was trade policy reforms which got underway and were accelerated in the 1980s in China and Southeast Asia, allowing exporters to have freer access to imported capital goods and imported inputs. Thus, the opportunity was created for firms in Northeast Asia, which were losing international competitiveness at home, to shift their operations to Southeast Asia, where they could continue to profit from their acquired know-how of producing and exporting labor-intensive manufactures.

Table 6-5
The Source of FDI in Selected East Asian Countries, 1986–1992
($ millions and percentages)

	China	Indonesia	Malaysia	Philippines	Thailand	Total
NIEs	21,123	1,573	4,123	580	3,565	30,964
	(70.9)	(25.2)	(29.8)	(17.9)	(35.4)	(49.0)
Taiwan	1,903	501	3,086	87	828	6,405
	(6.4)	(8.0)	(22.3)	(2.7)	(8.2)	(10.1)
Hong Kong	18,719	478	433	338	1,720	21,686
	(62.8)	(7.6)	(3.1)	(10.4)	(17.1)	(34.3)
Singapore	378	239	940	48	954	2,558
	(1.3)	(3.8)	(6.8)	(1.5)	(9.5)	(4.1)
Korea	123	355	755	108	64	2,558
	(0.4)	(5.7)	(5.5)	(3.3)	(0.6)	(4.1)
Japan	3,042	1,102	3,065	855	3,586	11,650
	(10.2)	(17.6)	(22.2)	(26.4)	(35.6)	(18.4)
U.S.	2,390	428	1,499	1,193	1,373	6,884
	(8.0)	(6.8)	(10.8)	(36.9)	(13.6)	(10.9)
Europe	1,316	1,009	2,711	378	1,108	6,522
	(4.4)	(16.1)	(19.6)	(11.0)	(11.0)	(10.3)
Total	29,785	6,250	13,822	3,235	10,071	63,163
	(100.0)	(100.0)	(100.0)	(100.0)	(100.0)	(100.0)

Note: The values for total FDI are taken from the IMF, *Balance of Payments Statistics Yearbook*. The shares of source countries are derived from recipient country data.

Source: Japan Institute for Overseas Investment, 1993, "Foreign Direct Investment in East Asia: Trends and Outlooks," as reported in Osamu Kawaguchi, *Foreign Direct Investment in East Asia: Trends, Determinants, and Policy Implications*, Report No. IDP-139 (Washington, D.C.: The World Bank, 1994), 4.

The fact that much of the FDI in East Asia is motivated by a reduction in trade barriers in the host countries, rather than by increasing trade barriers as was the case for much of the FDI in developing countries in the 1960s and 1970s, has profound implications for the costs and benefits of FDI for the recipient country. As is well known, FDI in highly protected economies is likely to be immiserizing, since protection distorts the market rate of return earned by foreign investors.[10] Some empirical support for this proposition is offered in a recent study of FDI from 1966 to 1988 in sixteen developing countries, including eight of the ten Asian countries considered here (Bangladesh and China excluded). Outside of Southeast Asia (defined to include Korea, Indonesia, Malaysia, the Philippines and Thailand), the study found that FDI lowered the rate of investment and growth, while in Southeast Asia it raised both. The author concluded from that evidence that, "The superior efficiency of FDI in Southeast Asian economies reflects not only less distorted financial conditions than in other parts of the developing world but also less distorted trading systems."[11]

The positive growth effects of export-oriented FDI in East Asia have been shown in a number of firm surveys to derive less from their financial contribution to raising level investment than from the infusion of technology and international business know-how that accompanies export-oriented FDI. A recent survey of 122 Taiwanese small- to medium-sized firms operating in Malaysia found that a large part of their invested capital was in fact raised in the domestic capital market.[12] The main benefit of the Taiwanese FDI to the local economy, aside from creating employment and generating export earnings, was found to be the commercial linkages that grew up between the Taiwanese firms and local (Bumiputra as well as Chinese) firms in Malaysia, which replicated to a large extent the complex networks of small- and medium-sized firms that characterize the manufacturing sector in Taiwan.[13] The contribution of export-oriented investment by Hong Kong and Taiwan firms in China is reportedly similar, deriving far more from the manufacturing and international business know-how they bring than from the financial inflow associated with their direct investments.[14]

There is no doubt that there is a significant amount of Japanese direct investment in East Asia. However, when one stops citing absolute levels of investment (i.e., X billion Yen), one realizes that for most recipient countries the amounts of FDI are not enormous relative to the sizes of their economies. Further, most of the FDI into East Asia is from Hong Kong, Taiwan, and the other Asian Tigers—not Japan. What attracts these direct investment flows? The boring answer is nothing more than loss of competitiveness in Japan and the Asian Tigers, and economic reforms in the recipient nations. Again, one can safely say that no mercantilist intrigue nor grandiose plots are need to understand Japan's financial involvement in Asia.

Fact of Life Number Four

The overall current account surpluses of Japan and deficits of the United States are related primarily to macroeconomic factors, and not to the industrial or trade policies of governments.

Recall our first two boring "facts of life." Resources endowments, comparative advantage, and other standard economic variables tell U.S. that Japan naturally runs a trade surplus with both the United States and most Southeast Asian countries. The same variables dictate that the United States will run a deficit with Japan and these same economies. Keep in mind that Japan runs trade deficits with natural resource rich countries (Saudi Arabia, Australia, Brazil, etc.), while the United States exports more than it imports to Australia, Central and South America, and certain European countries. All of these bilateral balances must balance out. If they do not, and they clearly do not in the cases of Japan and the United States, the reasons lie in the macroeconomic performance and policies of the country.

There is no free lunch. When a country, like the United States, consumes more than it produces, the excess consumption must be imported from other countries. Similarly, when a country, like the United States, invests domestically more than its people and government save, it must borrow from abroad to make up the difference. In contrast to the United States, Japan produces more than it consumes and saves more than it invests, therefore, it runs an overall current account surplus and capital account deficit. Boring? Of course. But the iron logic of balance-of-payments accounting is irrefutable.[15]

Data on gross savings and investment rates are crude, but tell the basic story. The true picture, nevertheless, is not as bleak as that painted by the gross data. The important alterations to the savings-investment picture can be broken down into two groups: first, cross-country differences in accounting conventions and other data collection issues; and second, underlying long-term trends driving the macroeconomic variables.

First, the gross data (see figure 6-1) indicate that the savings rate in Japan is roughly twice that of the United States. However, differences in accounting conventions between the two countries may cloud the picture. For example, Japan treats capital depreciation differently than the United States, and the U.S. accounts label all government expenditures as consumption, thereby failing to acknowledge the importance of public investment. The extent to which these and other accounting problems affect the saving rate gap between the two countries is still a matter of debate.[16] What does seem to be clear is that conceptual shortcomings in the national accounting frameworks appear to overstate the savings rate gap. A study that makes adjustments to the data that reclassify consumer durables and private research and development (R&D) spending, as well as standardizing for differences in tax regimes, reduces the gap by half— but does not eliminate it.[17] So, after being as careful as possible with the data, the simple, boring message remains: Japan's overall surplus is driven by its high savings rate and the low savings rate of the United States is behind its overall deficit.

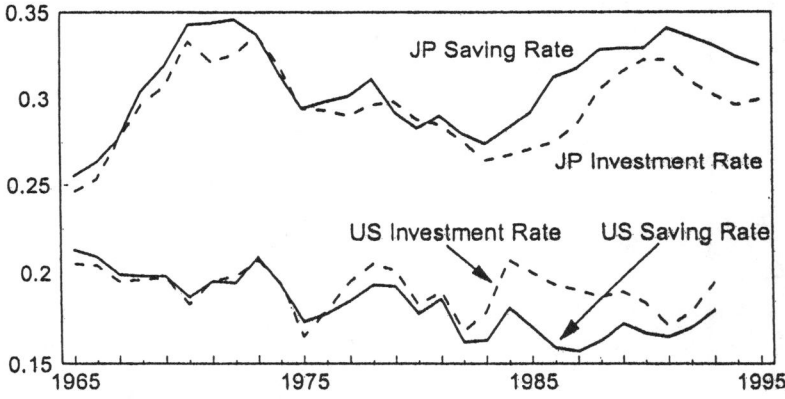

Figure 6-1. Gross Saving and Investment Rates, Japan and U.S.

Second, the long-run, underlying forces driving the macroeconomic variables. Saving rates in the United States are slightly lower, but basically where they were just after World War II. In contrast, Japanese saving rates, in particular household saving rates, rose substantially during the 1960s and early 1970s. Furthermore, households account for about two-thirds of the savings in Japan. Therefore, the key issue when analyzing the saving gap between the United States and Japan is: why did Japan's households start saving so much in the decades after World War II?[18] The standard economic explanation focuses on what are called "life-cycle" considerations. The simple life-cycle story implies that households' saving rates follow a bell-shaped pattern over their lifetime: rising during early-adult working years, peaking during high-earning middle age, and falling during retirement. To the basic life-cycle story is added the idea that households also take into account bequests that they leave to their heirs. So, as the members of the post-war generation in Japan matured, they saved more for their own retirement and to pass onto their children. That basically explains the high saving rate in Japan.[19]

This reasoning also gives rise to the hope that the savings gap will narrow in the future as Japan's population ages. Life-cycle analysis would predict that saving rates in Japan would fall and, therefore, the current account surplus may shrink.[20] However, there are reasons to believe that the turnaround may not be as severe as predicted. The recent sharp fall in asset prices, increases in the consumption tax, and increasing life expectancy could mean that Japanese saving rates may not fall so quickly in the coming decades. In any case, the main point is that it is these sorts of issues—demographics, tax policy, and the like—that are of primary importance when analyzing Japan's record of overall current account surpluses and the U.S. deficits. Stories of corporate espionage and government plots are not needed.

Conclusion

Once again, the dismal science disappoints the thrill seekers. In this particular story, the contention that Japan is outmaneuvering the United States in Southeast Asia is deflated by tried and true economic principles, such as comparative advantage and the savings-investment-current account identity. Yes, it is true that Japan is running large trade surpluses with the United States and East Asia. Yes, foreign direct investment is flowing from Japan into East Asia. And, yes, Japan continues to run large overall current account surpluses. However, all of these phenomena can be largely explained by standard economics models, without the need for more intriguing conspiracy theories. The economist's conclusion when looking at Japan's supposed "Southeast Asia connection" is boring, unexciting, perhaps disappointing, but ultimately true.

Notes

1. Walter Hatch and Kozo Yamamura, *Asia in Japan's Embrace: Building a Regional Production Alliance* (Cambridge: Cambridge University Press, 1996), 176.
2. Dennis J. Encarnation, *Rivals Beyond Trade: America versus Japan in Global Competition* (Ithaca, NY: Cornell University Press, 1995), 65.
3. Hatch and Yamamura, *Asia in Japan's Embrace*, 52, when discussing the results of economist Jeffrey Frankel remark, "The model... is able to produce sheet after sheet of statistical data about the impact on trade of different variables. But, in the end, it offers only [a] rather unsurprising and unrevealing conclusion. ..." ("Is Japan Creating a Yen Bloc in East Asia and the Pacific?," in *Regionalism and Rivalry: Japan and the United States in Pacific Asia*, ed. Jeffrey A. Frankel and Miles Kahler (Chicago, IL: University of Chicago Press, 1993). The quote nicely makes the point that sometimes the truth can be disappointingly unsurprising.
4. East Asian countries include Taiwan, South Korea, Singapore, Hong Kong, China, Thailand, Malaysia, Indonesia, and the Philippines.
5. F-tests reject the null hypothesis that the addition of the regional dummy variables adds nothing to the regressions. In other words, even taking into account the information conveyed by the standard gravity variables, the regional dummies are still important.
6. This section draws heavily on James Riedel, "Capital Market Integration in Developing Asia," in *The World Economy* (forthcoming, 1997).
7. United Nations, *World Investment Report 1994: Transnational Corporations, Employment, and the Workplace* (New York: United Nations, 1994), 41.
8. *Ibid.*, 68. The figures on FDI in China are inflated by some unknown amount due to "round-tripping" investment, in which investment capital which originates in China flows to Hong Kong and then re-enters China as foreign direct investment in order to take advantage of the favorable tax treatment and other preferences which are given to foreign investment.
9. The *caveat* in the previous footnote applies here as well.
10. R. Brecher and Carl Diaz-Alejandro, "Tariffs, Foreign Capital and Immiserizing Growth," *Journal of International Economics* 7 (1977): 317–322.
11. Maxwell Fry, *Foreign Direct Investment in Southeast Asia* (Singapore: ASEAN Economic Research Unit, Institute of Southeast Asia, 1993), 57
12. Mohamed Ariff and Tho, 1994
13. *Ibid.*
14. Yun-Wing Sung, 1994.
15. While the accounting identities are clear, it is important to realize that any causal chain linking saving-investment with the current account requires a macroeconomic model.
16. Some economists (Dekle and Summers) find that Japanese net national

savings is 15 to 30 percentage points higher than that of the United States, while others (Hayashi) report that the gap is only 10 to 15 percentage points. See Robert Dekle and Lawrence Summers, "Japan's High Saving Rate Reaffirmed," *Bank of Japan Monetary and Economic Studies* 9 (1991); and Fumio Hayashi, "Explaining Japan's Saving: A Review of Recent Literature," *Bank of Japan Monetary and Economic Studies* 10, no. 2 (1992).

17. Bela Balassa and Marcus Noland, *Japan and the World Economy* (Washington, DC: Institute for International Economics, 1988).

18. Of course, public savings is the other part of the story. The emergence of large fiscal deficits in the United States, particularly since the 1980s, has been an important drain on U.S. savings. At the same time, public savings was instrumental in increasing total Japanese savings in the 1980s—a time when private savings was declining. We refrain from elaborating further in this section of the paper on the role of fiscal policy, since this would only serve to reinforce our point that macroeconomic factors drive the overall external balances in Japan and the United States.

19. Other significant factors include the Japanese bonus system, tax incentives, high housing and land prices, the Social Security system, and cultural considerations.

20. Many of these studies are summarized by Charles Yuji Horioka, "Future Trends in Japan's Saving Rate and the Implications Thereof for Japan's External Imbalance," *Japan and the World Economy* 3, no. 4 (1992): 301–30. It is important to note that, even in the presence of a falling savings rate, the current account surplus may not shrink if investment also declines. Studies that try to take into account the evolution of both savings *and* investment as demographics and social policies change, generally find that Japan's current account surplus will decline (or become negative) around 2020; for example, Paul R. Masson and Ralph Tryon, "Macroeconomic Effects of Projected Population Aging in Industrial Countries," *IMF Staff Papers* 37, no. 3 (1990)

Chapter 7

The Structure of China's Changing Political Society After Deng Xiaoping: Its Paradoxical Dynamism

Satoshi Amako

China after Deng Xiaoping's Death

Confirmation of "the Post-Deng Xiaoping Era" Which Has AlreadyBegun

At the Fourth session of the Fourteenth Central Committee of the Communist Party of China (CPC) in Autumn 1994, it was declared that the central leadership was completed for transition to the third generation. In the following year, its Fifth session was to adopt a secret resolution deciding upon Jiang Zemin's guiding group which shall judge and decide without the older generation. This shows the beginning of the Post-Deng Xiaoping Era, which is the end of Deng's so-called cloister government. This government lasted since the first session of the Thirteenth Central Committee of the CPC in Autumn 1987 where it was decided that "Deng Xiaoping would decide all the important matters."

However, too much attention has been paid to Deng's lasting influence and the unpredictable political turmoil caused by his death because of his enormous presence. Nevertheless, the political leaders reacted as if Deng's death was on their schedule and, since February 19, 1997, the very day of Deng's death, have dealt with all national business indifferently. The National People's Congress, which began on March 1, was held in an orderly manner and did not make a great fuss over Deng's death.

When I visited Beijing on March 3, after a half year's absence, I felt the same atmosphere as I usually did. Beijing's peculiar atmosphere made by the people on the street and the crowds in the department stores and restaurants were also the same as usual. Even though it was still the middle of Deng's mourning period, there were no banners and ceremonies. What I did at last find were Deng-related books and photographs exhibited at the big bookstore. My Chinese friends welcomed me as usual and did not make any particular mention about Deng's death. These things made me forget about Deng's death and confirmed the fact that the Post-Deng Xiaoping Era has already started.

When comparing the formation of Hua Guofeng's leadership after Mao Zedong's death, the political circumstances after Deng's death are showing some differences, even though we can point out some similarities. After all, there is no explicit confrontation as that which occurred between Hua's faction and the Gang of Four and Deng's intention of returning to power.

Moreover, after Hua Guofeng took power, there was a serious struggle between the succession of Mao's line (i.e., placing priority on politics and continuation of the revolution), and the new line (i.e., emphasizing economic development and modernization). We cannot find this type of struggle at the moment of Deng's death. In addition, there is no evident rival to Jiang Zemin who can compare to the rivalry of Deng Xiaoping and Hua Guofeng. The most different factor is that Jiang Zemin has already been in power for eight years, unlike Hua Guofeng whose succession to Mao was realized just before Mao's death. These things can clearly explain the present political silence after Deng's death.

The Future of Jiang Zemin's Leadership

Then, can we predict that the same situation will last? I posed the following questions to several Chinese scholars: how does Deng's death impact Chinese society; and whether or not Jiang Zemin's leadership can sustain stability? They all answered (with one exception), that, first, Deng's death was taken into account even before his actual passing away. Second, political decisionmaking, excluding Deng had already been implemented. And, lastly, people pretended that nothing had happened. Only one young scholar, belonging to the Chinese Academy of Social Sciences, answered differently. According to him, the presence of Deng was enormous, while Jiang Zemin's political attitude sometimes swings between conservative and liberal. Therefore, we need to carefully look at the political situation at certain occasions, such as the retrocession of Hong Kong in July 1997, the Fifteenth session of the Central Committee of the CPC in October and the National People's Congress next year in order to judge the political stability.

I also agree that the performance of Jiang Zemin continues to be the "hot issue," even if the post-Deng political mechanism has already been set in motion. There would be three reasons to assert this: first, it is extremely difficult to conclude that Jiang's real political authority has already been built up; second, there would be a possible friction or crack within the CPC if he fails to deal with the personnel policy of the center of the CPC before the Central Committee; and, lastly, his leadership is challenged by contradictions caused by the policy of openness, such as corruption.

Jiang will probably continue to be in his present post until the Sixteenth Party Representative Congress in 2002, especially if he successfully overcomes such important events. However, in case he fails, no one can deny the possibility that he might have to step down before that.

The most important point in this future scenario is whether or not the new mechanism of changing the political leader—like an election among the members of the Political Bureau or the Central Committee—will be set up or if the obscene and secret political struggles which we have seen for years will continue. In the former case, not only the political stability but also the democratization of Chinese politics will be achieved. However, in the latter case, some degree of instability, including the development of leaders and democratization activists behind the scene, cannot be avoided.

National People's Congress with more Openness and Transparency

Even though, according to Chinese Constitutional Law, the National People's Congress (NPC) is the highest authority of power, it has been criticized as being nominal and nothing more than a rubber stamp. However, in this last decade, notably since Qiao Shi took the post of Chairman of the Standing Committee in 1993, the function of the NPC has been strengthened year-by-year. The last session was the most remarkable one because there were many "criticizing votes" against some draft bills.

The reports of activities of the Supreme People's Court and the Supreme People's Procuratorate were criticized the most. There were 431 votes and 331 abstentions (32.4 percent) against the former one with 1839 votes for it. For the latter one, there were 675 cons and 390 abstentions (40.4 percent) with 1621 pros. Among thirteen draft bills in total, more than 10 percent of the votes were against the four drafts. This indicates that even the members of the CPC, that is 68.4 percent of the total members of the Eighth session of the NPC, voted against. This is the most striking evidence of the dramatic increase in independent voting of the members and the strengthened NPC itself. According to the March 21, 1997, issue of *The Yomiuri Shimbun*, the correspondent in Beijing emphasized this as the biggest change in Chinese society in the last ten years.

It is also pointed out that the debates around each agenda recently became more substantial. One delegate from Fujian Province (former president of the Fujian Department Store) told the *People's Daily*,[1] that he realized the proceedings at the NPC could give a strong impression, judging from his experience at the NPC these last ten years. He also said that the number of people visiting the members of the NPC before the session were increasing and greater emphasis was being placed on the comments and proposals made by the delegates from the provinces with serious management and with appropriate feedback. Moreover, the meetings of the NPC were mostly reported by TV and newspapers.

Society and Provinces Becoming Independent from State and Center

Here, I would like to define State as the political power legitimized by some means for representing the people and the Center as the collective sense of political organizations composing the center of State power, such as the center of the CPC, the State Council, the Standing Committee of the NPC, and the Central Military Commission. In Mao's days, the CPC maintained its legitimacy by victory of the revolution and the overwhelming triumph of the people's independence, unification and liberalization. On this basis, the CPC almost perfectly equated the State itself. As a result, the State can be said to be deeply rooted, similar to the Cultural Revolution which affected many people, to the best, historically, of Chinese Society.

In Deng's era, the legitimacy of power was maintained by the improvement of the quality of life of the people suffering from poverty and the promise to high ranked officials of the restoration of confidence and self-respect through the realization of modernization. Moreover, he tried to reorganize State-Society relations and Center-Province relations by improving their competence and by giving incentives to the Society and to the Provinces which at that time had lost their independence and vitality. Needless to say, it caused new contradictions. But it is widely believed that such reorganization basically went well until the Tiananmen incident in 1989.

In the 1990s and especially after Deng's speech in 1992, however, Provinces and Society began to act within their own sphere occasionally neglecting the guidance and provisions made by Center and State. In some exaggerated way of expression, the general public started to live based on their own power and networking with the sense that it had nothing to do with Center and State.

It has been said that since the mid-1980s where there is a policy measure at the Center there is a countermeasure at the Province. I would like to explain this experience in due course.

The Structure of Changing a Politico-Economical Society: Its Paradoxical or Reactive Dynamism

Looking at the situation from a different perspective, the above direct observations are the basic factors composing the total picture of Chinese society which is now changing. How do we understand them? One might argue that, even though the maintenance of the dictatorial rule of the CPC has ensured political stability through the centralization of power, politics became democratized, pluralized and decentralized and the social order has become seriously damaged in actuality. Or, even though campaigns for cleaner politics and ethical leaders as well as the "Discuss the Politics" Campaign since 1995 which Jiang Zemin himself emphasized, have been organized, people are escaping from politics which has been polluted by corruption. Moreover, even though the necessity to observe the laws and procedures are urged, in reality, the law is sometimes neglected and the personal connection is now playing a big role.

These phenomena show paradoxical or reactive consequences. Moreover, paradoxically, such negative effects appear to be the driving force making the Chinese society more vitalized and developed. Here, I would like to analyze China's politico-economical changes by using the way of thinking resulting from this paradoxical or reactive dynamism.

Attempts by CPC's Dictatorial Ruling, the Enhanced Political Pluralistic Situation and Democratization

If I am questioned as to what the results of the Tiananmen incident mean, the answer would be that it was the turning point of the Deng-led modernization policy from the Western way to the Asian way. In other words, linkages between economic and political reform were abandoned and precedent was given to political stability and development in order to maintain economic reform.

Until now, the political squeeze is continuing with denying the political pluralism and placing emphasis on strengthening CPC's rule. Nevertheless, some examples show that substantial democratization is continuing. One is the change in the NPC which I mentioned above. A substantial number of the members of the CPC criticized the basic report made by the CPC and delegates of the NPC are beginning to represent and benefit each region. These things can be recognized as political diversity.

Another example is that the democratic election system by the farmers to elect the leaders of each village is spreading nationwide.[2] Whether it continues to go well or not is of greater importance than the case of the NPC when we think about the future of democratization in China.

The distinctive characteristic of the bottom level election is that it is regarded as a free election by the farmers in many areas, even though the position is taken that it is still under the CPC's guidance. Candidates, both self-nominated or nominated by others, who want to become the leader of the village are selected beforehand. And the new leaders are elected by the Village Congress in which all the villagers participate by secret ballot.

According to the Deputy Director of the Department for Bottom Level Government Construction of the Ministry of Civil Affairs, 50 percent to 60 percent of all the farming villages had done this bottom level election very or fairly well by the end of 1996. The remaining 40 percent was insufficient to determine. He also wants to complete the election under this scheme by 2000. Since 1991, I have been researching this bottom level election procedure and pursued research in six villages in 1996. In addition, I have continuously exchanged views with the person in charge of the Ministry. Judging from my overall impression, this bottom level election concept is rapidly spreading.

This so-called "Villager autonomy" comprised by such bottom level elections and the daily political life managed by the leaders elected in this manner are stimulating the restructuring of the relations between the farmers and the leaders and the formation of the leaders representing the farmer's benefit. Therefore, when researching the political consciousness, the behavior and the division of role and function between the top and the bottom of such bottom level leaders who stand between the party and the people is quite important in order to see the change of State and Society in the farming villages.

Here I would like to introduce the results of the research at the village near Chengdu and Chongqing cities in September 1996.

I emphasized the following points during the interviews. First, how were the preliminary candidates for the Chairman and the Member of the Committee of the village decided and what procedures were taken to select the final candidates from them. Second, what were the procedures of the election. Third, what was the structure of the Election Guidance Team and the role of the CPC member in the Team. Fourth, what were the concrete results of the election, e.g., who won the election with how many votes and who lost.

In sum, the local elections at the farming villages and the activity of the Committee of Villagers have developed dramatically in the last four years. According to the results of this research and the interviews with the officers of the Ministry of Civil Affairs, it may be safe to conclude that the more sophisticated process is rapidly spreading, while the policy speech by the candidates and the secret vote could only be found at a limited number of villages. The process and the content of the election also became substantial and it was not common for the CPC to intervene in the process of selecting the candidates.

For example, the Election Guidance Team, in which the CPC is directly involved, is comprised of the leaders of each village and the representatives of the Villagers Small Group. Moreover, the central role of this Team is to form the scheme for enhancing this election system and the selection process itself was not the purpose of the Team. At the election of the Chairman of one village, one leader, having knowledge of agricultural scientific techniques, won with 1400 to 1200 votes against the high ranked security officer (both were in their early 30s). It may well reflect the reality of the present situation of farming villages because economics won over politics.

The biggest reason why this bottom level election is being given more attention by the people and the election itself is starting to have substantial meaning is that the formation of the bottom level government has come to affect the interest of the farmers. This came about because of the enhancement of the market economy and their pluralized interest and behavior. If this pattern of formation of local government through elections becomes anchored in the Chinese society, it may be said that substantial democratization of the farming villages is occurring while guidance from the CPC and the Center is being emphasized.

Emphasis on Centralization and Spreading Decentralization

The "Releasing Rights and Transferring Interests" (*fang quan rang li*) policy led by Deng Xiaoping tried to revitalize the local economy and to urge overall economic development by giving responsibility to the local government. It played an important role in getting the openness policy on track. At the same time, center-local relations became a big issue because the presence of the local authority expanded. Now, this issue seems to have become much bigger than before the time of the post-Deng transitional period.

We cannot neglect the fact of an increased presence by local authority and the tension and contradiction between the center and local at the time of the changing pattern of political decisionmaking from the leadership of one strong figure to group-led policy management. I would like to introduce some new situations along with the results of the research at Xiamen, Hangzhou and Shanghai in March 1997.

Firstly, the Separate Taxation System employed in 1994, on the one hand, brought an increase in tax revenue to the central government. But, on the other hand, the local governments, especially those of the eastern coastal area, became frustrated because they had to pay more taxes to the center. They were also frustrated because the central government has the power to decide the amount of the local tax by asserting the macro-control through fiscal policy. Here local resistance against the center is growing. Among others, there are many attempts to increase revenue from outside the budget which is included in the local finance. I will come back to this point later because this is the conflict between "the measure" and "the situation."

Secondly, while, in order to maintain their authority and control, the central government wants to maintain its competence of personnel policy vis-à-vis the local authority, there is an apparent resistance from the local side against such decisions being made by the center. The decision about the personnel of the top ranked official of the local government was the sanctuary of the central government for years with no resistance. However, in recent years, the number of cases where the Provincial People's Congress has refused the Governor or the candidate of the leader of the Provincial Congress nominated by the central government and have elected a locally nominated candidate has increased. Moreover, even with the CPC's personnel policy, local high ranked members are increasingly chosen to the post of Secretary and Deputy Secretary of the Provincial Committee.

Thirdly, under the Separate Taxation System, even though the eastern coastal area has to pay more taxes to the central government, they receive less subsidies because the central government has to give more to the mid-western landlocked areas. This has caused friction between the eastern coastal areas and the central government and, moreover with the mid-western area as well. Therefore, the central government has had to give consideration to the eastern coastal areas by means other than subsidies. Choosing local top ranked officials to the central government and the affirmative action on investment are some examples. This would eventually cause criticism of inequality in the eastern coastal areas which may lead to an increase in friction and contradiction of the center-local relations and coastal-landlocked areas relations.

Fourthly, as a matter of fact, it can be found that local authorities are employing their own policies and, thereby, neglecting the regulations issued by the central government. It is officially maintained that, regarding the wholesaler of foreign capital, only two stores each in eleven cities open for foreign investments can be authorized. In reality, it is said that more than 400 stores have been authorized by the local level. The local governments assert that they are granting these authorizations in accordance with the Detailed Regulations of the Foreign Capital Enterprise Law. This law states that the local government can authorize, without permission of the State Council, the enterprise in cases where the total investment is less than $30 million. On the other hand, the central government argues that the local governments are issuing the authorizations without permission, though the case of the wholesaler is needed to do it. These actions by the local governments can also be seen in the rush of "construction of areas for development" in 1992 and in the immovable property trade boom in Shanghai and Guangdong in 1993.

When I raised this behavior of the local government that, in fact, it seems that they act on their own, one scholar in Hangzhou replied that this is a false obedience (*yang feng yin wei*). It seems to be an undeniable fact that the intention of the central government cannot be spread perfectly to the local level.

Emphasis on Political Idea and Depoliticization, "De-ideology" and Spreading Corruption

On September 27, 1995, just after the Fourteenth session of the Central Committee, Jiang Zemin made an important speech that "leaders should discuss politics" at the Convectors' Meeting of the Fifth plenum of the CPC Central Committee. In addition, more emphasis should be placed on political ideas which occasionally have been some consideration since the beginning of the era of reformation and openness.[3] After that *Qiushi* (Seeking Truth) on March 3, 1996, reported Jiang's "About Discussing Politics." It was reprinted in the *People's Daily* of July 1, 1996. Also, at the occasion of visiting the office of the *People's Daily*, he emphasized that leaders must "equip, lead and inspire" by utilizing the best things and personalities available and must also "strengthen the political idea."

His assertion and active campaign tried to place politics at the front against the atmosphere of depoliticization and "de-ideology" which could lead to decentralization and de-CPC through urging the highest unity with CPC to vigorously capture the local society.

Moreover, after the Tiananmen incident, they placed greater emphasis on the patriotic education movement. For example, in August 1994, the Propaganda Department of the CPC published the General Principle for Patriotism Campaign and called for its implementation. With the collapse of the USSR and East European socialist regimes, communist ideology was weakened. Patriotism was pursued as an alternative ideology. It is said that it brought forth the anti-foreign nationalistic emotion which can be seen in "China can say NO" by resonating with the issues from which people actually felt foreign pressure, like human rights, extension of the most favored nation clause, and the Senkaku islands.

An emphasis on the "Construction of Spiritual Civilization" has appeared through a process of "ideological tightening." It expresses an interest in and demand for an ethical and highly moralistic people and politics. This confronts the harsh reality of mammonism, an unjust economy, as well as the spreading collapse of an economy-centered policy. The mass media has launched a related campaign which urges people to learn from such models. This is one of the characteristics of Jiang Zemin's leadership. Importantly, at the Fourteenth session of the CPC, the "Resolution of Construction of Socialist Spiritual Civilization" was advocated and adopted as the concentration of such an advocate.

According to this Resolution, it points out their sense of crisis that : at some leading activities of some local provinces and field, people neglect the ideology education and spiritual civilization, ... [that] there can be found mammonism, epiculism and individualism in some level while morality lost its place, ... [that] political corruption caused the fall of CPC's authority and the change of political atmosphere, ... [and that] some lose their consciousness toward State and feel puzzlement toward the future of socialism. ... [Then, it emphasizes that] the patriotism, collectivism and socialism education will be broadly launched putting emphasis on study, politics and right and just attitude to serve to people, to make the socialism culture prosperous.[4]

However, despite such vigorous attempts, the numbers of crimes relating to power, such as political corruption, are increasing with no end in sight. According to the report of the Supreme People's Procuratorate submitted before the NPC, 56,491 cases in 1993 became 83,685 in 1995. While in 1996 the total number decreased to 82,356. Crimes committed by officials in positions higher than the prefectural office level have increased more than 10 percent compared with 1995.

The Jiang Zemin Government was gravely concerned with these facts and launched a series of anti-corruption campaigns in 1994 and 1995. In the course of this campaign, the structural corruption was disclosed in Beijing. Chen Xitong, then Secretary of the CPC Beijing Municipal Committee, and members of the Political Bureau of the Central Committee, were arrested and dismissed and the Vice Mayor committed suicide. However, as some opinion polls show, people are still frustrated with this corruption.

For example, according to the poll by Lingdian Co. in Beijing, Shanghai, Wuhan and Guangzhou, 33.2 percent think that the corruption in the CPC and social life is becoming worse and 22.4 percent think that it is not decreasing or is the same as before.[5] As I have pointed out already, many criticisms of the reports of the Supreme People's Court and the Supreme People's Procuratorate tell us that the local side is strongly criticizing the central government's reluctance to tackle this problem, or, in other words, to consider the seriousness of the situation.

Moreover, the tendency toward mammonism among the general public, such as non-licensed taxis or touters of souvenirs in the sightseeing area, could be felt at the time when I traveled in China during these years. Mr. Masaharu Hishida rightly observed as follows.

In the course of economic development, it is common that there appears the tendency of mammonism. In China, however, the situation is far beyond such level. It is the strong worship to mammonism that is the main reason of the Chinese illness such as the corruption of bureaucracy, drug, prostitution, slave trade and kidnapping of women.[6] These facts clearly show that, even the CPC and the Center vigorously advertise the importance of political and ideological education. People in the provinces and the general public are indifferent to these issues and political apathy and structural corruption are spreading.

The Rise of Legalism (Institutionalization) and Personal Rule (Situationalization)

Faced with so many problems caused by the excessive concentration and delegation of power in the Communist Party, Deng Xiaoping consistently advocated promoting legal rule and institutionalization after he assumed power. In fact, the level of institutionalization advanced significantly compared to the Mao Zedong period. Meetings for the Party, the People's Congress, the State Council and others all became regularized and decisions began to be made systematically through collective discussions. But there was some strong inclination on the part of Deng himself to make unilateral decisions without going through legal procedures when it came to major decisions. These instances of what may be called "personal rule" included such cases as the dismissals of two Party Secretaries, Hu Yaobang in 1987 and Zhao Ziyang in 1989, as well as the exercise of martial law and student crackdown by the military at the Tiananmen Incident. The decision to select Jiang Zemin as the successor to Zhao Ziyang in the wake of his fall was also made singlehandedly by Deng rather than through democratic discussions among the Party leadership.

Jiang Zemin had little Party experience in the central government. It would be fair to say that his prestige as the top leader was far from strong. As a result, Jiang made a conscious effort to stabilize a collective leadership system by further strengthening institutionalization while he relied on Deng's prestige once he assumed the top government position. Jiang proposed 10 major tasks in his "Political Report" at the Fourteenth Party Congress in 1992, amongst which was the objective to "greatly advance socialistic democracy and legal system."[7]

The most typical examples of personal rule can be found in the process of recruiting management level officials to which Party leaders of both central and provincial districts had exclusive prerogatives. But the situation changed in 1987 when Zhao Ziyang's "Political Report" set forth the introduction of the Public Official system which, after some trial period, resulted in the proclamation of the "Provisional Act of State Officials" in August 1993. This legislation provided a modern framework to recruit and appoint career bureaucrats by stipulating the types of offices, their job responsibilities, as well as the examination system.

Another important example of non-institutional rule can be found in the center-local relationship. While "the locals follow the center" would be a general rule, there existed a certain basic tendency which allowed more individual and situational responses to specific political and economic issues. In fact, it was this "Releasing Rights and Transferring Interests Policy" (local initiative), and a fiscal subcontracting system that proved to be one of the biggest factors that enabled a significant increase in local economic performance during the process of reform and openness. But this system was not without problems "of inequality among provinces of same conditions by reflecting the respective local government's bargaining power and the past performance, due all to the lack of subcontracting standards as well as their situational application." Moreover, it caused "local protectionism or redundant local constructions and others" because of "efforts by the local governments of different levels to pursue each of their own interests."[8]

It was in this context that the system of separate taxation was proposed in 1993 and then put into effect in 1994. Its purpose was to improve the situation by better institutionalizing central-local fiscal relations, and at the same time increasing the central fiscal revenues. The system was intended to separate the central tax (income tax of central government's own enterprises, tariffs, etc.), the local tax (income tax and business tax from local enterprises and individuals), and the common central and local tax (value added tax, resource tax and others). Administrative jurisdiction was also clarified. All in all, the situational relationship between central and local governments was considerably improved. Indeed, the introduction of the State Officials Act and the Separate Taxation System could be called a significant first step toward a more legalistic and institutional society.

What, then, were the actual results of these efforts at legalism and institutionalization? When the State Officials Act was enacted in 1993, the Party center and the State Council had put forward an idea of "establishing a fundamental public official system during roughly the next three years." But an article in the *Workers' Daily* three years later praised the system by saying "after the three years of implementation of the State Officials Act, the preliminary system of new recruitment in open, equal, competitive, and selective manners." But "in reality, the levels of its implementations differs at each local community or section. In some cases, certain frauds were reported. ... Therefore, the system was just set in motion toward its complete application."[9]

Other articles on the same subject published at almost the same time were more critical. They, for example, admitted that the examination system served an important role in recruiting promising people and promising a decline in fraud. They criticized that:

> the scope for competitive examination was so narrow that it was not yet well coordinated with other personnel system reform, and that the overall legal system for recruitment by examination was not a healthy one. Examinations were not scientifically made and many unjust attitudes were witnessed. ... After all, those who got high marks at examinations did not necessarily prove to be the best people.[10]

But if we look at this issue from a different perspective, we would wonder how much this institutionalization process, as represented by this public servant act, was actually penetrating into Chinese society. One article in *Qiushi* magazine which discussed "local protectionism," pointed out that "this recent tendency for protectionism never ceased to disappear. In reality, it is worsening." The author raised three factors in this regard. One was that both the examination and standards for recruiting Chinese officials were "unreasonable" because they were often based on simple short-term, numerical indicators and on nothing else. He summarized the issue by saying that "the numbers produce officials and officials produce numbers."[11]

Still other papers pointed out that while the development of a market economy did promote activities based on individual initiatives, they in turn encouraged the practice of making use of one's relatives, friends, and colleagues as an important system for engaging in economic activities. As a result, it warns that a similar sentiment of "brotherly sectionalism" is increasingly found in the appointment of senior officials.[12] This point is quite persuasive if we consider the strong personal relations which is generally considered a characteristic of Chinese society.

How, then, do we understand the actual implementation of a separate taxation system? According to an economist who responded to an interview conducted in Hangzhou in March 1997, the central government stresses the effectiveness of the Separate Taxation System. Indeed, central revenues went up and certain concentrations of power were achieved. But the local initiatives were adversely affected with a decline in tax revenues. Thus, local governments are not generally satisfied with this Separate Taxation System. In this regard, he said, local governments tend to evade or manipulate the tax system. Examples include the increase in a local agency's rather arbitrary charges of various fees, such as road repair fees, road/bridge tolls, inspection fees, education fees, waterway construction fees, etc.

It is often reported that the local governments do keep an equivalent amount of outside-of-the-budget revenue as that of budgeted revenue. But what is intriguing is the fact that even this outside-of-the-budget revenue may be divided into "open" and "closed" revenues (or it may be called "budget-outside-of-the-budget"), and that the latter's rise is significant in the wake of the introduction of the Separate Taxation System.

The Separate Taxation System was originally intended to resolve major tendencies of the so-called "three abuses" (i.e., abusive charges, abusive donations, and abusive fines), by replacing them with various kinds of newly enacted taxes, and to help organize and discipline overall fiscal situations which had been a perennial issue of central-local relations. But local governments maintain the view that "taxes" and "fees" are different, and protest that collecting "fees" has nothing to do with levying taxes. Thus, the people are obliged to pay an additional burden of various fees on top of taxes. It would indeed be paradoxical that through the introduction of the Separate Taxation System, which was aimed at fair taxation, as well as the legalization and institutionalization of center-local relations, one see's, in fact, an increase in the people's burden and a further situationalization through even more abusive fees.

Why the Paradox or the Reaction?

I have been trying to present an overview on the changing Chinese social phenomena by using "paradox" or "reaction" as key words for analysis. In fact, some social phenomena can emerge as a paradox or a reaction rather than an exception. We often witness or experience a "loss" when we seek to "win" the game or we end up "hating" each other even when we intend to "love" someone. Why then do these paradoxical phenomena occur?

What we first need to realize is the fact that there are generally two sides to a situation. The concept of goodness, for example, makes sense only when we have the concept of evil. The same can be said for the concepts of freedom and oppression. But at the same time, as it is easy to realize, one's good deed or an action to seek freedom does not necessarily achieve goodness or freedom. In this way, it may be considered as a natural phenomenon to witness the paradox of dictatorship enhancing freedom and institutionalization promoting situationalization.

Secondly, it should be pointed out that all the paradoxical phenomena share one common feature, i.e., the existence of a strong sense of objectives or orientations. Is it not considered a paradoxical phenomenon that those people who called for "true freedom" and "true liberalization" through the Marxist movement gave birth to a huge totalitarian dictatorship in our history?

Thirdly, when we look at these processes of generating paradoxes or reactions from the viewpoint of causality, we would explain that one's purposeful behavior under conditions in which such a purpose would prove to be quite difficult to achieve, can end up in a paradox or reaction of bringing about unwanted or unintended results. An expression like "things backfired" suggests this type of dilemma. The opposite to this is an expression like "smooth sailing." But it is fundamentally difficult to be objective about one's conditions because these include both structural/institutional and situational/spontaneous factors, while it always leaves a dynamic situation in which basic conditions can change in the entire process.

Why can we see so much paradoxical or reactive phenomena in today's changing Chinese society? First, one can say that the overall trend of reform and openness has liberalized people's materialistic desires, which drives the energetic economic activities. And this has now sufficiently accelerated so as to form a major trend in China. People are rushing to pursue a richer and more affluent life style. One extreme case of this trend was the rise of "money mongarism." These and other behaviors have strengthened their wills or decisions to create more plural values and behavior patterns in society.

Second, looking at this trend from the regime's side, it represents a decline of prestige of the central/state government and the eventual weakening of the Communist Party's centripetal force that was their organizational core. The general lack of charismatic leaders after Deng Xiaoping has accelerated this phenomenon. Also to be noted is the fact that communism as a regime ideology brought forth the collapse of the communist myth (or conviction) first by its own efforts to deny the people's sense of political participation and, subsequently, by the collapse of the

Soviet Union and other East European socialist governments. These are the main currents started in the late 1970s as the result of the policy of reform and openness.

Third, in spite of this, however, the Chinese government has stuck to the reconstruction of communist governance and has attempted to strengthen communist ideology by mending the rip with patriotism and moral education. In other words, the biggest cause of paradox or reaction can be found in their inclination to use old purposes and old methods, rather than fully utilizing new materials, at the time of fundamental changes in their situation.

This would explain the general phenomena in which dictatorship promoted democratization, centralization of powers brought about decentralization, the emphasis of politics and ideology caused the departure from politics and ideology, and institutionalization facilitated situationalization. The triad situation, in which old ideas/methods, new ideas/methods, and chaotic situations all coexist, will remain to be seen. And a clear picture of a new political and economic system that can depict an entire China has yet to emerge.

Basic Stance and Trend of Present Foreign Policy of China

Domestic Constraints to Foreign Policy

Let us next consider the implications of these changes in the domestic situation for China's foreign policy and identify the character of foreign policy in the Jiang Zemin era. The trends of democratization, decentralization, departure from politics and ideology, and the process of situationalization, are all supposed to be incremental, and if they go forward with some levels of adjustment with other opposing concepts, they will not greatly disrupt social stability. We can see that at present political and social trends are still within this range, namely, a relatively stable situation with some structural causes of instability.

Generally speaking, those paradoxical or reactive changes in the domestic situation could present an environment that makes the country's foreign policy more accommodating and moderate. But on the contrary, if the Chinese authority, which is aimed at maintaining the dictatorial regime and centralization as well as stressing the role of politics and ideology, should try to counter this paradox or reaction by using foreign policy to constrain domestic society, it is quite likely that attitudes toward foreign policy might harden. But, judging from the overall situation, it is not likely that domestic changes will directly influence foreign policy.

Having stated that, with the death of Deng Xiaoping, Jiang Zemin's regime may opt to place greater priority on the domestic situation rather than foreign policies due mainly to his not fully controlling internal political affairs. More specifically, the successful management of the Hong Kong reversion of July 1997 and the Fifteenth Party Congress are two key events. As to the former, China needs to proceed with the already set schedules of reversion without any significant chaos and to smoothly implement the "one nation, two systems" by maintaining Hong Kong's economic prosperity and political freedom. It is for this reason that China will try to avoid any situation that makes the Hong Kong issue sensitive from the foreign countries' viewpoint.

The latter will be most concerned with the handling of personnel matters in the central leadership. If China's relationship with the United States becomes tense over human rights or Taiwan issues, that might have a subtle affect on personnel changes. What is likely to occur, therefore, is that China will implement policies that will avoid friction in their dealings with foreign affairs. Thus, a more accommodating foreign policy and promotion of a peaceful environment will ensue.

Of course, China will maintain its foreign policy based on the strict sense of national interest and principle of non-interference in internal affairs. It may well make its policy even more clear as to its position of "joint development by shelving territorial issues" in relation to the disputes over maritime resources. Even on human rights issues, China has now shown more flexibility in engaging in dialogues as was seen during the visits of U.S. Vice President Al Gore and Japan's Foreign Minister Yukihiko Ikeda.[13] The most sensitive issue that needs the highest attention is the situation of Taiwan. Competition and friction between China and Taiwan are continuing over diplomatic relations with Latin American and South African countries, Taiwan's approach to North Korea, the Dalai Lama's visit to Taiwan, and others.

Probably what China wants least is the intervention of the West, particularly that of the United States, in all of these issues. We cannot disregard the question of Japan's direct and indirect involvement in the Taiwan problem. When Jiang Zemin visited Moscow in April 1997, the two governments clearly emphasized their "strategic partnership." This is not directed against Japan and the United States. But still it is thought to have the meaning of increasing the "cards in the game" that would restrain these two countries, particularly the U.S. If we summarize China's basic stance with respect to its foreign policy, based on these assumptions, it would be characterized by "the cooperation with the U.S. as the key pillar, coupled with the Sino-Japan friendship and good neighbor cooperation."

Actual Diplomatic Practices in the Post-Deng Era

It is only a few months since the death of Deng Xiaoping. But even during this short period of time, there have emerged several significant instances that can be useful in analyzing the future of China's foreign policy. Here, let us discuss the following four areas—namely, (i) the handling of North Korea's former Party Secretary, Hwang Jang Yop; recent situations of (ii) Sino-U.S. relations; (iii) Sino-Japan relations; and (iv) Taiwan. First, on Mr. Hwang's defection, China very carefully considered the North Korean situation, but still maintained the basic "China-Republic of Korea Cooperation." China still made conscious efforts to calmly resolve this matter by showing a willingness to cooperate with the U.S. Central Intelligence Agency (CIA) that had requested an investigation in Beijing. In other words, China did not take the attitude of employing Hwang as a diplomatic card in order to gain something from the U.S.

The main implication that can be found here is China's own inclination of staying out of chaotic issues of international society, and of resolving the matter, if it is involved, quickly and in a peaceful manner. It is also intended that China should appeal to the international community as a government actively supporting stabilization, rather than as a destabilizing force that has been reflected in the so-called "China threat" theory. China was also successful in demonstrating positive and cooperative relations with the Association of Southeast Asian Nations (ASEAN), especially the Philippines, with whom they have tense relations over territorial issues in the South China Sea, by choosing Manila as the destination for Hwang's departure.

Regarding the Sino-U.S. relations, encouraged by President Bill Clinton's message just after the death of Deng which stressed the necessity of strengthening bilateral relations, Beijing welcomed Secretary of State Madeleine Albright in late February as originally scheduled, and in March, accepted visits by Vice President Gore and House Speaker Newt Gingrich. The trend of improving their bilateral relations which began in the summer of the previous year continues. It may well be understood that it is China's desire not to ruin this momentum which could jeopardize the process of

Jiang Zemin's visit to Washington after the Fifteenth Party Congress in the autumn which is to be followed by President Clinton's visit to Beijing in the following year. In this regard, it is highly likely that bilateral Sino-U.S. relations will develop smoothly. China is placing a high priority on efforts to improve "Sino-U.S. cooperation." Though it was not really noticed, China did not loudly criticize Taiwan's active deployment of a large number of F-16 jet fighters from the U.S. It is remarkable for China to show this kind of restraint because China refrained from taking any concrete action against the U.S. when Washington and Taipei reached a contract in 1992 by saying that it would wait until the time of actual deployment. Furthermore, China has shown some willingness to talk on human rights issues.

Today the U.S. approach to China is basically a friendly one. But there are voices which still argue the theories of the "China threat" and "China as Evil Empire." The U.S. Congress is often very critical about such issues as "Taiwan, Tibet, Hong Kong, and human rights." House Speaker Gingrich traveled to Taiwan on his way back from Beijing and declared that the U.S. would defend Taiwan if it was attacked. But the U.S. administration showed a sense of frustration with this remark and were sympathetic to China. As we discuss later, the main point in this connection is what kind of action Taiwan will actually take.

If we turn our attention to Sino-Japan relations, the biggest issue was related to the visit of Foreign Minister Ikeda. One Japanese Foreign Ministry source was quoted as saying that the talk was conducted in a "surprisingly much more soft mood than had been expected."[14] And nothing is more representative of China's attitude than this atmosphere. During his visit, Ikeda reported to China that the freeze of grant assistance that Japan had decided upon in the wake of Chinese nuclear testing would be lifted soon. In addition, he promised mutual visits by Premier Li Peng and Prime Minister Hashimoto this year to commemorate the twenty-fifth anniversary of normalization between the two governments, and the state visit of Jiang Zemin to Tokyo on the occasion of next year's twentieth anniversary of the Japan-China Treaty of Peace and Friendship.

China's economy is developing rather smoothly as reflected in the total of over $60 billion of two-way trade relations between Japan and China. But when it comes to political matters, Sino-Japan relations deteriorated to "the worst relationship" since the normalization. It was caused by suspension of the Yen loan, the U.S.-Japan Security Joint Declaration, Prime Minister Hashimoto's prayer, and the question over the Senkaku islands. But what would be more troubling in the longer term is the mutual negative image between two people. According to a national opinion poll by the Prime Minister's Office in February 1997 which released the result of the "opinion poll on foreign affairs," for the first time, a little over 50 percent answered that Japan's relation with China today is "not so favorable." In an interview by *China Youth News*, Japan is ranked at the top as "a country you dislike the most." Moreover, the current heated discussion on "history recognition" may have its value, but China and Korea would strongly warn against the "revival of Japan's militarism."

Amongst these issues, what would prove to be the most sensitive one for China must be the Taiwan issue. Since the Taiwan Presidential election in Spring 1996, China has strengthened its hard and soft approaches of containment and engagement toward Taiwan. Some examples of this enhanced international containment would include, (i) China's approach to the Republic of South Africa which made it possible to establish diplomatic relations with the condition of securing the latter's Consulate General in Hong Kong after reversion at the expense of their long and friendly diplomatic relationship with Taiwan, and (ii) the dispatching of Foreign Minister Qian Qichen to Latin American countries in the latter half of 1996, where Taiwan maintains its largest pool of diplomatic relations, in order to undermine Taiwan's international base.

Still other examples can be found in such instances as, (iii) China's complaint about Democratic Party Chief Yukio Hatoyama's participation in an academic meeting on Japan, China, and Taiwan relations in Japan to restrain younger Japanese Diet members from approaching Taiwan, and (iv) the recent allegations of political monies being contributed to President Clinton's election campaign, in which the Chinese Embassy was reportedly involved, can be interpreted as Beijing's ploy to negate the influence of the Taiwan lobby in the United States. In this way, China has made steady efforts to "contain" the expansion of Taiwan's international space.

Parallel to these efforts are the movements to engage Taiwan which include (i) the enhancement of China-Taiwan exchanges. In 1996, the number of people visiting the mainland from Taiwan marked over 1.57 million which was the highest since the lifting of the ban against the Taiwanese visits to their Chinese relatives in 1987; (ii) Overall China-Taiwan trade has expanded considerably to reach $19 billion (9.4 percent increase from the previous year). Indeed, China-Taiwan trade has entered a new stage as represented by the inauguration of the direct service of regular freighters between China and Taiwan, though the vessels used are still limited to those of third-world countries; and, furthermore, (iii) on March 31, while China reaffirmed its position to unify Taiwan based on the

"8 point proposal of Jiang Zemin" of January 1995, it also made clear to Foreign Minister Ikeda that China would be willing to "prepare a China's Vice Chairman's position to the Taiwan President in the wake of unification" and to "maintain Taiwan's military without sending Chinese forces to Taiwan."

In spite of these steps, instability surrounding the Taiwan issue will not be solved soon. First, Taiwan's inclination to independence is steadily increasing. For example, Taiwan decided to "abolish Taiwan Province" in December 1996 at the occasion of the bipartisan National Development Congress which included opposition parties like the Democratic Progressive Party (DPP). Even though the decision was later "frozen" in view of the political situation, it still reflected the will to advance the Taiwanization of the Republic of China. In addition to this, according to an opinion poll in Taiwan which was released in February this year, support of the DPP surpassed that of the ruling Kuomintang (KMT) to the top. Hsü Hsin-liang, Chairman of DPP, stressed that people were beginning to accept moderate "self-reliance of Taiwan," but these remarks will necessarily concern China.[15]

On the foreign policy side, Taiwan has demonstrated a "roll over diplomacy" against the above mentioned Chinese move for "containment." In December 1996, Foreign Minister Chang Hsiao-yen visited South Africa to maintain substantial relations and then went to Latin American countries to strengthen their ties. Taiwan received the Dalai Lama in 1997. Even the contract between Taiwan and North Korea regarding the disposal of low level nuclear waste in January 1997 can be interpreted as counter to Chinese diplomacy.

If the tension between China and Taiwan should rise again, coupled with the destabilization of the situation due to the "failures" of personnel affairs or policies on the part of China, there is always a possibility of the rise of a "hard-line course" against Taiwan. Success or failure of Hong Kong after reversion would subtly influence the future of China-Taiwan relations. In view of these possibilities, U.S. House Speaker Gingrich repeatedly said that the U.S. would defend Taiwan if it was attacked militarily and that the U.S. would not be silent about human rights issues, all to restrain China's option to attack Taiwan.

In any event, the most sensitive issues in the immediate future would be (i) the internal "establishment of Jiang Zemin's leadership system," based on the personnel matter, at the Fifteenth Party Congress, and (ii) foreign policy issues, such as coping with Taiwan's active diplomacy to shake China through tensions and negotiations, and with the United States which considers Taiwan as the major issue while linking it to such issues as human rights, China's entry to the World Trade Organization (WTO) and trade friction.

Notes

1. *People's Daily*, 14 March 1997.
2. cf. *The Asahi Shimbun* (Tokyo), 15 April 1997; which reported on democratization in the agricultural areas in China.
3. *People's Daily*, 17 January 1996.
4. *People's Daily*, 14 October 1996.
5. *She Hui Lan Pi Shu 1996–7* (Bluebook on Society), ed. Jiang Liu, Lu Xue Yi (Beijing: Zhong Guo She Hui Kexue Chu Ban She, 1997), 85.
6. *Chu Go Ku wa Kyoi Ka?* (Is China a Threat?), ed. Satoshi Amako (Tokyo: Kei So Sho Bo, 1997).
7. *Chugoku Nenkan* (China Yearbook), (Tokyo: Tai Shu Kan, 1993), 215.
8. Takahara Akio, "Chugoku no Zaisei Seido to Chuo-Chiho Kankei," in *Ajia Shokoku no Chiho Seido* (Tokyo: Institute of Local Government, 1995), 122.
9. *Zhong Quo Zheng Zhi* (China Politics), 9th Period (Beijing: China People's University Press, 1996), 100.
10. *Ibid.*, 101–102.
11. *Ibid.*, 10th period, (1996), 34, 40.
12. *Ibid.*, 92.
13. *Asahi Shimbun*, 31 March 1997.
14. *Ibid.*
15. *Asahi Shimbun*, 29 March 1997.

Chapter 8

The United States, Japan, and Post-Deng China: A Contextual Approach

H. Lyman Miller

In the United States today, there is perhaps greater dissension over policy toward China than at any time since the late 1940s. In that period, a Democratic Truman administration and a Republican Congress contended over what approach to pursue toward a crumbling Kuomintang (KMT) regime led by Chiang Kai-shek that retained the sympathy of the American public, and toward a rising revolutionary communist regime under Mao Zedong. Contention over China policy took place in a larger setting of American uncertainty at facing the complications of establishing a postwar world order and the onset of the Cold War. Dissension over China policy was ultimately resolved with the beginning of the Korean War, bringing U.S. denial of recognition to the Beijing regime, the extension of containment to Asia, intervention in the Chinese civil war, and, soon thereafter, direct military conflict with Chinese forces.

Today, dissension over China policy is also waged in a setting of uncertainty. The end of the Cold War has brought ambiguous implications for the United States domestically and its role in a post-Cold War order.

The demise of the Soviet Union has left the United States in a position of relative primacy in the international system. But the United States does not dominate the international economy nor does it have the preponderant military strength to the degree that it did in the late 1940s. As in the late 1940s, dissension over China policy takes place now in the context of a Democratic Clinton administration and a Republican Congress. But divisions over China policy do not cleave neatly along party lines. Instead, divergent constituencies contend within each party and collude across party lines.

This complex setting has produced starkly divided American views of China and its approach to the international order. Some see China as a renegade power that presents a rising threat to international peace and stability. Beijing, on this view, seeks to establish hegemony over Asia that China supposedly enjoyed in its long past and is bent on transforming the broader international system to its own purposes.[1] Others see China as an increasingly system-affirming partner whose domestic transformation is bringing ever greater linkages to the international economy and political order. Beijing, in this view, is gradually accepting the perforations of a hard-won national sovereignty that interdependence brings in the contemporary international system.[2] Still others predict the collapse of the Beijing regime and the fragmentation of China into separate, probably warring regions, recapitulating the warlordism of the early Republican era, now with attendant international dangers of mass emigration, uncontrolled nuclear weapons, and ethnic conflict.[3]

These divergent American reckonings of China's international outlook and ambitions frequently rest on assessments of the undeniably impressive changes in China domestically in the past 20 years. But these assessments of China's domestic evolution and its import both for China internally and for Beijing's future approach to the broader international order are also contradictory. Specifically at issue is whether the Beijing regime has been strengthened or weakened by the reforms of the Deng era.

Some of those who see China as a rising threat trace what they see as China's assertive—even aggressive—posture in the 1990s to new-found national strength and confidence unleashed by the transforming reforms of the post-Mao era. Others attribute what they characterize as Beijing's truculent foreign policy behavior to domestic weakness. By this line of argument, the Beijing leadership can no longer contain the domestic tensions unleashed by the Deng era reforms. It therefore tries to mobilize Han nationalism and to deflect internal social tensions outward as a means of rallying allegiance to a declining and discredited regime and hanging on to power.

Those who see China as an emerging, essentially conservative, system-maintaining participant in the international system are similarly divided with respect to China's domestic scene. Some describe a domestic context that has been fundamentally internationalized by Deng's reforms, giving growing domestic constituencies in China an increasing stake in regional stability and a corresponding interest in accommodating international norms. Others argue that China's reforms have weakened the regime, confronting it with an intractable dilemma. Regime legitimacy now rests solely on the leadership's ability to deliver continued high rates of economic growth, but continued growth increasingly means that the regime must make previously unacceptable social and political changes that portend its own demise. Still others argue that Beijing's political fragility and weakness portends fragmentation, with altogether different implications for the region and international system. Deng's reforms have triggered central-provincial tensions that portend the breakup of China into separate political entities or chaos.

The premise that most of these assessments share, however divergent, is that China's domestic evolution has been and will remain the primary determinant of its posture toward the prevailing international order. The argument of this paper is just the opposite. As impressive as the changes in China's domestic scene have been and will probably continue to be, the most important factors in the evolution of China's international outlook have been external. They are, first, Beijing's assessment of the larger security context it faces—the global balance of power, the constellation of powers in the Asian region, and the military threats it perceives on its borders and off its shores—and second, its access to the international economy.

A contextual review of China's international outlook from this perspective shows that Beijing's foreign policy behavior has largely been reactive, not assertive, and cautious, not adventurist. In addition, the strategies by which Beijing has pursued national strength have been shaped and skewed most fundamentally by the realities of China's external context. These patterns remain valid today, and, granting the relative growth of Chinese national strength, they are nevertheless likely to remain so for the foreseeable future. The implication of this analysis is that Washington and Tokyo—the two most powerful actors in Asia—together with other capitals in the Asian region, will continue to play a major role in shaping China's approach to the international system.

China and the International System: The Long Perspective

From a historical perspective of China's place in the international system, 1971 is arguably the most important date in modern Chinese history since the Opium War. The People's Republic of China's (PRC) entry into the United Nations in October that year marked China's acceptance into the international system as a fully sovereign and nearly universally recognized member for the first time since Britain forcibly began the long, difficult process of incorporating China into the international order created by the West and imposed on East Asia in the nineteenth century.

For most of the period since the Opium War, China's position in the international system was subordinate and less than fully sovereign. The Treaty of Nanking, which ended the Opium War in 1842, the Treaty of Tientsin (1858) and the Convention of Peking (1860), which ended the Arrow War, imposed on China Western conventions of international relations through the treaty port system, the mechanism by which Western interests and rights were secured at the expense of Chinese sovereignty. Through the Anglo-American "Cooperative Policy" of 1862, the American "Open Door" policy of 1899–1900, and the Washington Conference treaties of 1921–22, the treaty port system of Western (and eventually Japanese) collaborative imperialism in China survived the collapse of the Qing dynasty and imperial order in 1911–12.

Throughout this period the Western powers committed themselves, in principle, to aiding Chinese reform, with the object of transforming China into an equal, eventually fully sovereign, and ultimately "civilized" partner in the international order capable of and committed to upholding treaty commitments according to prevailing norms. After the Nationalist revolution of 1927–28, Chiang Kai-shek's Nanjing regime made progress toward this goal, first recovering tariff autonomy in 1928–29 and, in the context of Allied collaboration against Japan in World War II, abolition of extraterritoriality in 1943. Finally, the communist revolution establishing the People's Republic in 1949 expelled the remaining vestiges of the former treaty port presence.

China's recovery of domestic sovereignty in the 1940s did not, however, lead to China's acceptance as a full-fledged member of the international order. Because of Beijing's lean toward the Soviet side and Washington's policy of actively discouraging international recognition of the PRC and the economic embargo it imposed after the onset of the Korean War, China remained on the outside. In the first year of its existence, the PRC was recognized by 18 countries in the world, most of which were its partners in the Soviet bloc. Even in the late 1960s, Beijing was recognized by considerably less than half of the nation-states in the international order, and the rival Republican regime in Taipei still held China's seat in the United Nations.[4] China in the 1950s had extensive trade with the Soviet bloc, with some Third World states, and, after trade with the Soviet bloc declined in the 1960s, with Japan and Europe. But the place of trade in China's economy was extremely limited.[5]

The impact of Beijing exclusion from the international order on its pursuit of its national agenda was fundamental. Beijing's lack of legitimate international standing denied it recourse to normal diplomatic mechanisms through which to pursue its interests on the international stage. The PRC's formal treaty of alliance with Moscow enhanced its security in the face of a hostile United States, but by 1959 the treaty was defunct in fact if not principle. Beijing in the 1960s pursued a "dual adversary" strategy of confrontation against both the United States, which escalated its potentially dangerous military involvement in Vietnam in 1965, and the Union of Soviet Socialist Republics (USSR), which accelerated its buildup on China's northern borders in the same year. The shrillness of Beijing's revolutionary international rhetoric bespoke a sense of weakness and insecurity in this dangerous setting, an impression reinforced by the abiding caution in most of Beijing's foreign policy behavior.[6] China's "people's war" defense posture testified to the regime's recognition of its military weakness in the face of enemies holding a vastly superior technological edge, as did its launching of its "Third Front" industrialization of the deep interior.[7]

Without access to the international economy, Mao Zedong's development strategy of self-reliance reflected as much an effort to make a virtue out of a necessity as it did Mao's imputed preference for autarky. And with respect to reunification, Beijing's policy of seeking Taiwan's "liberation" comported with the international reality that Taipei represented China in the international order and, after 1954, maintained a security alliance with Washington that afforded the United States military bases with which to "contain" the PRC.

After its acceptance into the international order, symbolized by its entry into the United Nations in 1971, the context in which China could pursue its national goals of security, development, and reunification changed fundamentally. It could thereafter use conventional mechanisms of diplomacy and international organizations to maintain its independence, security, and international prestige. It could pursue national development with access to the resources of the international economic order. It could also address its long-standing civil war with the Nationalist regime on Taiwan from a reversed position of international legitimacy, with itself the insider and Taipei the outsider.

Beijing's foreign policy and international outlook changed in step. Beijing dropped its previous class-based foreign policy rhetoric of opposing imperialism in favor of a nation-state-based vocabulary that focused on state interest and opposing the "hegemony" of the "superpowers"—terms it had not used before. It diluted its long-standing development strategy of "self reliance" with a significant expansion of foreign trade. In 1975 Premier Zhou Enlai, aided by a rehabilitated Deng Xiaoping, restored the "four modernizations" to the national agenda after a decade's disruption by the turmoil of the Cultural Revolution.

But Beijing's progress in the 1970s toward its national goals on the basis of its new position in the international order was slow for a variety of reasons. Beijing still was not formally recognized by the United States, which impeded its entry into international economic organizations. Although both Beijing and Washington anticipated full normalization of U.S.-China relations relatively soon after President Richard Nixon's February 1972 visit, domestic political changes in the United States—Watergate, the transitional Ford presidency, and the preoccupation of the early Carter years with other foreign policy issues—distracted U.S. action. Over the same period, leadership succession conflict—as the health of both Mao Zedong and Zhou Enlai declined, culminating in 1976 in the death of both men and the purge of Deng Xiaoping for a second time—paralyzed movement on the Chinese side. Only after his political rehabilitation and a successful campaign in 1977–78 to seize control over the Party agenda could Deng Xiaoping begin to transform China's domestic landscape and foreign outlook on the basis of China's changed position in the international order.

China's Transformation Under Deng Xiaoping

The policies of "reform and opening to the outside world" that Deng Xiaoping inaugurated in the late 1970s as the framework of Beijing's approach to economic development and foreign relations rested on two interlocked assessments. One was that China's rapid economic modernization is essential to the survival of the PRC in the contemporary world and therefore must become the foremost priority of the Communist Party of China (CPC). The other was that China's domestic modernization requires a stable international context over a prolonged period of time.

These priorities reflected Deng's assessment in the late 1970s of both China's international situation and its domestic circumstances. Internationally, Deng recognized on China's periphery a resurgent Japan that was beginning to translate its spectacular economic growth into international political influence. Also emerging around the East Asian rim were the "four little dragons" (Hong Kong, Korea, Singapore and Taiwan), newly-industrializing cultural cousins of China that had found ways to develop with impressive speed. More broadly, Deng saw on the global level a new scientific and technological revolution in lasers, microelectronics, computers, biotechnology, satellite communications, and atomic energy that was radically changing the criteria by which national strength would be measured. China itself was still paralyzed by the unrelenting domestic political conflicts launched by Mao Zedong over the previous two decades. All of these trends indicated to Deng that China was not only not overtaking the advanced nations of the world but was falling farther behind.[8]

Both of the twin premises that drove Deng's policies were registered at the Third Plenum of the Eleventh Central Committee in December 1978, which fundamentally altered the Party's guiding ideology and moved China into its post-revolutionary phase. Marking a watershed change in Chinese politics, the plenum subordinated waging a "class struggle"—the foremost political priority under Mao—to expanding the "forces of production," that is, to economic growth and raising the livelihood of the Chinese people. Henceforth economic performance became the criterion against which the success of policies in most other sectors would be measured.

On the basis of this revision in the Party's "basic line" emerged the array of economic policies that dramatically transformed China's domestic scene in the 1980s and that provided the basis for present projections of China's growing national strength. Deng and collaborators in economic reform decollectivized agriculture, dismantling Mao's communes in favor of a return to family-based market-driven farming. Deng stimulated growth in the urban economy both through gradual reform of the state-owned enterprise sector and by spurring the growth of the private and collective sectors in consumer goods and services. The massive system of state planning built with Soviet assistance in the 1950s was dismantled, and the system of state-set prices steadily gave way to market pricing. Deng opened first the coastal provinces and then the interior to foreign investment and pressed for a mammoth expansion of foreign trade, taking China into the international economy and bringing the international economy into China's development.

The Deng regime also pressed for political and social changes that abetted the direction of his economic reforms. Deng worked to restore Party discipline and institutional routine to China's political processes. Under Deng's leadership the Party altered the criteria by which it evaluates cadres, recruiting and promoting those who suited the technocratic bent of Deng's policies and demoting and purging those who advanced under the "leftist" criteria of Mao's years. Beijing resumed the late 1950s project of setting down codes of law to provide a legal basis for the economic reforms and to regulate the social conflicts that modernization inevitably brings. Deng also engineered a deliberate retreat of the Party and state from society, tolerating a legitimate private sphere and flourishing resurgence of public associations, professional groups, and religious organizations. A revised Chinese society, in Deng's view, would both bind China's polity together again after years of fragmentation and alienation under Mao's policies of class warfare and also provide new platforms for mobilizing society behind the regime's larger developmental goals.

Deng also moved in the late 1970s to secure a stable international environment for China's development which, amid perceptions of a growing Soviet threat, meant cooperation with the West. Under his leadership Beijing normalized relations with Tokyo and Washington in 1978, not only completing processes begun in the early 1970s but also opening the way to China's entry into international economic organizations important to China's development, such as the World Bank and the International Monetary Fund (IMF). Normalization of these key relationships served Beijing's larger purpose of deterring the USSR, a convergence of strategic interest with Washington and Tokyo that was reflected in their common commitment to oppose "hegemonism" in the East Asian region. This anti-Soviet focus was a major area of continuity in foreign policy orientation from the late Mao years. Even though Beijing offered Moscow new talks in April 1979 to improve relations as it notified Moscow of its intention to allow the already empty 1950 bilateral alliance to expire, it continued to see the USSR as the main threat to PRC security and to seek collaboration with the United States, Japan, and other countries in the West as its main strategic goal. The Soviet intervention in Afghanistan in December 1979 only sharpened this focus. Perceptions of a shifting superpower balance in favor of the United States, and perhaps new differences over Taiwan with the new Reagan administration, led Beijing to alter its tactics but not its overall goal of securing a stable international context for domestic modernization. In 1982, then Party General Secretary Hu Yaobang enunciated Beijing's "independent foreign policy line," an approach that softened its stridently anti-Soviet focus and dropped its previous insistent call for an "international united front" with Washington and Tokyo against Moscow. Building on minute initial steps taken in late 1980 and 1981 and responding to Leonid Brezhnev's overture at Tashkent in March 1982, Beijing began a cautious and carefully calculated exploration of improving relations with the USSR. This approach was premised on Soviet satisfaction of Chinese security concerns—the "three obstacles" of the Soviet build-up on China's borders, the Soviet intervention in Afghanistan, and Soviet support for the Vietnamese intervention in Cambodia. After the accession to power of Mikhail Gorbachev, Moscow moved on each of these issues, culminating in a full-fledged Sino-Soviet reconciliation during Gorbachev's visit to Beijing in May 1989, the first by the top Soviet party leader in 30 years.

Normalized relations with Moscow did not come at the expense of continued good relations with Washington and Tokyo. Bilateral ties with both the United States and Japan expanded in several areas, filling out relationships that in the 1970s had been built mainly on strategic collaboration against the USSR. U.S. ships made port calls at Shanghai and Qingdao, and a pattern of routine military exchanges flourished through the 1980s. Chinese trade with both the United States and Japan grew rapidly, achieving a total trade volume in 1988 nearly six times that of 1980. Beijing's "independent foreign policy line" in the 1980s framed relationships with Washington and Tokyo on one hand and Moscow on the other that remained asymmetrical, not equidistant.

Complementing these shifts in foreign and domestic policy was a major alteration in its approach toward Taiwan. On the same day that it normalized relations with Washington, Beijing dropped its previous campaign calling for Taiwan's "liberation"—a theme theretofore enunciated annually at observances of the anniversary of the February 27, 1947, KMT massacre of Taiwanese. In its place Beijing put forward a new pitch for "peaceful reunification." It began to use the lunar new year Spring Festival holiday, the traditional Chinese occasion for celebrating ties of kinship and patriotic brotherhood, as the annual occasion for authoritative statements on Taiwan issues, and stopped marking the anniversary of the February 27, 1947, massacre in Taiwan. Beijing called for steps to open communications, tourism, commercial enterprises, transports, and other ties across the Taiwan Straits that would gradually lay the foundation for substantive dialogue on reunification later. Subsequent statements by the Beijing leadership—Ye Jianying's eight points in 1981 and Deng Xiaoping's comments on a "one country, two systems" approach in 1982—stipulated that Taiwan might become a "special administrative region" retaining extensive autonomy over internal affairs and foreign representation under the umbrella of PRC sovereignty. Thereafter the "Fujian Front" People's Liberation Army (PLA) and the Fuzhou Military Region opposite Taiwan were abolished in a major 1983 reorganization of military region commands.

China's defense policies changed in step with the priorities of the early Deng years. In 1985, a Central Military Commission (CMC) meeting decided on the reduction of PLA forces by a million troops, down to about 2.5 million. It also formally inaugurated a new effort to upgrade and modernize the PLA under a new doctrine of "people's war under modern conditions." This doctrine departed sharply from Mao Zedong's "people's war" strategy which had called for maintenance of huge numbers of active and reserve forces and diffusion of industrial development throughout the country. In the event that foreign invaders occupied some part of China, the remainder could survive militarily and economically to continue the war, despite China's technological weaknesses. In keeping with Deng's developmental emphasis on the coastal provinces, China would now need a technologically more modern military capable of defending its maritime industrial centers farther from China's shores and fighting "limited wars" on its periphery. Funding for military modernization, however, could not come from increased state budget allocations, which would have to follow progress in overall economic development. Instead, money for defense modernization would have to come from other sources, including savings from the reduction in forces, production of civilian goods by defense industries, and arms sales abroad.

The success of Deng Xiaoping's policies in achieving fundamental domestic and foreign policy goals over the first decade under his leadership is in most respects beyond dispute. Beijing successfully normalized relations with all three of the major powers that had traditionally threatened its security, and by 1989 China faced no immediate security threat of the kind that it had faced after 1949. China established itself as a major presence in the international economy even though it was still outside the General Agreement on Tariffs and Trade (GATT). Domestically, China's gross domestic product between 1979 and 1988 grew at an annual average rate of 9.8 percent, producing a visible impact on living standards of the Chinese people both in the cities and the rural areas. On reunification issues, by the end of the 1980s, thanks to a pathbreaking domestic change in Taipei, a pattern of growing cross-Straits economic and unofficial exchanges had begun. In 1984 Beijing successfully concluded an agreement with London on the reversion of Hong Kong in 1997.

China, in short, seemed to be on the right track by the late 1980s. Even at a time of significant change elsewhere in the socialist world, China seemed the front-running and most progressive of the reforming communist states. China was enjoying its most secure and prosperous period since the beginning of the encounter with the West in the Opium War. From the perspective of the broader international system, Beijing's participation in multilateral disarmament forums and the growing place of foreign trade and investment in China's domestic development suggested that Beijing was gradually accepting the "perforations" of national sovereignty that interdependence in world affairs demands.

Post-Cold War Uncertainties

As promising as China's circumstances seemed after a decade of relative successes under Deng Xiaoping's policies, events both inside China and out combined rapidly to cloud China's domestic scene and its foreign policy horizons in unanticipated ways. These new dilemmas led the Chinese leadership more than once to reassess whether or not the fundamental premises of Deng Xiaoping's reforms and the approach he pursued toward the international system would continue to hold.

Domestic challenges emerged along two fronts. First, the advance of Deng's economic reforms aroused social tensions that deepened visibly throughout the 1980s and that culminated in the popular demonstrations in Beijing and several other cities in the spring of 1989. Though widely perceived as a "democracy movement" in the West, the 1989 demonstrations reflected an outpouring of diverse anxieties, frustrations, and ambitions—including fears of surging inflation, jealousies aroused by the reforms' uneven impact on different groups, and anger at spreading corruption—alongside genuine calls for political liberalization. The demonstrations erupted in the context of a split in the Party leadership over economic policy that paralyzed its ability to respond. The leadership's indecisive and halting responses to the demonstrations served only to swell the demonstrators' ranks and focus their animus on the regime itself. In the end, the leadership's decision to crush the demonstrations with lethal force dissipated the atmosphere of optimistic progressivism that a decade of reforms had fueled and presented a still reformist leadership with new problems of domestic governance and legitimacy.

Second, these social tensions and conflicts erupted as the Party's top leadership was entering a critical phase of succession and generational turnover. In August 1989 Deng Xiaoping turned 85, and in November and the following spring he relinquished his only remaining official posts, as chairman of the Party and State Central Military Commissions. These steps brought to conclusion a nearly decade-long attempt by Deng to retire his own generation of revolutionary veteran leaders from the front rank of the Party and state leadership and to promote in their place younger leaders committed to the reform policies he had launched. This effort began at the 1982 Twelfth Party Congress with the creation of a Central Advisory Commission (CAC). Thus establishing an institutional back bench from which retired leaders could still provide advice to younger front-line leaders. Deng's effort was fulfilled by the retirement of his veteran colleagues in two groups, one at the September 1985 national Party conference and another at the Party's Thirteenth Congress in 1987. In their place emerged a younger, post-revolutionary generation of leaders who lacked their elders' experience as professional revolutionaries but whose technical educations, foreign training, and bureaucratic experiences better suited the administration of a rapidly modernizing society. The retiring elders continued to have significant influence and impact on politics and policy, sometimes blunting or altering the thrust of new reforms. But after veteran retirements at the 1987 Thirteenth Party Congress and a series of corresponding state leadership changes at the Seventh National People's Congress in 1988, Deng's efforts appeared to be on track. Successive waves of leadership changes at lower levels of the Party and state apparatuses in the 1980s brought about a comparable transformation there.

Nevertheless, the fall of Zhao Ziyang as Party general secretary in May 1989, in the midst of the Tiananmen crisis, was a major setback to Deng's efforts to provide for a stable leadership succession. Zhao himself had reluctantly become the Party's top-ranking leader in 1987 when Deng's first choice, Hu Yaobang, was removed from that position. Deng's succession arrangements were also complicated by the appointment of Jiang Zemin—a Beijing outsider without a strong base of central power—as Zhao's replacement. Meanwhile, both Zhao's fall and the eruption of leadership differences over Tiananmen gave the retired elders new opportunities to intervene more actively in day-to-day leadership decision-making, effectively undermining the thrust of Deng's efforts over the previous decade.

Challenges on the foreign policy front emerged in conjunction with the end of the Cold War and the collapse of the Soviet Union in three ways. First, the decline in Soviet-American tensions in the late 1980s marginalized China at the global level of international politics. China's position as a strategic counterweight in the U.S.-Soviet balance of power declined as Washington and Moscow, beginning with the 1987 treaty on intermediate nuclear forces, demonstrated a capacity to make breakthroughs on fundamental questions. Moscow's readiness to support American efforts in 1990 to rally a broad international coalition against Iraq's annexation of Kuwait visibly dismayed Beijing. China's strategic value dissolved altogether when the USSR collapsed in 1991. With the global bipolar balance of power gone, China no longer mattered as much as it had previously, and with respect to many of the larger issues that remained—such as the Middle East and German reunification—China's influence had never been significant.

The demise of the bipolar structure of world power therefore presented Beijing with a fundamental dilemma. Since the inception of the PRC in 1949, Beijing had invariably leaned to the side of the weaker of the two main powers in the global bipolar system. In the 1950s it had leaned to the side of the Soviet Union against the predominate power of the United States. In the 1960s, at a time of growing perceptions of superpower parity, Beijing had pursued a "dual adversary" approach, opposing both superpowers. In the 1970s it had leaned toward the United States at a time of rising Soviet power and U.S. decline. In the 1980s, as the United States reasserted itself, Beijing enunciated its "independent foreign policy line," distancing itself from Washington at the global (but not the bilateral) level while pursuing a cautious reconciliation with Moscow.

Beijing's shifts accorded with its perceptions of the changing superpower balance. At the same time, since the early 1970s Chinese analyses also described an emergent multipolarization in the structure of world power, with the bipolarism of the Cold War giving way to a gradual evening out of power among five centers of power—the two superpowers plus a unifying Europe, a resurgent Japan, and China. The superpowers would retain their predominant position over a long period, Chinese assessments projected, but gradually the gap between them and other rising centers of power could be expected to narrow.

As it did everyone else, the sudden collapse of the Soviet Union shocked Chinese analysts, who now saw major consequences for China in the international system. Instead of a gradual, long-term evolution toward multipolar balance, Beijing now saw the emergence of a potentially hegemonic system dominated by the remaining superpower, the United States, to whose purposes all other powers and states would have to bend their international agendas. In an increasingly multipolar order, China's power would be enhanced—it could resist any single power's pressure by building coalitions of common interest with the other centers of power using a traditional balance of power politics. In a unipolar hegemonic system, this would be much harder to do. Accustomed to ensuring maximum strategic latitude for itself by leaning to the weaker side in a bipolar system, Beijing now had no clear counterpart to U.S. power with which to align.

A second way in which the end of the Cold War and the demise of the USSR complicated Beijing's foreign policy horizons is paradoxical: at a time when China seemed to grow smaller on the global stage, it seemed to grow bigger on the regional stage of East Asia. With the Soviet Union gone and the United States far away, many Asian states—especially in Southeast Asia—now began to see China's growing strength no longer as a useful counterweight but as a rising threat. Before the end of the Cold War, some non-communist states of Southeast Asia linked Vietnamese efforts to establish domination in Cambodia and Laos to its alignment with USSR. In that context China's emerging strength in the region was useful in opposing a perceived larger threat to the region. With the collapse of Soviet power and with Hanoi's withdrawal from Cambodia, China's rising strength appeared more threatening by virtue of the changed regional context. For Beijing, this development enhanced China's stature and enhanced its security. But its also complicated relationships in the region and encouraged alignments to balance China's power. Vietnam, whose own regional ambitions made it an object of suspicion among some ASEAN (Association of Southeast Asian Nations) states, now found common ground with them.

This shift in regional perceptions of China did not stem from new trends in China. China's high rates of economic growth and its program of military modernization began well before the end of the Cold War. China's gross domestic product (GDP) grew at an average annual year of nearly ten percent over the 1979-1988 period, slowed considerably during a three-year effort at economic retrenchment to curb inflation and restore sectoral balance in the 1989-1991 period, and grew at more than double-digit rates thereafter until 1996. Its military modernization effort began in 1985, and state budge allocations for defense began to rise at double-digit rates in 1989. Even so, while the absolute size of China's overall defense spending has risen, its relative size as a proportion of gross domestic product as actually shrunk.[9] In the 1980s, when the broader U.S.-Soviet competition polarized the region's politics, China's economic growth and military modernization made Beijing useful to Washington and its allies. In the altered landscape of the post-Cold War world, China's rising power, despite its earlier origins, now seemed threatening.

Third, the end of the Cold War and the decline of strategic collaboration against the Soviet Union complicated Beijing's key bilateral relationships. This has been nowhere more the case than in Beijing's relations with Washington. From the early 1970s through the 1980s, U.S.-China relations had rested on a convergence of strategic interest in opposing the Soviet Union. As the Cold War ended, the strategic basis of the relationship dissolved. Increasingly, bilateral differences that previously had been subordinated to the overriding strategic interest began to surface. In the 1990s problems have dominated the U.S.-Chinese bilateral agenda: complaints about Chinese human rights abuses; mounting Chinese trade surpluses; complaints about access to Chinese markets; violations of intellectual property rights; Chinese exports of goods produced by prison labor; Chinese exports of nuclear and missile technology to Pakistan and Iran; Tibetan autonomy; and complaints about China's one-child policy. Frequently, such problems have overshadowed remaining common interests.

From a broader perspective, some of these problems are simply manifestations of a growing bilateral relationship. The United States and China in the 1970s had few problems in bilateral trade because it was virtually non-existent. In the early 1980s, the trade balance was in the U.S.'s favor. Only in the 1990s did the annual trade balance swing strongly in China's favor, in part because of a structural shift in regional trade as Hong Kong, Taiwan, South Korea, and other East Asian businesses began to use the China coast for export-processing bases. Other problems—American sympathy for Tibetan autonomy and revolution against Chinese family planning practices, for example—festered beneath the surface of U.S.-PRC strategic collaboration against the USSR in the 1980s and gained prominence as that strategic basis of the relationship dissolved.

In addition to the foreign policy challenges brought by the end of the Cold War, Beijing has faced a new dilemma with respect to Taiwan, stemming mainly from domestic changes in the island's politics and its consequences for Taipei's approach to the international system. The death of Chiang Ching-kuo in 1988 and the appointment of Lee Teng-hui as KMT chairman and Republic of China (ROC) president completed a process of "Taiwanization" of Taiwan's politics. In this process, the Mandarin-speaking mainlanders who emigrated to the island in 1948–49 with the Chiang Kai-shek's Nationalist regime and who monopolized the island's politics for the next 30 years were gradually succeeded by politicians drawn from among the much larger population of descendants of the island's indigenous Chinese, who speak a Minnan sub-dialect. This "ethnic" transition in the island's politics reflected broad social changes brought about by Taiwan's economic success, in which a rising Taiwanese business class steadily competed first for local office and then for higher positions in the ROC government and Kuomintang party apparatus.

In addition, Taiwan's burgeoning middle class brought pressure to bear on the ROC's martial law authoritarian rule over a broad range of local issues and eventually over much more fundamental issues—specifically KMT domination of the political process and Taiwan's relationship to a unified China. In 1987, Chiang Ching-kuo lifted the ban on the formation of political parties and on an opposition press, inaugurating a process of democratization of the island's politics that culminated in the popular elections for the office of ROC president in March 1996.

These changes emerged in the context of the PRC's "peaceful reunification" campaign, launched in 1979 when Beijing normalized relations with Washington. Beijing clearly saw the Taiwanization of ROC politics coming, perceptions which lent urgency to its effort to get a process of reunification started. Beijing therefore applauded Chiang Ching-kuo's lifting of the ban on cross-Strait contacts and exchanges in 1987, making possible Taiwan tourist visits, business operations and investments, and cultural and educational exchanges with the mainland that have since flourished. Beijing was also undoubtedly encouraged by the beginnings of political contacts in 1993 with the formation of quasi-official negotiating bodies (Taipei's Straits Exchange Foundation and Beijing's Association for Relations Across the Taiwan Straits) and talks between these bodies' directors in Singapore.

But Beijing has also been alarmed at other consequences of the Taiwanization of ROC politics. One has been the growing expression of political sentiments for Taiwan independence, especially as espoused in one form or another by the KMT's rival, the Democratic Progressive Party (DPP). The other has been Lee Teng-hui's pursuit of upgraded standing and legitimacy in the international system, both in international organizations, including the United Nations (to which, in 1995, Taipei offered to make a billion dollar contribution in exchange for a seat), and with individual countries. Beijing has seen this "flexible" or "pragmatic" diplomacy by Taipei not simply as an effort to strengthen the ROC's position in reunification negotiations with the PRC but as fundamentally challenging the "one China" foundation on which reunification rests.

All of the above factors—the Tiananmen crisis, the changes in the international setting brought about by the end of the Cold War, and the Taiwan dilemma—emerged simultaneously in the short span of 1989–1991. They also converged in Beijing's relationship with the United States. The Tiananmen disaster precipitated a sweeping reversal in American public impressions of China, from the unrealistically rosy optimism to the unrealistically comprehensive revulsion of the post–1989 present. China had seemed the foremost reforming communist state in the world, whose adoption of market economics and progressive leadership promised a China that at last might resemble America after all. After Tiananmen, and after the revolutions in Eastern Europe and the collapse of the USSR, China seemed like a political fossil; an authoritarian state dominated by an aging communist leadership out of touch with the demands of the people it ruled and with the wave of democratization sweeping the rest of the communist world. The dramatic political transformation of Taiwan only underscored the new antipathy toward China and won new sympathy for Taipei's cause.

These problem have been compounded by uncertainties in the United States itself about the American role in a post-Cold War world. Without an overarching anti-Soviet framework, American foreign policy has lurched unpredictably among priorities, interests, and ideals. With respect to China, this lack of consensus has exacerbated a much more politicized policy context. Diverse interest groups pursue disparate China agendas in Washington, forming frequently surprising coalitions and antagonisms both between and within the Congress and the Executive branches. This disarray has come to the fore in the politics of China policy during the Clinton administration under a president and foreign policy team that has at times pursued contradictory policies in China or has allowed competing foreign policy bureaucracies to pursue their own agendas without coordination and without the hierarchy of priorities that leadership should provide.

The foregoing analysis leads to several general conclusions. First, China, the world's largest political community, joined the international order only very recently, overcoming a position of prolonged subordination in and then general exclusion from the international order. Many of the issues that the international system confronts today with respect to China are reflections of the fact that China joined the international order very late. Second, the complications bought about by China's late entry are compounded by its coincidence with the last stages of the Cold War, whose end has revised the frameworks and attendant expectations by which China's place in the international system and its progress in accommodating international norms is judged. Third, China in this period has undergone and continues to undergo a profound transformation in the manner in which it has pursued national security and prosperity. The change in national leadership from Mao to Deng—paramount leaders with very different outlooks—was instrumental in this transformation. But the primary determinant in this transformation has been the transformation in China's international setting and the possibilities that it afforded Chinese leaders to pursue their national agenda. Despite their highly divergent ideological priorities, Mao and Deng shared a common agenda of security and development; their different approaches to fulfilling this agenda reflected to a large degree adaptations to different international context.

Responses to Post-Cold War Domestic Challenges

The policies of "reform and opening" that Deng pursued in China's new position in the international order allowed the PRC to make major progress toward its national goals of security, development, and reunification in the 1980s. By the end of the 1980s, they also brought new complications and dilemmas, partly of China's making and partly brought on by the end of the Cold War order. The Chinese leadership that sought to address these new complications and dilemmas is the same leadership that survives Deng Xiaoping's passing on February 19, 1997. A broad assessment of how this post-Deng leadership has dealt with China's national goals in a post-Cold War setting before Deng's death therefore will suggest the most likely prospects for continuity and change in China itself and in its international outlook.

At three points the Beijing leadership appears to have reassessed whether the fundamental premises of Deng's reforms and the policies based on them continue to hold. In 1989, immediately following the Tiananmen disaster, Party conservatives challenged the Dengist strategy of economic reform and questioned the wisdom of working in an international order dominated by a United States committed to a strategy of "peaceful evolution" against the socialist states. In 1991 the collapse of the USSR briefly renewed doubts about the premises of Deng's policies. And since 1995, the Beijing leadership has appeared to debate the feasibility of working with a United States whose actions in the East Asian region suggested a new strategy of containment against China.

In the first two of these episodes, the leadership debated but ultimately reaffirmed the main tenets of Deng's reform strategy. In the first instance, the Central Committee's Fourth Plenum, held on June 24, 1989, immediately after the Tiananmen disaster, explicitly endorsed the correctness of the Thirteenth Congress' "basic line"—the "one center" of taking economic development as the foremost task and the "two points" of "reform and opening up" and "upholding the four cardinal principles"—despite the deviations in leadership under deposed Party General Secretary Zhao Ziyang. It also reiterated that Beijing's "independent foreign policy" line remained "unchanged."[10] In the fall of 1989, at the Fifth Plenum, the leadership did constrain elements of Deng's economic policies as they had been implemented by Zhao Ziyang and formally adopted a plan of economic retrenchment (the "39 points") associated with Deng's conservative rival, Chen Yun, stressing overall administrative regulation and coordination of the economy to redress sectoral imbalances and bring the surging inflation of 1988 under control. But in other respects, conservative efforts to reassert their own priorities—through criticism of "peaceful evolution" and the campaign against "bourgeois liberalization"—were waning by 1990. In addition, statements at the Seventh Plenum in December 1990 on the need to maintain "a certain rate of economic growth" suggested that Deng and his allies were moving to reassert their economic reform agenda, criticizing the economic downturn brought about by the retrenchment package of 1988-89 and harnessing sentiment among some provincial leaders in the politics of formulating the Eighth Five-Year Plan adopted in 1991.[11] In the second instance, the occasion of the collapse of the Soviet coup appears to have stimulated debate over the premises of Deng Xiaoping's policies that Deng ultimately overcame with his landmark tour of the south in early 1992.[12] The third instance will be discussed below.

Once Deng and his allies had reasserted clear-cut control over the Party agenda, politics and policy proceeded strongly on the basis of the twin premises that guided Deng's policies in the 1980s—economic modernization and maintenance of a stable international environment in which to pursue it. The Fourteenth CPC Congress in 1992 was the most politically lopsided congress in the Deng era, endorsing strongly reformist guidelines for Party policy. In particular, the Party congress designated as the goal of economic reform the creation of a "socialist market economy," a landmark conclusion to a decade-long leadership debate over the role and scope of market-based economics at the expense of state planning. The Party's November 1993 Third Plenum followed up this abstract redefinition with a 50-point set of more concrete guidelines for specific reforms of the state-owned enterprise system, taxation and finance, and foreign trade intended to achieve the goal of "socialist market economy." Implementation of the taxation reforms began in 1994, and initial steps in the other areas were also begun but interrupted by efforts to control the unanticipated high spike of inflation in 1994–96.

The Fourteenth Congress also put in place a Political Bureau and Secretariat leadership whose bureaucratic careers, coastal associations, and relatively liberal political lineage strongly disposed them toward extending Deng's reforms as he withdrew from active, day-to-day decisionmaking.[13] The consolidation of this younger technocratic, reform-inclined leadership centered around Party General Secretary Jiang Zemin and was abetted by his own steady efforts to build a base of power drawing on former associates from Shanghai, constituting what is sometimes called the "Shanghai gang" in central leadership politics. Jiang also broke the long-standing bastion of conservatism in the Beijing municipal Party organization, using the popular anti-corruption issue to topple Chen Xitong in 1995. Consolidation of the Jiang leadership has also benefited from the steady decline and demise through the 1990s of the conservative Party elders who tempered and at times impeded Deng Xiaoping's reform policies in the 1980s. These include the passing of Nie Rongzhen, Hu Qiaomu, and Li Xiannian in 1992, Yao Yilin in 1994, Chen Yun himself in 1995, and Peng Zhen in early 1997—a major depletion of the elders' ranks followed by the demise of Deng himself at nearly the end of this sequence.

These developments have contributed to an overall stability in leadership politics and consistency in domestic policy direction, despite (or perhaps because of) the stresses of succession and the long anticipated passing of Deng Xiaoping and the daunting problems of governing the regime faces. Although the present Political Bureau leaders certainly differ among themselves over political issues, their overall cohesion has been impressive. There is no visible evidence of the ferocious factional conflict and divergent policy agendas that characterized the last year of Mao Zedong's life and the power struggle that followed his death in September 1976. Instead, the present leadership has appeared to operate according to a clear-cut division of labor, with none of the public kibitzing or outright intrusion into other leader's policy portfolios. The leadership has closed ranks and weathered unanticipated domestic crises—such as the worst episode of inflation since the early years of the PRC, in 1994–96—without public sign of discord. There have clearly been debates and controversies among the broader political elite—such as between the coastal provinces and the interior ones over future central state investment and revenue transfers in the context of formulating of the Ninth Five-Year Plan in 1995. In addition, a strident "neo-conservative" voice has been audible in some publications such as *Zhenli de Zhuiqiu* (Pursuit of Truth). But these strains appear to reflect contending interests and residual ideological divisions at lower levels of the elite and do not appear to have fractured the cohesion of the central leadership.

In addition, the leadership has appeared secure enough to undertake reforms that entail significant risk of social unrest and political opposition. This is most recently evident in the leadership's resumption of action on the problem of the state-owned enterprise sector in April this year. The 1993 Third Plenum's 50-point decision had called for a process of enterprise reform through corporatization for some and merger and bankruptcy for others. Thereafter, the legal groundwork for this process was placed under the supervision of National People's Congress Chairman Qiao Shi, with the passage of a new corporation law and revised bankruptcy legislation and the State Council began trial point experiments in several cities. But the unexpected surge of inflation after the summer of 1994 sidetracked broader state-owned enterprise reform as Vice Premier Zhu Rongji worked to bring inflation within acceptable levels using monetary and credit controls. Once the annual national economic work conference in December 1996 declared that a "soft landing" had been achieved, the State Council announced a resumed push to accelerate the process of enterprise reform.[14]

A number of pressures help explain the leadership's evident readiness to move on this front—the inflationary impact of unrestrained lending to enterprises that operate in the red, persistent deficits in the central budget, the impossibility of establishing a true central bank and other indirect levers of guiding an increasingly marketized economy without tackling enterprise reform first, and the requirement for acceding to GATT/WTO (World Trade Organization). But reform of the state sector also portends massive unemployment and significant political opposition from among those wedded to the idea that the state-owned enterprise sector is the heart of socialism in China. These contending priorities have made enterprise reform a terrible dilemma in the past and help explain the gradualism of the leadership in approaching it. In this context, the leadership's announced resolve to deal with it now is an indication of leadership cohesion over a potentially highly divisive question.

That the top leadership appears ready to move on state enterprise reform now is all the more remarkable in light of the other potentially difficult issues it has faced and will face in 1997. Aside from the passing of Deng Xiaoping in February 1997, Beijing must manage the reversion of Hong Kong on July 1, 1997, and convene the Party's Fifteenth Congress, scheduled for the fall of that same year. Party congresses are the supreme public event in Chinese politics, affecting the political careers of the Party elite and laying out authoritative guidelines for work in virtually every significant policy sector. Preparations for Party congresses normally begin to heat up the political atmosphere at least 18 months ahead of convocation. In 1997 the congress must deal with the question of a new post for Premier Li Peng, anticipating his stepping down from that position in the spring of 1998 following constitutional stipulations, and of designating his replacement. Although these questions have already produced visible indications of bargaining, reflected in the Beijing and Hong Kong rumor mills, there have been as yet no signs of a leadership split approaching the summer leadership retreat at Beidaihe, where key decisions on the upcoming Party congress appointments will likely be made. Quite the contrary, we have seen a veneer of business as usual.

These and other indications suggest that the Party leadership has maintained a consistent facade of cohesion and unity through the course of an important generational transition, a striking departure from the failure of other communist states to manage succession crises. The Beijing regime nevertheless faces immense problems of governance that have invited skepticism about its endurance. The collapse of the communist regimes in Eastern Europe and then the USSR itself provided impressive evidence of the fragility of such political systems. China has regional disparities, ethnic tensions, and emergent minority nationalisms reminiscent of those that brought about the fragmentation of the Soviet Union.

Trends through the mid–1990s suggest, nevertheless, that prospects for full-scale regime collapse and regional fragmentation have receded, at least in the near term, from what seemed possible in the 1989–1991 period.

- The economic bases for regional fragmentation are beginning to be counterbalanced by nationally integrating and recentralizing trends. Efforts by some provinces to shelter their own markets against competing goods from other provinces and to hoard their resources and higher-skilled labor—what was called "socialist feudalism" in the 1980s—are declining as a more rational division of provincial and regional labor is developing. The 1994 taxation reforms have made initial progress in redressing the decline in the central portion of revenue while also providing for the needs of local and regional governments.

- Beijing has never ceded nor lost control over regional political and military appointments. Since the 1992 Fourteenth CPC Congress, 28 provincial Party secretaries and 26 provincial governors have been replaced. Military region and district commanders and political commissars have been rotated frequently.
- Beijing has repeatedly demonstrated its readiness to use whatever force necessary to suppress ethnic and religious unrest in the autonomous western regions of China. Tensions will remain in these regions, and uprisings and unrest will continue. But demographic trends, economic development, and Beijing's foreign policy priority on stable relations with the Central and South Asian states all work increasingly against efforts by these regions' minorities to break away. As in 1911–12, only full-scale collapse of the center will change this prospect.

Prospects for other forms of radical political change also seem to have receded. Understandably, given the events of 1989, the regime has focused on suppressing potential dissidence in the cities, moving quickly to stamp out the slightest manifestation of political agitation that might blossom into larger mass protest. The heaviest hand of suppression has fallen on urban workers, where the regime has been particularly ruthless. Crackdowns have been evident particularly over the past year, prompted not only in anticipation of 1997's crowded agenda (the reversion of Hong Kong and the Fifteenth Party Congress) but also by the regime's decision to press ahead with state enterprise reform and its attendant risks of mass unemployment and urban unrest.

The potential for military praetorianism may also have diminished. The top military leadership has undergone the same generational transition as has the civilian political leadership. The revolutionary veteran leaders who dominated the PLA's politics in the post-Mao era up through the

1980s have given way to younger, increasingly professional military leaders whose careers began after 1949. The impact of this transition on the relations between the civil and military leaderships is profound and potentially unstable. Before the 1990s, military influence in PRC politics was felt first and foremost through the long relationships between senior military leaders and the paramount leaders of the CPC who themselves had long service in military leadership posts. When PLA leaders had reason to approach the top political leadership in the past, they had immediate informal access to Mao, to Deng Xiaoping, and to other top leaders like "Uncle Ye" (Jianying) on the basis of those leaders' long experience in military positions. None of the "third generation" leaders, who emerged in the 1990s, have such experience or ties in the PLA.

Deng Xiaoping recognized this potential gap in civilian-military leadership ties and, particularly since the late 1980s, took steps to counter it. Military access to the Party now runs more through institutional channels and professional routines than at any time since the mid–1950s, during the heyday of Soviet assistance in professionalizing the PLA. In addition, the General Political Department has ceaselessly spawned indoctrination campaigns since 1989 emphasizing the Party's "absolute authority" over the army. Jiang Zemin has worked hard since becoming the Central Military Commission chairman in 1989 to establish cordial relationships with the military top brass, visiting central PLA bureaucracies, regional units, and military academies frequently. In addition, a major turnover of PLA leaders down through division levels has been carried out under his leadership. More PLA generals owe their promotions to Jiang than to Deng. The promotions of Zhang Wannian and Chi Haotian as CMC vice chairman at the Fifth Plenum in September 1995, both of whom appear to be closely tied to Jiang, appear intended to facilitate his relationship with the PLA after the probable retirement of Liu Huaqing and Zhang Zhen at the Fifteenth Congress in the fall of 1997.

All of the trends suggest that the post-Deng leadership around Jiang Zemin remains committed to the basic premises that guided Deng Xiaoping's domestic policies before the 1989–1991 transition to a post-Cold War era. The Jiang leadership continues to see economic modernization along the lines of economic reform pioneered by Deng as the best approach to increasing China's national strength and prosperity. It continues to uphold the policy orientation signaled by the 1992 Fourteenth CPC Congress' designation of China as a "socialist market economy" and to act on the concrete reforms derived from that orientation set out in the 1993 Third Plenum's 50-point decision, as the current phase of state enterprise reform suggests. And it appears ready to apply whatever coercion is required to maintain the domestic stability needed for these reforms.

Response to Post-Cold War International Challenges

Beijing sees the most significant challenges to continuing Deng Xiaoping's interlocked domestic and foreign policies in the post-Cold War setting context not in China's domestic scene, but in its international context. Changing political circumstances and atmospheres in Tokyo, Taipei, and, especially, Washington have produced uncertainties in those capitals' policies toward China. In turn, these have raised questions in Beijing over whether or not it can continue the foreign policy approach set down and pursued by Deng Xiaoping over the previous decade.

In authoritative public pronouncements, Beijing continues to reaffirm the tenets of Deng's approach—that China's economic modernization requires a stable international environment and China's integration into the broader international system. In key areas Beijing's approach to the international order continues to act on the "independent foreign policy line" built on these premises. Its linkage of China's economic growth to the international economy is clear in the continued growth of PRC foreign trade—in 1995 it was the world's tenth-ranking trading nation—and in its efforts to attract foreign direct investment. It continues to press for membership in GATT/WTO, demonstrating a grudging but still clear-cut readiness to make painful domestic political adjustments in order to respond to foreign pressures to meet WTO requirements regarding subsidies to state enterprises, transparency of its trade regime and market access, gradual lowering of tariffs, and intellectual property rights protection. It also appears to recognize and increasingly accept the ambiguities of economic interdependence as China becomes a net importer of oil. It may eventually do the same with respect to the similarly sensitive question of dependence on foreign sources of food.

Similarly, it continues to recognize, as it has since the early 1980s, that participation in multilateral forums on such questions as disarmament serves critical Chinese national interests. This was reflected most recently in its declaration of readiness to sign the draft comprehensive test ban treaty last year. In most regions on China's periphery, Beijing has seen its economic and security interests best served by policies promoting stability. With Russia, the new Central Asian states, and India, Beijing has sought to defuse tensions through diplomatic means, set aside territorial disputes, and promote mutual economic development.[15] It continues to collaborate cautiously in international efforts to defuse tensions on the Korean peninsula, serving its foremost interest in stability and gradual change.

The exception to this overall hierarchy of foreign policy priorities is in the Spratlys, where Beijing appears ready to risk arousing Southeast Asian and other international suspicions in order to establish a presence that will lend substance to its claim to sovereignty over the islets. Beijing has worked hard in the 1990s to expand its ties with the Southeast Asian states, but it has also resorted to a strategy in the Spratlys that combines "ambiguity, incrementalism, tactical timing, selective use of force, and 'divide and dominate' tactics."[16] Although Beijing's ultimate goals in the Spratlys remain unclear, its actions at least in part respond to efforts in the 1980s by the Southeast Asian claimants, and especially Hanoi, to occupy parts of the islet group to substantiate their own claims.

The most serious challenges to the foreign policy approach Beijing has been following have emerged in its relations with Washington, Tokyo, and Taipei. With respect to Japan, Beijing's uneasiness in the early 1990s with what it perceived to be an increasing activism in Tokyo's foreign policy in East Asia and in global affairs was exacerbated by the demise of the Liberal Democratic Party's (LDP) domination of Japan's party politics. Increasingly, Beijing has claimed to see a more fragmented political arena in Tokyo in which more extremist political voices gain greater hearing and affect Japanese foreign policy in unpredictable and potentially disturbing ways. In Taipei, Beijing has become alarmed at a domestic political evolution on the island that threatens its goals of an ultimate reunification with the mainland. The rise of the DPP, the splintering of KMT commitment to the principle of "one China," and the "elastic diplomacy" of President Lee Teng-hui in the 1990s have all complicated and ultimately reduced prospects for fulfilling Beijing's reunification goals. In Washington, the politicization of China policy has accelerated in the administration of Bill Clinton, the vagaries of whose China policy reflects both his own lack of interest in Asia, in general, and China, in particular, and his efforts to satisfy diverse political constituencies at home.

Some of these trends converged in the 1995–96 Taiwan Straits crisis. In May 1995, after repeated assurances that it would not do so, the Clinton administration bent to Congressional pressure and granted Lee Teng-hui a visa to visit his alma mater, Cornell University. Although the purpose of the visit was private—to receive an honorary degree—it also suited Taipei's larger international purpose of establishing itself as a recognized independent entity deserving official representation in the international system. Beijing saw the Clinton administration decision as a further step in the erosion of the "one China" principle at the foundation of U.S.-PRC relations. Having foregone confrontational responses despite apparent debate over previous encroachments of this kind—such as President George Bush's sale of 150 F16s to Taipei in 1992—Beijing decided it could no longer tolerate incremental challenges to its claimed sovereignty over Taiwan. Its series of military exercises from August 1995 to the ROC presidential elections in March 1996, together with Washington's response in positioning two aircraft carriers off Taiwan, marked the most serious confrontation across the Straits since 1958.

Beijing's response in this crisis is frequently portrayed in the American press as an example of Chinese belligerence and assertiveness, traits that are then generalized as indicating Beijing's emergent attitude toward the international system as a whole. In the crisis, however, Beijing was clearly the conservative power, seeking to restore the status quo ante that had been undermined by political dynamics in both Washington and Taipei.

The impact of the Taiwan Straits crisis in Beijing was to rekindle a smoldering leadership debate over the implications of an uncertain American post-Cold War foreign policy, and specifically its China policy, for Beijing's pursuit of its security and development goals. If Washington, despite the ups and downs of U.S.-China relations in recent years, was continuing the generally collaborative policy toward China that it had followed over previous administrations since the 1970s, then the Dengist approach to Chinese security and development could continue. If, however, Washington was moving toward a new, confrontational policy resembling "containment," then Beijing could no longer pursue that approach without major adjustment.[17]

Since 1995 the former view—presuming a collaborative United States, despite the unpredictable impact of the American domestic political process on Washington's China policy—has seemed to prevail. This has been abetted by the effort of the Clinton administration—burned by the confrontation in the Taiwan Straits—to re-stabilize U.S.-PRC ties since the summer of 1996. Repeated affirmation of the "one China" principle by authoritative administration spokesmen (including the President himself), the Beijing visits of Secretaries Warren Christopher in November 1996 and Madeleine Albright in early 1997, and the effort to resume bilateral summits and routine exchanges of other high-level officials, despite the political pressures and controversies, have helped improve the relationship but not entirely reassured Beijing about Washington's long-term intentions after the deep erosion of trust over the preceding several years.

In the meantime, therefore, some adjustments have emerged in Beijing's foreign policy. The most interesting of these has been the diplomatic effort to find common cause with other states against American unipolar domination of the post-Cold War order. Beijing's "strategic partnership" with Moscow, as expressed most recently in the joint statement issued during Jiang Zemin's April 1997 visit to Moscow, is intended to "promote multipolarization of the world" and to resist efforts by any country to "seek hegemony, practice power politics, or monopolize international affairs."[18] Similarly, the recent Sino-French joint declaration issued during President Jacques Chirac's visit to Beijing registered both sides' desire to "foster the march towards multipolarity" and "oppose any attempt at domination in international affairs."[19] PRC media now routinely cite Chinese leaders reiterating comparable statements with visitors to Beijing and on international visits.

At first glance, such diplomatic efforts are reminiscent of Beijing's efforts to build an "international united front against U.S. imperialism" in the late 1950s and a comparable united front against Soviet "hegemonism" in the 1970s. But in fact they differ significantly, not only in rhetorical formulation but also approach, even though the object in all cases was to tilt what Beijing saw as the prevailing strategic balance. Beijing's international united fronts in both the 1950s and the 1970s were targeted at a superpower that it had explicity identified as "the most dangerous threat" to world peace and China's own security. The present effort thus far stops well short of identifying the United States that way. It is instead intended, first, as a hedge on preponderant American leverage in an international system in which China is now an increasingly well established and important player. Second, it seeks to redress through diversification Beijing's weak position in the bilateral ties with Washington that it continues to need and desire.

Implications for the United States and Japan

The foregoing discussion suggests several conclusions that are important for American and perhaps Japanese policies toward China. These are as follows:

- Beijing continues to follow a strategy towards national development and security premised on interaction with and further integration into the prevailing international system.
- The Beijing regime is not weak, divided, and without resources in dealing with the immense problems of governance that it faces. Prospects for radical political change, sudden collapse, or regional fragmentation and break-up are not high.
- Beijing's foreign policies are not adventurist, aggressive and assertive; they are cautious and largely reactive to a dynamic and uncertain international context.
- The most serious challenges to Beijing continuing along the approach that it has followed since the beginning of the Deng Xiaoping era and that it continues to follow today with only slight modification are external. Most particularly, they are the policies of Washington and Tokyo toward China. The Taiwan question, and Taipei's efforts to establish itself as a recognized political entity independent from the PRC, also have the potential to disrupt Beijing's approach to the international order along present lines. But that is true only to the extent that Washington and Tokyo respond to Taipei in ways, as Washington did in 1995, that threaten directly or by implication the symbolism, but not necessarily the substance, of Beijing's claims to sovereignty over the island.

To the extent that the above conclusions are valid, Washington and Tokyo play key roles in determining the context in which Beijing addresses its fundamental national goals now and for the foreseeable future. Above all, this circumstance requires clarity in both capitals in their China policies. Engagement rather than containment is the policy best suited to bring to successful and constructive conclusion the effort begun in the 1970s to bring China into the prevailing international order. Both the United States and Japan share an overwhelming interest in bringing such a policy of engagement to bear.

Successful engagement of China will require consistency in application over a prolonged period of time. Consistency in turn will require enduring political consensus in each capital behind such China policies. At present, such consensus does not exist and, in the American case, seems nowhere in sight. The sensationalistic, narrowly partisan, intensely ideological debate in Washington over China policy, driven far more by quarrels over domestic values and interests than differing perceptions over realities in East Asia, offers no easy resolution but resort to reason and argument on the basis of fact or appeal to prudence. Nevertheless, the potential consequences for failure to establish consensus may prove disastrous in the long run, creating confrontation and enmity with China where present trends do not warrant it.

Notes

1. The most prominent exposition of this view recently is the highly sensationalistic book by Richard Bernstein and Robin Munro, *The Coming Conflict with China* (New York: Alfred A. Knopf, 1997). Other exponents of this viewpoint include Paul Wolfowitz, Dean of the School of Advanced International Studies (who likens China's rise to that of Nazi Germany), and Professors Samuel Huntington of Harvard and Arthur Waldron of the Naval War College.

2. Among those who argue all these lines and who urge an American policy of engagement toward China are former National Security Advisers Henry Kissinger and Zbigniew Brzezinski, Ambassadors Arthur Hummel and Charles Freeman, former National Intelligence Officer for East Asia Ezra Vogel, and Michel Oksenberg, Robert Ross, David Shambaugh, and Michael Swaine. As will become clear, the author agrees with these views.

3. This viewpoint is expressed by Gerald Segal, "China Changes Shape," *Foreign Affairs* 73, no. 3 (May/June 1994): 43–58; and Jack Goldstone, "The Coming Chinese Collapse," *Foreign Policy*, no. 99 (Summer 1995): 35–52.

4. A convenient listing of the successive recognition of Beijing by other states is appended to Han Nianlong, ed. *Diplomacy of Contemporary China* (Hong Kong: New Horizon Press, 1990), 584–594; and in Tian Zengpei, ed., *Gaige Kaifang yilai de Zhongguo Waijiao* (Beijing: Shijie Zhishi Chubanshe, 1993), 638–645.

5. For annual foreign trade statistics since 1950, see PRC State Statistical Bureau, *China Statistical Yearbook 1989* (New York: Praeger, 1990), 546.

6. The classic analysis on the gap between Beijing's revolutionary foreign policy rhetoric and its more discriminating and cautious actions in this period is Peter Van Ness, *Revolution and Chinese Foreign Policy: Peking's Support for Wars of National Liberation* (Berkeley: University of California Press, 1971).

7. On the "Third Front" construction, see Barry Naughton, "The Third Front: Defense Industrialization in the Chinese Interior," *China Quarterly*, no. 115 (September 1988): 351–386.

8. See in particular Deng's speeches to a national science conference on March 18, 1978, and to a cadre conference on January 16, 1980, "The Present Situation and the Tasks Before Us," in *Selected Works of Deng Xiaoping, 1975–1982* (Beijing: Foreign Languages Press, 1984), 101–116 and 224–258.

9. International Institute of Strategic Studies, *The Military Balance 1995/96* (London: Oxford University Press, 1995), 266. The size of China's defense

spending is a subject of tremendous controversy. In Western press and popular discussions, the figures in the annual budget for defense presented each year to the National People's Congress—which have grown at double-digit rates in recent years—are often erroneously taken to indicate growth for defense spending overall, which has also grown but probably not at such spectacular rates. See also Karl W. Eikenberry, "Chinas Challenge to Asia Pacific Regional Stability," in *Southeast Asian Security in the New Millennium*, ed. Richard J. Ellings and Sheldon W. Simon (Armonk, New York: M.E. Sharpe, 1996), 92–93.

10. Communique of the Fourth Plenary Session of the 13th CPC Central Committee, *Beijing Review*, 3–9 July 1989, 9–10.

11. Communique of the Seventh Plenary Session of the 13th CPC Central Committee, *Beijing Review*, 7–13 January 1991, 31–33.

12. For a brief summary of this episode, see Joseph Fewsmith, "Reaction, Resurgence, and Succession: Chinese Politics Since Tiananmen," in *The Politics of China: The Eras of Mao and Deng*, 2nd ed., ed. Roderick MacFarquhar (Cambridge: Cambridge University Press, 1997), 493–496.

13. The subsequent discussion of leadership politics summarizes conclusions offered in H.L. Miller, "The Post-Deng Leadership: Premature Reports of Demise?" in *Washington Journal of Modern China* 2, no. 2 (Fall/Winter 1994): 1–16; and *idem*, "Overlapping Transitions in China's Leadership," in *SAIS Review* 16, no. 2 (Summer-Fall 1996): 21–42.

14. The April 1997 State Council circular includes a number of concrete provisions that indicate central resolve to act after years of caution and tentativeness. These include creation of a supra-ministerial "leading group" under the State Economic and Trade Commission to guide the process, detailed stipulations for disposition of failing enterprise debts and liquidation of remaining assets, and creation of re-employment centers to aid workers losing jobs in the process. Xinhua News Agency in Chinese, April 20, 1997. See also the commentator article "Standardize Bankruptcy, Encourage Merger, Vigorously Carry Out the Project of Re-Employment," *Remin Ribao*, 21 April 21 1997.

15. With respect to Russia, Jiang Zemin has visited Moscow twice (1994 and 1997) and President Boris Yeltsin has visited Beijing twice (1992 and 1996). The Russian Parliament ratified the agreement resolving most border problems soon after the dissolution of the USSR. The largest sector remaining from the former Sino-Soviet border dispute is in the Pamir mountain range, which is now claimed by the Tajik Republic. Beijing has not pressed this dispute with Dushanbe, urging that it be set aside indefinitely. The border military reduction negotiations begun after Mikhail Gorbachev's 1989 Beijing visit have progressed in the post-Soviet era, producing 5-nation agreements on demilitarizing their common borders. Diplomacy between Beijing and New Delhi has produced two agreements, in 1993 and 1996, stabilizing the Sino-Indian boundary dispute and establishing confidence-building measures in border regions pending a permanent resolution.

16. Mark J. Valencia, *China and the South Sea Island Disputes*, Adelphi Paper No. 298 (London: International Institution for Strategic Studies, 1995), 23.

17. Indications of this debate are discussed briefly in Miller, "Overlapping Transitions in China's Leadership," 39–40.

18. "Joint Statement by the People's Republic of China and the Russian Federation on the Multipolarization of the World and the Establishment of a New International Order," April 23, 1997, in *Beijing Review*, 12–18 May 1997, 7–8.

19. "Sino-French Joint Declaration," May 16, 1997, *Xinhua* (in English), 16 May 1997, FBIS via WNC (Foreign Broadcasting Information Service via World News Connection).

Chapter 9

Changing U.S. Perspectives on Human Rights

Akira Iriye

The literature on human rights is enormous. The bulk of it, however, deals with the subject ahistorically, abstracting the concept from its history and elaborating on its legal implications or philosophical foundations. Many writers have discussed the relevance of a presumably Western-originating legal concept (or moral precept) such as human rights to a non-Western society. Samuel Huntington, to take just one example, discusses the human rights question in his *The Clash of Civilizations and the Remaking of World Order*[1] and argues that, because the human rights doctrine is a product of Western civilization, any attempt to spread, let alone impose, it on other lands is bound to fail. What is lacking in such an analysis is an attempt at examining how human rights have come to be seen as an important aspect of international affairs, and how governments, in particular the United States government, have sought to promote the cause, and with what consequences. Human rights may be an eternal verity in the West and nowhere else, but human rights diplomacy in the international context is something else. By tracing the history of human rights as an issue in international affairs, we may gain a perspective into how that diplomacy has come to affect U.S. relations with other countries, including China and other nations of Asia.

In 1919 a group of Vietnamese expatriates gathered in a Parisian apartment and drafted a "declaration of Annamite people," to be presented to President Woodrow Wilson and other foreign dignitaries who had assembled for the peace conference. The document set forth an eight-point program including a general amnesty for political prisoners, freedom of the press, and the right to form political associations. The document was submitted to Wilson and other world leaders, who simply ignored it.[2]

This episode illustrates some important aspects of the human rights question. First, the Vietnamese nationalists presented their argument for freedom and autonomy in the universal language of human rights. The vocabulary may have come from the West, but they ardently believed that the principles they asserted were universally applicable. Second, the United States, arguably the most committed to the human rights principle of all nations, did not share the Vietnamese perspective, that is to say, the Vietnamese view about the universality of human rights. (Disappointed by the cool reception by the West, some of the Vietnamese, the most famous of them being Ho Chin Minh, were to turn to Marxist-Leninist anti-imperialism as the solution, giving up on a liberal construction of human rights for a more radical one.) Third, generalizing from these observations, one may note that, quite apart from the doctrinal foundations of the human rights principle, its practice has varied from time to time, from country to country.

To elaborate further on this last point, the gap between principle and practice, or profession and execution, has constituted an important part of the history of human rights in international affairs. Historians agree that the concept of human rights in modern times became embedded in the vocabulary of political affairs in the last decades of the eighteenth century and the beginning of the nineteenth. Often referred to as the "age of the democratic revolution," the period was notable not simply because of profound domestic transformations in Europe and North America, but also because various forces combined to create an Atlantic community, forces that transformed the ways in which people behaved toward one another. People of different ranks, classes, ages, and occupations developed patterns of civility, politeness, and respect for each other; in short, they became "civilized." This "civilization," of course, was intimately linked to the economic and social transformation that was being brought about by the rapid development of industrialization, urbanization, and trans-Atlantic commerce. Human rights, in such a context, were essentially a principle of civilized behavior in which an individual's autonomy, freedom, and dignity were respected.

That was the principle. It is not surprising that the Americans, perceiving themselves as members of the Atlantic community, should have readily accepted and identified with it. But how about the areas of the world outside the Atlantic community? Did human rights literally mean the rights of all humans, not just North Americans and Western Europeans? That in practice this was never the case was clearly seen in the institution of slavery or the treatment of native Americans in the United States. Despite the profession of the ideal of spreading the "blessings of liberty," moreover, neither the United States government nor the American people seriously entertained the thought of bringing the idea and practice of human rights to other countries. United States foreign relations throughout the nineteenth century were primarily concerned with territorial acquisition and the expansion of trade, while individual Americans were far more preoccupied with internal affairs than with events in distant parts of the globe. Those few who did profess an interest in foreign affairs outside the Atlantic world were merchants, missionaries, travelers, and others with no grand vision of playing a role in the social transformation of other lands.

When, then, did Americans begin to view the promotion of human rights as an objective they would seriously pursue abroad? This may have coincided with the emergence of the United States as a world power at the turn of the twentieth century. Both American leaders and people wanted their nation to be a new kind or power, not merely a traditional sort of great power defined geopolitically, in terms of economic resources and military force. Of course, exceptionalism had been there from the founding of the United States, but until the twentieth century, it had not meant that the nation had a special task to transform other societies. But now, as the United States was beginning to view itself, and was being viewed as a world leader, it needed to define its *raison d'être*, an image of what it meant to the world, and what it could do in the international arena that was different from what other great powers had done.

Not surprisingly, civilization emerged as a possible answer. As Frank Ninkovich argues in *Modernity and Power*,[3] Theodore Roosevelt, William Howard Taft, and Woodrow Wilson were all keen to envision the United States playing its role as a civilizer, bringing civilization to less civilized parts of the globe. Civilization meant, as it had a century earlier, civility, politeness, and mutual respect, but now, in the age of rapid technological development and modernization, these values seemed to be in need of greater reinforcement than ever before. The United States could be a model of a nation that was technologically and materially modernized but at the same time spiritually civilized. And the nation could show the way to others so that they, too, would come to approximate its achievements. Such a vision was historicist in that there was little expectation of a quick transformation of a society. Rather, as a country undertook modernization, it was expected to come to appreciate the values of modern spiritual civilization, including human dignity and freedom, namely human rights. But the process would take time. Such a view explains why Wilson was cool to Ho and his Vietnamese colleagues as they sought to obtain his support for their struggle for colonial autonomy. Human rights, Wilson implied, were not something that one could acquire out of context; they had to be preceded by laborious preparation, which, Wilson believed, Ho and others had not undertaken.

Up to this point, therefore, one may note that human rights had not yet been viewed as a universally applicable doctrine or as a foreign policy objective of the United States. While modern civilized nations dealt with one another in a framework defined by human rights, they would not expect other societies to do likewise, at least not until they, too, became civilized. If such a view had persisted, it might have led to historical relativism and, hence, moral relativism, the idea that different societies had their own ethical standards and, consequently, that one society should not try to impose its standards on another. Such a relativist view, should it prevail today, would be content with the protection of human rights in the United States and certain other countries but not in all nations; it would have little trouble living within a world in which some societies suppressed human rights.

Obviously, that is no longer the case. Something must have happened in the course of the last several decades to make human rights more than just a historical phenomenon and to turn it into an objective of the foreign policy of the United States and of certain other countries as well. In seeking to locate the origins of human rights diplomacy, we do have to go back to Wilson, for despite his cool response to the Vietnamese nationalists, he did espouse a universalistic foreign policy, as best exemplified by the League of Nations. As he conceived of the world organization, the same principles and rules of behavior applied to all nations, powerful and weak, Western and non-Western, that belonged to it. (Vietnam, of course, was not a member, being a French colony.) The League of Nations, therefore, despite its ineffectualness as a peace-keeping body, set an important precedent; a universal body was being established, and its members were to share certain basic principles. Human rights were, to be sure, not specifically mentioned, but the important thing was the principle of universalism. Contents could be added and amplified later. (Article 23 of the League Covenant referred to "fair and humane conditions of labour for men, women, and children" as an objective to be pursued "in all countries," a statement that may be taken as one of the first international agreements on universalism.)

The human rights principle was severely challenged during the 1930s, as anti-democratic states denounced the League's alleged universalism and began proclaiming their own standards of behavior. But this very crisis, in retrospect, served to reinforce universalism. Even before the Second World War ended, the United States and its allies had defined their war objectives in universalistic terms, citing their commitment to what Franklin D. Roosevelt called the "four freedoms": freedom of speech, freedom of religion, freedom from want, and freedom from fear. The other nations, in the meantime, sought to reestablish world organization on the basis of even more sweepingly broad principles than the League. To be sure, for the principal powers such as the United States, Great Britain, and the Soviet Union, the postwar peace was envisaged geopolitically, something to be preserved through big-power cooperation against the resurgence of Axis militarism. At the same time, however, there was a keen interest in basing the postwar world order on broad principles of freedom, justice, and human rights. The preamble to the United Nations (U.N.) charter declared the member states' reaffirmation of "faith in fundamental human rights, in the dignity and worth of the human person, in the equal rights of men and women and of nations large and small." An Economic and Social Council was established within the United Nations so as to promote "respect for, and observance of, human rights and fundamental freedoms for all." It is notable that a separate body, UNESCO (U.N. Educational, Scientific & Cultural Organization), was created within the U.N. in December 1945, so as to focus on human rights and other "cultural" and "moral" issues. As the UNESCO constitution stated, "a peace based exclusively upon the political and economic arguments of governments would not be a peace which could secure the unanimous, lasting and sincere support of the peoples of the world. [Peace] must therefore be founded ... upon the intellectual and moral solidarity of mankind." It is difficult to find a better expression of the new universalism at that time; the idea that only through the preservation and promotion of human rights and freedoms could a durable peace be achieved.

The United States fully supported such universalism; indeed, its inspiration was unmistakably Wilsonian, but Wilsonianism now appeared more likely to be globalized than after the First World War. The United States in 1945, even more than in 1918, was the undisputed world leader. Its officials often spoke of "one world," "the American century," and "the century of common man," implying that under U.S. leadership tides of democratic change were about to envelope the entire world. The fact that one of the first postwar objectives pursued by Washington was to bring democracy to Germany and Japan, hitherto self-consciously anti-democratic states, suggested an optimism that this indeed was the case. As if to reconfirm that the optimism was truly global, the 1948 Universal Declaration of Human Rights, adopted by the United Nations, declared that the principles contained in the declaration (such as freedom, equality, and dignity) were to be seen as "a common standard of achievement for all peoples and all nations ... without distinction of any kind, such as race, color, sex, language, religion, political or other opinion, national or social origin, property, birth or other status." Although in reality human rights were being abused all over the world, the declaration served as a statement of universal aspirations, a vision for the future. To ensure "universal respect for, and observance of, human rights and fundamental freedoms for all," a Commission on Human Rights was established within the Economic and Social Council in 1947. It is clear that at this stage the vision was that of the unity of humankind, united in terms of the struggle for human rights and freedom for all people. Such a vision was accepted by an America that was emerging as the world leader. Just as it had at the turn of the century, the United States would define its world role in terms of certain ideals, but this time those ideals would have the support of the rest of the world. Eleanor Roosevelt was one of the most active participants in human rights activities through the United Nations.

In the absence of the Cold War, the United States government might have actively conducted a foreign policy in pursuit of human rights. Of course, to the extent that the confrontation with the former Union of Soviet Socialist Republics (USSR) was defined ideologically, human rights were never far removed from official thinking; the bipolar confrontation was seen as a struggle between freedom and totalitarianism. The United States would wage a Cold War to defend freedom and human dignity against a brutal ideology that subordinated individual freedoms to class interests or state power. At the same time, however, as the Cold War became increasingly militarized and globalized, human rights considerations became subordinated to the larger dictates of military strategy and balance of power. In a worldwide contest of will, it seemed to matter less whether a country protected human rights than that it was anti-Communist. Thus the United States initially did not join the majority of the United Nations in condemning apartheid in South Africa, and it rejected U.N. investigations into human rights abuses in the Dominican Republic in the wake of the U.S. expedition of 1965. Conservatives in the United States, in fact, attacked the U.N.'s human rights advocacy as an interference in the domestic affairs of member states. It was not until 1977 that Washington appointed its first full-time representative on the United Nations Human Rights Commission. It was also then, under the Carter presidency, that the State Department created the post of assistant secretary of state for human rights affairs. Even President Jimmy Carter, however, supported the Pol Pot regime in Cambodia as the rightful government with a seat in the United Nations, despite the widely recognized human rights abuses the regime had perpetrated. The decision was made for geopolitical reasons, to contain Soviet influence in the Indochinese Republic.[4]

However, it was not just the Cold War that played havoc with human rights diplomacy. The independence of more than a hundred new countries after the Second World War introduced a new element, a new challenge to international affairs. Initially, they—those that were already independent or achieved independence shortly after the war—endorsed the Declaration on Human Rights and other documents, viewing them as an enunciation of the principle of non-discrimination. By the 1960s, according to Ian Brownlie, "the principle of respect for and protection of human rights had become recognized as a legal standard."[5] Soon, however, many Third World countries came to question the universalism of the human rights doctrine. In the 1970s, they began to develop their own identity, sometimes referred to as a "new international economic order" when involving global economic relations and as a "new international cultural order" when considering cultural exchanges, information dissemination, and related matters. Several of these countries cavalierly violated human rights as defined by U.N. documents, but, commanding a majority in the United Nations, they were often immune from attack. Instead, they spoke in the name of anti-imperialism, implying that Western principles were a form of cultural imperialism. Imperialists, they argued, were the chief violators of human rights. Rejecting the universalism of human rights and other doctrines, they emphasized diversity, separateness, and distinctions among peoples and cultures of the world, rather than common, shared aspirations of all.

The United States did not have an effective response to these instances of Third Worldism, except to show its displeasure by withdrawing from such organizations as the International Labor Organization (ILO) and UNESCO, in a sense abdicating its role as world leader in promoting human rights. It did not, however, abandon universalism or retreat to moral relativism. Interestingly enough, as Henry Kissinger has noted, during the 1970s human rights came to "rank among the principal goals of American foreign policy."[6] This took the form, not of a self-conscious response to Third Worldism, but of a concern with the internal affairs of the Soviet Union and its allies as a policy of detente was being pursued toward them. As the Nixon and Ford administrations pushed for arms limitation agreements with the Soviet Union, and as U.S.-USSR relations improved, there inevitably arose the question of liberalization and democratization within the Iron Curtain, for it could be argued that no durable detente was possible without economic and political reforms in the socialist countries. It was not surprising that from the beginning the Conference on Security and Cooperation in Europe (CSCE), established in 1972, should have listed human rights and cultural exchange among the objectives to be promoted jointly by the North Atlantic Treaty Organization (NATO) and the Warsaw Pact nations. The CSCE's Helsinki accord of 1975 was a ringing endorsement of human rights and laid the basis for what would come in the 1980s, the sweeping transformation of Soviet-bloc nations economically and politically.

Despite what some saw as a return to the Cold War in U.S.-USSR relations in the late 1970s and the early 1980s, the momentum, once set in motion, could never be reversed. An important byproduct of the thawing of Cold War tensions was the growing irrelevance of the Third World's anti-imperialist rhetoric. Non-Western countries could no longer dismiss human rights and democracy as mere imperialist rhetoric when the Soviet Union and other Eastern European nations were beginning to embrace these values. Moreover, in the same years several Third World countries began to undertake rapid economic development, in effect ceasing to be Third World. Thus was created an opportunity for the United States and other advocates of human rights to promote the cause in these fast-changing economies. Not surprisingly, it was precisely in those countries that were beginning to undertake rapid economic transformation—South Korea, Singapore, China, and several in Latin America—that the United States showed special interest in promoting human rights. Because these nations were modernizing themselves in the economic realm, they could be encouraged to carry out political reforms. In a way, this faith in political modernization provided the framework for a reinvigorated human rights diplomacy. It was intended to ensure that an economically modernized nation would also protect the rights of its citizens. One sees the same concern with modernization that was evident at the turn of the century. But now there were more and more countries joining the global economy as mass producers and consumers. It would be of real concern to the United States, and to international relations as a whole, that these countries should be creating modern citizens with all their rights and freedoms. Otherwise, they would remain politically underdeveloped, unruly, and inherently hostile to world order and to democratic societies. And it did seem as if democratic tides were spreading to many lands in Asia, Africa, and Latin America. Then came Tiananmen.

It is remarkable that the suppression of student movements in China occurred in the same year that saw the coming down of the Berlin Wall, ending the Cold War. It was as if the principle of human rights were emerging triumphant in Europe, while at the same time it was being suppressed in China. The end of the Cold War magnified the human rights crisis in China and elsewhere, precisely because the principle seemed to help define the agendas for the post-Cold War world.

For the United States the new agenda could be conceptualized by reverting to traditional values. President George Bush asserted that the post-Cold War world order must seek "to increase democracy, increase prosperity, increase the peace, and reduce arms."[7] The juxtaposition of democracy, prosperity, and peace is important; the American leader was reiterating the traditional liberal internationalist perspective now transposed onto the world arena to give it direction. It was as if, now that the dictates of the Cold War strategy, necessitating the need to deal with the Soviet challenge by all methods in all parts of the world, had been removed, the United States could promote its liberal visions with less embarrassment and with greater consistency than earlier. Not just liberal internationalists, but nationalists and conservatives could applaud the new emphasis on human rights and market economies, for they could see these as traditional American principles producing a world environment that served the national interest.

The fundamental significance of the human rights diplomacy in the post-Cold War era lay in the fact that the concept suggested a promising approach to a world which, precisely because the Cold War had ended, was in a state of uncertainty. What would now determine the shape of international affairs? Would the world revert to being an arena for the traditional game of power politics, pitting nations against each other?

Would there emerge newer forces that made such reversion to the past unlikely? For instance, various regional entities, ranging from the European Union to the North American Free Trade Agreement (NAFTA), could add new meaning to international relations by introducing regions, not just states, as actors in the drama. There were also an increasing number of multinational organizations which, added to such existing institutions as the International Monetary Fund and the International Atomic Energy Agency, impinged upon the sovereign rights of individual states. They were joined by non-state actors within each nation and across national boundaries. Organizations such as Greenpeace and Physicians without Frontiers actively pursued their own agendas, sometimes with the support or connivance of governments, but frequently to the annoyance of the latter. In the meantime, economic forces were linking all parts of the globe with greater speed than ever before. The end of the Cold War served to link former adversaries together economically, and the reduction in the military budgets of the United States, the former Soviet Union, and other powers had the effect of enhancing the role of economic transactions in world affairs. Power tended to be defined by economic rather than by military indices.

In such a situation, some guiding principles were needed to reconceptualize international relations, and human rights was one of them. It did not really matter that the concept had originated in the West; what was important was that human rights seemed to provide a vision, an organizing principle, for the world in the wake of the Cold War. Because the collapse of communist totalitarianism had been very much part of the story of the end of the Cold War, and because the United States, as a self-proclaimed champion of human rights, emerged as the only super-power in the wake of the disintegration of the Soviet Union, it was natural that the principle should be looked upon as the key to the new world order.

By the same token, countries that were not ready or willing to accept an American-defined new world order resisted the incorporation of the human rights principle into the post-Cold War system of international relations. It is not surprising that China should have emerged as the main opponent of the United States in this regard. The Chinese leadership was loathe to accept the U.S. initiative for a number of reasons. For one thing, they saw the human rights diplomacy as an interference in Chinese domestic politics; at a time when Chinese politics after the passing of Deng Xiaoping was likely to be in a state of flux, the Communist leaders had to try to minimize uncertainty and turmoil at home. Thus, for them to oppose human rights was a way of preventing undue foreign influence upon the mass of people. Moreover, the Chinese leadership saw the U.S. promotion of human rights as a device for retaining its power in an area of the world where Chinese power was bound to increase. In other words, in Beijing's perspective, the human rights diplomacy was another way through which the United States was seeking to prevent China's emergence as a great power. To the Chinese, to emerge as a great power was to return to the past, a hundred and fifty years ago, when China had enjoyed influence and prestige as the undisputed leader in the east Asian region. To invoke such a memory was to be persuaded of the distinctive Chinese civilization with its own codes of ethics, quite apart from the West's. Thus it was impossible to accept the Western definition of human rights as if this were applicable to an area with its own philosophies and patterns of behavior.

Above all, China's continued resistance to the human rights diplomacy suggests that the country still views itself as a sovereign state in a world of sovereign states. In other words, despite all the changes taking place in world affairs, the Chinese still consider the concepts of the nation, nationalism, and national interest as the key guides to international affairs. Not individuals, non-state organizations, cross-national entities, or transnational economic interests, but the nation is still the focus of policy. In such a framework, the U.S.-Chinese contention about human rights may be seen as an aspect of the sharply contrasting images of the world after the Cold War. Whereas proponents of human rights believe the world is entering a new stage in which sovereign states will not be the sole actors, the opponents believe nothing has really changed, that sovereignty, power, and national interests must still provide the basic vocabulary of international affairs.

In a sense both contentions are right. On the one hand, there is little doubt that transnational economic and cultural forces are reshaping the world; but, on the other hand, national entities are not disappearing but in some instances, such as China, strengthening themselves. We would be mistaken to accept only one of these possibilities as the reality. Rather, we should see both the continued existence of independent states, some aspiring to a great-power status, and the emergence of non-state actors and cross-national forces, as providing the momentum for world transformation.

If such an analysis makes sense, then it follows that there will no easy resolution of the human rights question so long as it is dealt with within the traditional framework of interstate relations. That is, so long as the United States and China treat the question as a diplomatic issue between two sovereign states, there is a limit to what can be accomplished.

Washington may press Beijing for greater protection of the rights of prisoners, for instance, threatening to deny China certain trade privileges otherwise; and the latter might accede to such pressure by making a few concessions but not really throwing open the country to democratization. The record of such governmental negotiations has been meager. Samuel Huntington writes that as far as the human rights issue is concerned, U.S. policy has been a case of "unconditional surrender" to China.[8] This may be an exaggeration, but it is certainly true that the United States has conceded many commercial privileges China has coveted without obtaining more than a modicum of human rights reforms in the country. But the above analysis suggests that human rights today are not something that can be negotiated among states as if this were still a traditional world of sovereign nations. We live in a world in which non-state actors, ranging from private individuals to various cross-national organizations, are increasingly assertive, and human rights are something that is properly promoted by them, not by states or governments. Rather than the United States government negotiating with the Chinese government about the freedom of the press or fair trials of dissidents, individuals and non-governmental organizations are the appropriate agencies for seeking change. It is they, for instance Amnesty International and the International Red Cross, that have been active in the cause and gained some significant results. They are the forces for reshaping international affairs, not tradition-bound states. For this very reason, the sovereign regime in Beijing will persist in resisting pressures for human rights reform, because they will tend to strengthen non-state actors which are by definition subversive of state power. Just as persistent, however, will be the forces for reform.

In his recent essay on the "Americanization" of postwar Japan, historian Olivier Zunz notes, "More than other people, [Americans] have put on the world agenda their understanding of the relationship among national wealth, individual freedom, and personal well-being."[9] Even if at present China may be focusing on the first of these three principles, it will never be able to detach this from the other two, which are both human rights issues. The U.S. State Department now has an under secretary of state for human affairs; the office handles environmental, drug, migration, and human rights problems. The title, "human affairs," is very apt, for human rights are part and parcel of the global human concern with problems that go beyond such traditional national affairs as security and prosperity. Not even the most closed of societies, or the most authoritarian of regimes, would long be able to ignore the relationship between security, economics, and "human" affairs. And so long as the United States views itself as world leader, its espousal of human rights is bound to continue, even to intensify. It may be, as G. John Ikenberry argues in a recent article, that "the world does not need hegemonic leadership in the way it did in the past." The world today, he suggests, is much more homogeneous than fifty years ago, and to that extent "America's liberal hegemonic work has largely been accomplished—at least the work that requires the most concentrated mass of material capabilities and military power."[10] Not through economic resources or military power, but through its advanced communications and information technology linking all parts of the globe, and through the ideals with which it has identified itself as a nation among nations, the United States still serves its role as world leader. Just as likely, China may persist in resisting such assertions by U.S. leadership. But in a rapidly changing world environment, the contest will not, luckily, lead to military conflict but to a heterogeneous, interdependent Asia-Pacific region.

Notes

1. Samuel Huntington, *The Clash of Civilizations and the Remaking of World Order* (New York, Simon & Schuster, 1996).
2. Mark Bradley, "Imaging Vietnam and America" (unpublished doctoral dissertation, Harvard University, 1995), 8.
3. Frank Ninkovich, *Modernity and Power* (Chicago: University of Chicago Press, 1994).
4. For data on U.S.-UN relations, I am indebted to Gary Ostrower, *The United Nations and the United States* (forthcoming).
5. Gerrit W. Gong, *The Standard of "Civilization" in International Society* (Oxford: Claredon Press, 1984), 91.
6. Henry Kissinger, *Diplomacy* (New York: Touchstone, 1994), 752.
7. *Ibid.*, 805.
8. Huntington, *The Clash of Civilizations*, 194.
9. Olivier Zunz, "Modernization and Individualism," *Seikei University Asia-Pacific Studies*, no. 14 (1997): 70.
10. G. John Ikenberry, "The Future of International Leadership," *Political Science Quarterly* (Fall 1996): 400–401.

Chapter 10

U.S.-Japanese Relations, Democracy and Human Rights Issues in Asia

Tadashi Aruga[*]

Introduction

Joint statements issued at the closing of U.S.-Japanese summits usually mention that the two nations share basic liberal democratic values and emphasize this fact as the foundation of their global partnership. The Hashimoto-Clinton Declaration on Security of April 1996, for example, emphasizes the common commitment of the two nations to "freedom and democracy." Their joint message to the Japanese and American peoples listed the promotion of democracy and human rights in the world among the purposes for which the two nations should work together.[1] Since differences between them have tended to be overemphasized in recent bilateral trade conflicts, it is very important to remind the Japanese and the Americans of the basic common values that they share. Liberal democratic values have not prevailed yet in Asia. Japan is a rare Asian nation which has practiced parliamentary democracy and maintained extensive civil liberties and rights during the latter half of this century. Besides, economic and social benefits are more equitably distributed in Japan than many other nations, because Japan has succeeded in combining its remarkable economic development with the creation of a "middle-class society." The United States has not found any serious human rights violations in Japan. The U.S. State Department's Country Reports on Human Rights have devoted very few pages to Japan, because there has been little to criticize about the Japanese government's human rights record. Human Rights Watch, a leading human rights NGO (non-governmental organization), in the United States, rates Japan's human rights record as "generally ... good."[2]

Since the 1980s, liberal democracy has been ascending in the world. In many countries, dictatorships and other forms of repressive government have been replaced by liberal democratic regimes. The collapse of the Communist dictatorship in the Soviet Union and Eastern European countries was the most dramatic of these changes. According to a recent survey of political and civil liberties by the Freedom House, more than 60 percent of all countries are now democratic, whereas less than 30 percent of them were democratic in 1974.[3]

In East Asia, South Korea, Taiwan, the Philippines, and Thailand transformed themselves from military or one-party dictatorships to liberal democratic regimes. Mongolia, a former Soviet satellite, followed the example of Russia. But the other Asian communist states retain a one-party dictatorship, while both China and Vietnam have introduced a partially market-oriented economy and have greatly increased their involvement in the international economy. Most Southeast Asian countries have some kind of authoritarian government. In South Asia, India is the only country which has practiced parliamentary democracy since its independence. But its democracy has been marred by remnants of the caste system. Since a world composed of liberal democratic nations which respect human rights is the most agreeable world for both Japan and the United States, it is certainly desirable for both that Asian nations move towards liberal democracy.

Given the common commitment of the two nations to liberal democratic values, the promotion of democracy and human rights in Asia seems to be an issue most suitable for U.S.-Japanese cooperation. But the matter actually is not so simple. The United States has made the promotion of human rights one of its foreign policy objectives since the mid-1970s and has vigorously pursued human rights diplomacy in a number of cases since then. Although Japan's commitment to the cause of international human rights has become much clearer in recent years, its approach to human rights diplomacy remains very timid, particularly in Asia. Major reasons for this contrast, which will be discussed later, still remain. Although it is possible to mitigate this contrast to promote U.S.-Japanese cooperation on this issue of democracy and human rights in Asia, it seems to be difficult for Japan and the United States to work closely together in this area.

Backgrounds for Contrasting U.S. and Japanese Approaches

It should be said first that the encouragement of democracy and of human rights are interrelated but not the same. Democracy can be practiced without due regard to minority rights. An authoritarian regime can be very repressive but also can be relatively lenient and allow a degree of individual freedom.

Since the days of Woodrow Wilson, the United States has promoted the spread of democracy in the world. But President Wilson did not practice human rights diplomacy. It was only during World War II that the United States began to mention respect for human rights as a universal principle. The term "human rights" first appeared in the Declaration by the United Nations issued in January 1942, The Charter of the United Nations made it an objective of the organization to achieve international cooperation "in promoting and encouraging respect for human rights and for fundamental freedoms for all without distinction as to race, sex, language, or religion." It was in 1948 that the United Nations (U.N.) adopted the Universal Declaration of Human Rights which defined the universal standard for respecting human rights.[4] Liberal delegates of the United States contributed to drafting these memorable documents. However, there was considerable uneasiness among white Southerners towards these documents which included the principle of racial equality. The United States government subdued their uneasiness by emphasizing the principle of sovereignty and non-intervention in domestic affairs. To counter their attempt to curtail the treaty-making power of the president, President Eisenhower promised the Southern conservatives that he would not support the ratification of international covenants on human rights the drafting of which was in progress in the U.N. The United States, therefore, opted for a passive role in the drafting.[5]

In was only in the mid-1970s that the United States began to pursue human rights diplomacy. By that time, the United States had succeeded in calming domestic racial tensions on the new social and legal principle of racial equality. Because of this success, the Americans were able to look abroad and make the promotion of human rights one of the purposes of their foreign policy. The promotion of human rights was thus combined with that of democracy in American foreign policy. The number of private organizations dedicated to the international protection and promotion of human rights greatly increased in the 1970s. In the mid-1970s, members of the U.S. Congress, particularly Congressional Democrats, wanted to reassert their will in foreign policymaking dominated by the chief executive. The reorientation of U.S. foreign policy away from the old cold-war framework after the Vietnam debacle had been carried out under Richard Nixon's initiative. Because of this, Congress wanted to inject some new elements into American foreign policy to regain its own initiative. The insertion of human rights conditions in foreign aid bills was a means of this self-assertion. Human rights diplomacy was also a reflection of the desire of many Americans to reestablish the moral foundation of U.S. foreign policy that had been shaken by the Vietnam War. When President Jimmy Carter announced the promotion of human rights in the world as one of the pillars of his foreign policy, stating "our commitment of human rights must be absolute," his speech was favorably received by the American public.[6]

U.S. human rights diplomacy employed the method of quiet diplomacy—attempts to persuade through various diplomatic channels. It also used the methods of applying public pressure and threatening or imposing sanctions. Such high-handed tactics as public criticism and threatening or applying sanctions were annoying to and resented by governments friendly to or allied with the United States. Towards its allies and friends, the United States used the method of quiet diplomacy in most cases but sometimes used public diplomacy as a means for advocating human rights diplomacy when it seemed effective. For countries where the United States had economic, political and security interests, the United States chose methods of human rights diplomacy most compatible with the protection of those interests, thus inviting the criticism that the U.S. human rights diplomacy lacked consistency. Successive U.S. administrations tried to balance U.S. interests in human rights with its interests on other issues. But U.S. human rights diplomacy has been much more vigorous than that of any other Western democracy, because the United States is by far the most powerful among the Western democracies and therefore most influential in shaping the world order. It also reflects the national tradition of the United States to emphasize its mission in the world.[7] It is natural that Japanese human rights diplomacy has been much less vigorous than America's. But it has been strangely weak if the rise of Japanese economic power and its well-established liberal democracy are taken into account.

There are several reasons for this weakness. Yasuaki Onuma suggests two cultural reasons: the emphasis on modesty in Japanese culture tends to discourage the practice of proselytizing for a high cause, and legalistic thinking is foreign to many Japanese. Onuma also points out that for the Japanese government in the postwar era, the term diplomacy meant bilateral diplomacy with particular countries. Japan simply wanted to make the most of the existing international order created and maintained by the United States in the post-World War II era. It did not regard the job of creating and maintaining a world order as its own job, but as someone else's. Onuma also thinks that Japanese human rights diplomacy has been hindered by the lack of interest of the Japanese business community in the human rights situation in developing countries.[8] In this writer's view, these factors may also be related to Japanese culture. The Japanese attitudes towards interpersonal relations have been particularistic, not universalistic. They have accepted the principle of respect for certain human rights as a code of behavior to maintain harmony in Japanese society in the postwar era. But their commitment to human rights has been somewhat ambiguous, since these rights were given to them by the occupation authorities, not something they gained through their own efforts. Their respect for individual rights has been fuzzy, particularly where the assertion of such rights seems to disturb social harmony. Nor has their interest in human rights, because of this particularism, been strong outside their own society.

Onuma also points out that the failure of Japan to confront the problems of Japanese guilt in its aggressive wars and colonialism has prevented Japan from taking a leading role in Asia in matters involving moral issues. "Had Japan openly criticized China or Korea for their failure to secure human rights," he says, "there would have been a hard reaction, being that Japan had not yet taken full responsibility for colonialism replete with human rights abuses." The Chinese and Korean governments might have tried to mobilize anti-Japanese mass movements by reminding their peoples of the past aggressions and colonialism efforts conducted by Japan. Even if Japan had made declarations expressing sincere repentance in stronger terms for its aggressions and its repressive colonial rule, Japan would not have been free from the burden of its past. But Japan's frank self-criticism of its own imperialist past and its emphasis on the fresh departure of a postwar Japan as a liberal democratic nation seem to be prerequisites for a more vigorous Japanese leadership on democracy and human rights issues.

U.S. Policy on Democracy and Human Rights in Asia before 1989

When President Carter started his human rights diplomacy, its major focus was set on rightist dictatorial regimes in Latin America. While East Asia was not its major focus, Carter tried to soften the repression of the democratic movement by the conservative regime under President Park Chung Hee in South Korea. Since the United States had considered it most important to have a strong leader in South Korea, as the country was confronted with the hostile Communist regime in the North, it had tolerated Park's repressive policy, including the trial of democratic movement activists. Carter's human rights diplomacy encouraged the democratic movement in Korea. In 1979, when the democratic movement was gaining strength in Korea, President Park was assassinated by his bodyguard. Encouraged by the Carter administration, South Korea seemed for a while to move towards democracy. But the young hard-line army generals led by General Chun Doo Hwan increasingly got the upper hand, and they went on to create a military government led by Chun in 1980. Thus Carter's diplomacy ended in failure in Korea. Carter was much chagrined, but the only thing his diplomatic pressure was able to bring forth was the suspension of the execution of Kim Dae Jung, who was sentenced to death in the military trial. The Japanese government, too, pressured Chun Doo Hwan's government not to execute Kim Dae Jung. This was unusually strong human rights diplomacy directed against its neighbor; and it reflected the unusually strong interest of the Japanese public in the fate of Kim Dae Jung, who had once been kidnapped in Tokyo and secretly transferred to Korea by the Korean intelligence agency.[9]

President Ronald Reagan had been very critical of Carter's human rights diplomacy before he became President. Reagan contended that Carter's policy simply destabilized several authoritarian, but friendly, regimes and in one case led to the emergence of a pro-Soviet, Communist-oriented dictatorial regime. Because of the strong public and Congressional interest in human rights diplomacy, Reagan responded with his version of human rights diplomacy which featured the aspect of a democratic ideological offensive against the Soviet Union and its satellites. Reagan seemed to favor the policy of "standing pat" with friendly, authoritarian, and anti-Communist regimes. In reality, however, the Reagan administration pursued the policy of attempting to transform several friendly, but authoritarian, governments to democracy. In East Asia, the Reagan administration continued to apply strong pressure on Chun Doo Hwan to introduce a democratic constitution and step down from the presidency. Although Chun yielded primarily to the rising democratic movement, Washington's diplomatic pressure was instrumental in the political transformation towards democracy in South Korea in the 1980s. In the Philippines, initially Washington got along with Ferdinand Marcos's dictatorial government. When the force of democracy gained ascendancy in 1986, however, Washington gave the last push to his downfall by persuading him to leave the Philippines to make way for a democratic government. In both cases, political realism led Reagan to favor the peaceful transfer of power to a democratic government in the wake of an ascending democratic movement. It seemed to be the only way to secure political stability and long-term friendship in those countries.[10]

In both cases, the Japanese government supported U.S. policy and welcomed the birth of a democratic government. In the case of the Philippines, Tokyo increased its economic aid to help the Aquino government manage its fragile economy. In those days, there was no visible difference between Washington and Tokyo over the problems of human rights and democracy in Asia. If there was any possible friction between Tokyo and Washington over human rights issues, it was over sanctions against the apartheid system in South Africa. While the Reagan administration favored "constructive engagement" with the South African government, various anti-apartheid citizens' groups instituted severe non-governmental economic sanctions, and Congress legislated an act of economic sanctions much stronger than that which

Reagan had proposed. Although Japan had clearly stood against racial discrimination, Japan favored milder sanctions against South Africa. While abiding by the U.N. sanctions against South Africa, Japan, whose nationals were treated as "honorary whites" in this country, was lenient in the actual application of the sanctions because of Japanese interest in South African trade. Therefore, there was considerable criticism of Japan in the U.S. Congress and among the anti-apartheid public.[11] But U.S.-Japanese friction did not develop over the anti-apartheid sanctions because a great transformation towards non-racial democracy was about to take place in South Africa.

The Changed Global Landscape for International Human Rights Affairs

The year 1989 was literally an epoch-making year in world history. Remarkable events which took place in that year changed drastically the global landscape of democracy and human rights. That year witnessed the collapse of the Communist regimes in East European countries and progress in economic and political liberalization of the Soviet Union. The Berlin Wall, the symbol of a divided Europe since 1961, was pulled down by the people's power, and its fall symbolized the end of the Cold War. Remarkable changes in Eastern Europe and the Soviet Union seemed to exemplify the global trend towards pluralist democracy and the market economy. President George Bush spoke of creating the "new world order" based on democracy and the market economy. There was conservative action in the Soviet Union. But the coup attempt by conservatives failed in 1991, and Boris Yeltsin as the Russian President proceeded to restructure the Soviet Union into a democratic Russia and a number of independent states, all of which parted with the Communist dictatorship. Since 1989, it has been an important purpose of U.S. and West European foreign policies to help Eastern Europe, Russia and other members of this CIS (Confederation of Independent States), to stabilize their fledging liberal democracies and facilitate their transition to capitalism. The remarkable events of 1989 and after changed the global landscape of human rights and democracy issues. The collapse of the former Soviet bloc greatly strengthened the structural power of the United States and other Western democracies to define the international standard in human rights. The United States began to promote democracy and human rights more vigorously in its foreign policy. Countries in Western Europe, too, adopted more vigorous human rights diplomacy. Without these changes in 1989, the 1993 World Conference on Human Rights would not have been possible.

Because of these major changes in Eastern Europe, in the Soviet Union, and also in South Africa, the focus of human rights diplomacy of the United States and other Western democracies shifted to Asia, where many nations still maintained some form of authoritarianism in spite of great strides in their economic development. The collapse of the Soviet bloc did not shake the one-party rule of most of the socialist countries in Asia. Having lost Soviet aid, Vietnam introduced a market-oriented economy and adopted a more peaceful foreign policy; but it retained basically the communist one-party rule. North Korea remained an unusually seclusive militarized socialist state, very hostile towards the West. In the People's Republic of China, the movement for democracy was suppressed by military force in the Tiananmen Square Incident in June 1989. Western democracies were much dismayed to see that the wind of freedom in the socialist world was halted in China. The events of 1989 in the Soviet bloc hardened, instead of softening, the attitude of the Chinese rulers towards democracy activists.

Until 1989, the United States had not pressed the Beijing government to improve human rights or liberalize its rule, because it had not wanted to embarrass the Chinese government which the American leaders had regarded as a tacit strategic partner in the Cold War against the Soviet Union. China, led by pragmatic Deng Xiaoping, had developed a quasi-market economy, encouraging private enterprises and foreign investment in the 1980s. In addition, China had advocates of political reform, such as Hu Yaobang, within the top leadership, although Deng forced him out in 1987. The United States had therefore considered China more liberal than the Soviet Union, until *glasnost* began to liberalize the Soviet system. The Tiananmen Square Incident, which contrasted sharply with the trend in the Soviet bloc, shocked the public in the United States and other Western democracies. In response to the incident, the United States and other democracies imposed measures of sanctions upon China.

The Bush administration, however, did not want to cut all ties with China, which had been developed since 1972. As James Baker, his Secretary of State wrote later, "no matter the gulf between our two systems, China is not Cuba. Overriding strategic interests of the United States require engagement, not isolation."[12] In spite of considerable criticism in Congress, the Bush administration renewed the term of China's most favored nation (MFN) status. It also sent two high-ranking officials to Beijing in December 1989 to convey its interest in improving U.S.-Chinese relations and proceeded to soften sanctions imposed on China. When their mission became publicly known, it was dubbed "kowtow diplomacy" by critical Congressmen and commentators. Because criticism of Bush's China policy was strong among the Congressional Democrats and the constituencies of the Democratic party, Bill Clinton, Democratic presidential candidate in 1992, criticized it and promised to take a tougher stance on human rights issues in China during his presidential campaign.[13] In 1993, Clinton renewed China's most favored nation status for another year but declared that the next renewal would depend on the improvement of human rights conditions China should make in several aspects.[14] Thus, the Clinton administration chose to pursue a more vigorous human rights diplomacy towards China. Japanese foreign policy had responded slowly to the increasing weight of human rights issues during the 1980s. Japan had ratified the two U.N.-sponsored international covenants on human rights in 1980, and had gained a membership in the U.N. Commission on Human Rights in 1982. In 1984, the Japanese Ministry of Foreign Affairs established the Human Rights and Refugees Section. Japanese diplomacy began to play some role in the U.N. Commission on Human Rights, but otherwise it had not pursued what could be called human rights diplomacy. Japan did not list the international promotion of democracy and human rights among the purposes of its foreign policy.[15]

When the changed landscape of international human rights affairs made China the major target of human rights politics in 1989, Japanese diplomacy was confronted with a challenging situation. Japan had to avoid isolating itself from the United States and other Western democracies in human rights politics, but also had to avoid antagonizing China. An antagonized China might start a massive anti-Japanese campaign. Because of the history of Japanese imperialism in China, Japan seemed to be most vulnerable to anti-foreign nationalism in China. In this situation, Japan began to include the international promotion of democracy and human rights among the official purposes of its foreign policy, and followed the Western countries in imposing sanctions on China after the Tiananmen Square Incident. But Japan limited its sanctions to a level milder than other Western countries. Japan defended its position in G-7 conferences, arguing for the special necessity of maintaining a friendly relationship with its great neighbor. Japan also recommended the softening of the G-7 position towards China for the benefit of keeping China engaged with Western democracies in the interest of the international community. Since the United States and European nations, too, were aware of the benefit of keeping China engaged, Japan was able to avoid becoming itself isolated.[16]

It may be said that Japan practiced a sort of human rights diplomacy towards China. In quiet diplomacy, Japan expressed its concern with the gap between the human rights condition in China and the international standard of human rights, and advised China to narrow the gap. Japan presented itself to China as the developed capitalist country most concerned with maintaining a friendly relationship with China and working to mitigate international sanctions against China. Anticipating the moderation of Western sanctions, Japan cautiously took gradual steps to normalize its relations with China. Japan and China worked together to complete the normalization of their relationship with the visit of the

Japanese royal couple to China in October 1992. Thus, Japan's diplomatic stance had a special value to China, because the latter could make use of its improved relationship with Japan as a lever to induce the Western democracies to lift their sanctions. Therefore, the Japanese policy was to stand with Western democracies in emphasizing democratic values and international human rights, but to keep a distance from them in the practice of human rights diplomacy. In 1991, for instance, the Japanese government followed the examples of Western countries by introducing the human rights conditions of a recipient country as a criterion for offering Official Development Assistance (ODA) programs. But the Japanese government rarely applied this criterion in the actual allocation of its ODA programs.[17]

Asian Self-Assertions in International Human Rights Politics

Because of the disintegration of the Soviet Union, China's security environment was much improved. But the collapse of the Soviet bloc weakened China's ideological position. Regardless of the power rivalry between China and the Soviet Union, the existence of the powerful Soviet bloc had been useful to China as an ideological counterforce against the United States and other Western democracies. With the disappearance of the Soviet bloc, China felt the stronger structural power of the Western democracies in the issue area of human rights. Their human rights diplomacy, particularly that of the United States, seemed to be subversive to the Chinese system of a Communist dictatorship. At first the Beijing government invoked the doctrine of sovereignty and non-interference as a defense against this human rights diplomacy. But it also started a publicity campaign which stressed that human rights were respected in China.

A number of other Asian governments, too, felt annoyed or threatened by the strengthened structural power of the Western democracies on human rights issues. The Deputy Secretary of Singapore's Ministry of Foreign Affairs, for instance, expressed his displeasure at the "aggressive Western promotion of democracy, human rights and freedom of the press to the Third World at the end of the Cold War."[18] Thus the Chinese government was able to form an Asian coalition with other Asian governments on international human rights politics. No Asian country argued that the idea of human rights, which originated in Europe, was alien to Asians or defined human rights affairs as a purely domestic matter which was not a legitimate field of concern for the international community.

Instead, they attempted to present their own views of human rights to defend their practice in human rights affairs. For this purpose, they set up offices and institutes to handle or to do research on international human rights. It may be said that the structural power of the Western democracies at least forced the Asian countries to define their own views on human rights.

China began its defense of its human rights practice in November 1991, by publishing the "Chinese White Paper on Human Rights Conditions."[19] This white paper endorsed the principles declared in the Universal Declaration of Human Rights and recognized that human rights were a matter of universal concern. The human rights condition of each nation was part of the process of historical evolution, it was argued in the white paper. It was inevitable that nations had different human rights conditions in accordance with their respective historical backgrounds, stages of their economic development, their cultural traditions and political systems. The People's Republic of China had achieved genuine independence from foreign imperialism and had made great strides in improving the nation's human rights conditions. Since China was still a developing country, the human rights conditions in China might leave much to be desired, it was admitted in the paper. The People's Republic was a socialist state governed by the dictatorship of the people's democracy. The Chinese citizenry enjoyed extensive political rights under this system, it was maintained. The white paper stressed the importance of the right of independence for each nation without which even the right to life, the most basic of the human rights, cannot be secure. With national independence comes the right of national development, without which the economic, social and cultural rights of the citizens cannot be fulfilled. Thus, China regarded the rights of the Chinese nation as a whole more fundamental than the rights of its individual citizens.[20]

While defending the human rights condition in China, Chinese publicists continued to criticize the self-righteous human rights diplomacy of the West. They posed such questions as: Could the Western nations, which had exploited non-Western peoples for so long, be qualified to lecture about human rights to those who had suffered from imperialism? Were not the developed Western nations structurally responsible for the poverty of the developing nations? Could the Western nations be justified in practicing cultural imperialism in pressuring non-Western countries to accept the Western version of human rights? Did not Western nations, particularly the United States, have serious human rights problems in their own societies? Could the American standard of human rights be universal when the United States had not ratified major U.N.-sponsored human rights covenants and conventions?[21]

With the restoration of domestic order, the progress of normalization of its relations with Western democracies, and the resurgence of its economic growth, a more confident China strengthened its counterattack on the human rights diplomacy of the West towards China and other Asian nations. In resisting the Western structural power on human rights affairs, China found a number of Asian allies. Lee Kuan Yew, the founding father of the thriving city-state Singapore, emerged as the most outspoken defender of the Asian way, that is, emphasis on communitarian values.[22] Lee and other Singaporean spokesmen considered it the Asian way to recognize the importance of society—family, local community, and national society—in human life and interpret human rights within the context of this philosophy. Individuals have the obligation to serve and work for the societies to which they belong. They should be trained in self-discipline through education, and anti-social behaviors should not be tolerated by the state. Thus, they defended the continuing paternalistic rule of the dominant People's Action Party (PAP) in Singapore. This Asian way, which stressed social discipline, they argued, had been the source of recent Asian success in economic development.

Excessive individualism tends to create social maladies and economic stagnation; there are a number of symptoms of its evils in the Western societies. Excessive individualism should not be allowed to spread in Asian countries. They hinted about the superiority of the Asian way over the Western way, citing Asia's great leaps in economic development. Because of great economic success, they argued that Asian nations have become better able to challenge the Western tendency to universalize its own values.[23] Singapore's Asian way collided with the American way when President Clinton intervened diplomatically on behalf of an American teenager who was sentenced to whiplashing for his misbehavior in Singapore. Among Southeast Asian countries, Singapore and Malaysia have emphasized the Asian culture and the Asian way, while the Philippines has held a view of human rights much similar to the Western one. Thailand is somewhere in between. Indonesia has justified its authoritarian rule with the theory of development dictatorship and has defended its human rights conditions in terms of the nation's stage in economic development and its need to preserve national unity.[24]

Since most Asian governments, regardless of their respective political systems, felt displeased or uncomfortable with the Western human rights diplomacy and wanted to place human rights issues in their national cultural backgrounds, the representatives of the Asian governments produced a declaration when they met in Bangkok before the U.N. World Conference on Human Rights, which took place in Vienna, in June 1993. This declaration was critical of the Western human rights diplomacy and emphatic on the primacy of the national rights and on national and regional variations in human rights practices. In addition, this Bangkok declaration expressed the opinion that "the promotion of human rights should be encouraged by cooperation and consensus, and not through confrontation and the imposition of incompatible values." It was specifically opposed to the linkage of human rights issues with the ODA programs. The declaration also included a statement that the Asian states recognize that:

> while human rights are universal in nature, they must be considered in the context of a dynamic and evolving process of international norm-setting, bearing in mind the significance of national and regional particularities and various historical, cultural, and religious backgrounds.[25]

At the U.N. World Conference on Human Rights, there was a "clash of civilizations." But it is more accurate to describe it as an intercultural dialogue. It must be remembered, moreover, that many NGOs, in addition to states, sent representatives to Vienna. When Asian governments met in Bangkok, Asian human rights NGOs had a separate meeting there. Asian NGOs favored more liberal views on human rights than Asian governments.[26] It may be possible to dismiss the Vienna Declaration and Programme of Action as an ambiguous document of mere verbal compromise which conceals divergent and conflicting views. But it is remarkable that the conference of more than 170 countries was able to adopt, through a painstaking process of consensus building, a declaration which reconfirmed the commitment of all the states to human rights and fundamental freedoms for all and reiterated "the universal nature of these rights and freedoms." This writer would like to commend highly the process of international dialogue stimulated by the Vienna Conference. Conceding to the view expressed in the Bangkok declaration, the Vienna declaration stated the following (and thereby weakened the meaning of that Bangkok sentence by changing the structure of the sentence):

> While the significance of national and regional particularities and various historical, cultural and religious backgrounds must be borne in mind, it is the duty of States, regardless of their political, economic, and cultural systems, to promote and protect all human rights and fundamental freedoms.[27]

In these human rights conferences, Japan naturally did not support the majority position of the Asian countries. In Bangkok, Japan argued for the universal nature of human rights, was opposed to the development-first doctrine, and defended the policy of considering democracy and human rights conditions of recipient nations in offering ODA programs. Although Japan voted for the Bangkok declaration in the spirit of cooperation and compromise, it published an explanation of the position of the Japanese government which clarified the Japanese reservations to the declaration. Japan reiterated its position in Vienna.[28] Thus Japan clearly sided in principle with the Western democracies in multilateral forums on human rights. At the same time, Japan was very cautious in conducting its human rights diplomacy. Although it used pressure tactics to improve human rights conditions in several African states in providing them with ODA, it refrained from such tactics in its ODA programs towards Asian countries. In spite of the basic similarity between Japan and the United States in their human rights philosophy, there was a wide gap between the way each respectively conducted human rights diplomacy.[29]

U.S. and Japanese Human Rights Diplomacy Since 1994

In 1994, President Clinton changed the U.S. policy of linking China's most favored nation status with improvements in certain apects of the human rights conditions in China.[30] Although the United States had considerable bargaining power against China, China too had considerable reciprocal bargaining power. China's political weight was already great in Asia, and Washington often needed China's cooperation in the conduct of its foreign policy. The North Korean problem was a case in point. It was not in U.S. interests to antagonize China, a potential superpower in the twenty-first century. To be more specific, the attraction of the great China market had increased enormously as China's economic growth had been very rapid. During the 1993–94 period, China had apparently been engaged in an effective publicity campaign directed towards American multinational corporations and indirectly towards the U.S. Congress. Business groups had begun to urge the administration to continue China's MFN status, warning it of Chinese economic retaliation which might result in the loss of many American business opportunities in China and many jobs at home. The climate of opinion in Congress had changed considerably within one year.[31] Clinton wanted a compromise settlement on the conditionality he had imposed in the previous year, but China was unwilling to cooperate because such a compromise would seem to mean a compromise by China on its national right to defend its political system. Only after Clinton had decided to retract the conditions imposed in the previous year, did China make symbolic concessions in human rights issues to lend some credibility to the effectiveness of Clinton's new policy of a more positive constructive engagement.[32] Clinton abandoned the linkage diplomacy he had announced in the previous year and returned to the policy practiced by the Bush administration. But this did not mean that the United States had abandoned its human rights diplomacy towards China. The Clinton administration continued to raise human rights issues in its dialogues with China. China made angry verbal responses to U.S. human rights diplomacy, but did not use punitive measures against the United States in deference to the latter's power. Towards smaller European nations critical of human rights violations in China, Beijing sometimes employed punitive measures. Thus, China was engaged in reverse human rights diplomacy towards weaker powers.

Although U.S.-Chinese human rights politics has been significantly stabilized, there may be some fluctuations in U.S.-Chinese tensions in the future. When these tensions increase, both the American and Japanese societies will become more keenly aware of U.S.-Japanese gaps on Chinese human rights issues. If, in addition, the United States is also engaged eagerly in human rights politics with other Asian countries—Indonesia and Myanmar for example—these U.S.-Japanese gaps will be highlighted even more. Japan has conducted quiet human rights diplomacy towards Indonesia, mentioning its concern with the human rights condition in East Timor. But Japan has never used its ODA towards Indonesia as a diplomatic lever to apply pressure. Japan and the United States took the same position towards the military regime in Myanmar by imposing sanctions. After the military regime released opposition leader Daw Aung San Suu Kyi in 1995, Japan moderated its sanctions and allowed the expansion of Japanese business activities in Myanmar, despite the continuation of the suppression of her democracy movement by the military regime.[33] When the United States and European countries expressed their opposition to ASEAN's (Association of Southeast Asian Nations) immediate admission of Myanmar, Japan also expressed concern, but did not openly object.[34] ASEAN states have expressed some criticism of the harsh dictatorship of Myanmar's military regime. But they do not think it a sufficient reason to keep Myanmar outside their organization. Towards Western democracies, they emphasize the importance of engaging Myanmar. The main reason for their eagerness in Myanmar's affiliation is probably their desire to make their regional union geographically complete and to avoid driving Myanmar to form a closer relationship with China.

If the American public becomes emotionally engaged in human rights issues in Asia, the psychological distance between the American and Japanese societies will be widened. There is in the Japanese populace considerable sympathy towards "the Asian way" because of its own communitarian tradition. Many Japanese are afraid of what they regard as excessive individualism in contemporary American culture and its contaminating influence. Besides, Japanese like to have an Asian identity. Because of the great economic development of Asian countries, their desire for an Asian identity has become strong. Because of cultural habit, Japanese find the American style of missionary diplomacy meddlesome and self-righteous, particularly because they know of the widely reported social maladies in American society. If Japan has some much politicized economic issues with the United States, both the Japanese and American societies may be further alienated from each other. The Japanese have found U.S. human rights diplomacy towards Asian nations to be quite similar to U.S. trade diplomacy towards Japan. Both diplomacies have employed pressure tactics with the threat of sanctions. Such a perception of American arrogance towards Asians may gain strength again in Japan in the future. On the American side, the image of Japan as a non-Western nation which is not "like us" may be invoked again. Japan's own human rights problems, such as Japan's slow response to the wartime "comfort women" issue, social discriminations against minorities and foreigners, and job discriminations against women, might increase the criticisms of Japan by human rights groups in the United States.[35]

The Possibility of U.S.-Japanese Cooperation on Democracy and Human Rights Issues in Asia

Although there is some danger of U.S.-Japanese frictions over democracy and human rights issues in Asia, as described above, we should not be overly pessimistic about the possibility of U.S.-Japanese cooperation on democracy and human rights in Asia. Japan and the United States can cooperate in conceiving and implementing better foreign policy strategies to build up the socio-economic basis of a liberal democratic political system in Asian and other developing countries. Japan and the United States may increase or decrease their ODA programs as an incentive for political reform. But such a policy of giving or denying rewards is effective only in some special circumstances. The same can be said of other forms of direct diplomatic intervention. It is far more fundamental for both countries to structure their respective ODA programs for the purpose of building the socio-economic basis of democracy. For this purpose, Japan should develop a policy science which combines development studies with democratization studies. Japanese universities and think-tanks should cooperate with ODA-related governmental and quasi-governmental agencies in developing such a policy science.

If a country changes its political system from authoritarianism to liberal democracy, greater respect for human rights will follow. When there is no such systemic change, however, it is desirable to mitigate human rights abuses under an authoritarian regime. Human rights diplomacy serves this purpose. Even when Japan and the United States do not employ the same means, they can work for the same goal. Japan will employ quiet diplomacy of persuasion in most cases, but it should not shrink from using public diplomacy of open criticism in some cases. In any case, Japan must repeatedly declare its unequivocal commitment to human rights. The international protection of human rights should be included in the major objectives of Japanese foreign policy. To be more specific, Japan must establish international credibility for its commitment to international human rights. This will require the Japanese people to have a view of history appropriate for a liberal democratic nation; a view of history that criticizes their imperialistic, militaristic past and emphasizes the significance of the development of postwar Japan as a peace-oriented liberal democratic nation. It will also be necessary for its credibility to eliminate discrimination against ethnic and historical minorities, develop greater gender equality, attend more carefully to the human rights of non-Japanese residents, and give more humane treatment to asylum seekers. It is important to increase the public awareness of human rights issues both at home and abroad through human rights education in schools. Unless there are a number of influential organizations dedicated to the international protection of human rights, Japan will not be able to conduct credible human rights diplomacy. It should be noted that the presence of influential international human rights organizations in the United States has made it possible for the United States to conduct vigorous human rights diplomacy. Thus, there are several preconditions for successful U.S.-Japanese cooperation in democracy and human rights issues.

There is also something to be desired on the part of the United States. First, the United States should take a long-term view of the development of democracy in Asia. If the American people are confident of the future of liberal democracy, the United States can take a long-term view and be more patient. Second, the United States should make greater efforts to fight such social maladies as its numerous violent crime cases, the spread of illicit drugs, and the presence of an impoverished "underclass." The United States is very worthy of international admiration because it is trying to develop and maintain liberal democracy in a multi-racial, multi-ethnic society. But such social maladies as have been mentioned above are detrimental to America's efforts to be the champion of liberal democratic nations. If the United States could convey to the world its image as an energetic nation combating these social maladies, it would certainly enable U.S. human rights diplomacy to gain more respect from Asian peoples.

It is often said that as the United States enters the age of global and information capitalism, the middle class, the mainstay of stable liberal democratic politics, is beginning to disintegrate in American society. If the middle class is going to disintegrate under the dual impact of the globalized economy and the information revolution not only in the United States but in other Western democracies, the future of liberal democracy will not be bright. This writer hopes liberal democracy is a form of government which has considerable resilience. A policy science is needed to study not only the future triumph of liberal democracy in developing countries but also the future of seemingly triumphant liberal democracy in advanced countries.

Notes

*This final report was written by Tadashi Aruga on behalf of the study group on human rights issues, which also consisted of Fumiko Fujita and Motoyuki Takamatsu. The author also served as its coordinator. This writer acknowledges his great indebtedness to the views and knowledge on this subject by these colleagues. This paper is based on discussions with them. However, this writer alone is responsible for any faults in this final product.

1. Gaimushô, *Gaikô seisho 1997* (Tokyo: Gaimushô, 1997), Part I, 234-37. This year's *Gaikô seisho* (Diplomatic Blue Book) also summarizes Japanese contributions to protecting human rights and promoting democracy in the global community. See pages 110–112.

2. "Human Rights in the APEC Region: 1995," *Human Rights Watch/Asia* 7, no.15 (November 1995): 30.

3. Strobe Talbott, "Democracy and the National Interest," *Foreign Affairs* 75, no. 6 (November/December 1996): 50.

4. *The Major International Treaties, 1914-1973* (New York: Stein and Day, 1975), 212, 247–48.

5. Paul Gordon Lauren, *Power and Prejudice: The Politics and Diplomacy of Racial Discrimination* (Boulder: Westview Press, 1988); Natalie Hevener Kaufman and David Whiteman, "Opposition to Human Rights Treaties in the United States Senate," *Human Rights Quarterly* 10, no. 3 (1988): 309–337.

6. *Public Papers of the President: Jimmy Carter, 1977* (Washington, D.C.: USGPO, 1977), I, 2.

7. For general discussion on U.S. human rights diplomacy, this writer relied mostly on Sandy Vogelgesang, *American Dream, Global Nightmare: The Dilemma of U.S. Human Rights Policy* (New York: Norton, 1980); Jushua Muravchik, *The Uncertain Crusade: Jimmy Carter and the Dilemmas of Human Rights Policy* (Washington: American Enterprise, 1988); A. Glenn Mower, Jr., *Human Rights and American Foreign Policy: The Carter and Reagan Experiences* (New York: Greenwood, 1987); Michael Ross Fowler, *Thinking about Human Rights: Contending Approaches to Human Rights in U.S. Foreign Policy* (Lanham, NY: University Press of America, 1987). Available in Japanese is Tadashi Aruga, ed., *Amerika gaikô to jinken* (Tokyo: Nihon Kokusaimondai Kenkyûjo, 1992) and his article in *Ajia no jinken: Kokusaiseiji no shiten kara*, ed. Akio Watanabe (Tokyo: Nihon Kokusaimondai Kenkyûjo, 1997), 153–176. *Ajia no jinken* is the only Japanese book that discusses human rights in Asia as an issue in international politics. For a historical discussion of U.S. efforts in promoting democracy in the world, see; Tony Smith, *America's Mission: The United States and the Worldwide Struggle for Democracy in the 20th Century* (Princeton: Princeton University Press, 1994).

8. Yasuaki Onuma, *In Quest of Intercivilizational Human Rights: 'Universal' and 'Relative' Human Rights in an Asian Perspective*, Occasional Papers, No.2/ 1996 (San Francisco: Asia Foundation's Center for Asian Pacific Affairs, March 1996), 4–5

9. Motoyuki Takamatsu, "Kankoku ni taisuru jinken gaikô no tenkai," in *Amerika gaikô to jinken*, 210–29.

10. *Ibid.*, 231–38; Takamatsu, "Kâtâ-Rêgan bei ryôseiken ni yoru tai-Firipin jinken gaikô no tenkai," *Tezukayama Daigaku Kyôyôgakubu Kiyô*, no. 31 (July 1992): 367–92.

11. Aruga, "Minami Afurika seisaku to Aparutoheito taisei," in *Amerika gaikô to jinken*, 265–314.

12. James A. Baker, III, *The Politics of Diplomacy: Revolution, War & Peace* (New York: Putnam, 1995), 97–111, 594.

13. Robert I. Bernstein and Richard Dicker, "Human Rights First," *Foreign Policy* 94 (Spring 1994): 37; Robert A. Manning, "Clinton and China," *Orbis* (Spring 1994):195.

14. *Congressional Quarterly* (May 29, 1993): 1349; *Public Papers of the Presidents: Clinton, 1993*, I (Washington, D.C.: USGPO, 1993), 770–73.

15. Onuma, "In Quest of Intercivilizational Human Rights," 5–6.

16. Seiichiro Takagi, "Tenanmon jiken to Nihon no jinken gaikô," *Ajia no jinken*, 183–92. (Its English version is "Human Rights in Japanese Foreign Policy: Japan's Policy toward China After Tiananmen," in *Human Rights and International Relations in the Asia Pacific Region*, ed. James T. H. Tang (London: Pinter, 1995), 97–111.)

17. *Ibid.*, 193–94; Onuma, "In Quest of Intercivilizational Human Rights," 6.

18. Cited in Christina M. Cerna, "Universality of Human Rights and Cultural Diversity: Implementation of Human Rights in Different Socio-Cultural Contexts," *Human Rights Quarterly* 16, no. 4 (November 1994): 746.

19. A Japanese translation of China's first white paper on human rights, "Chugoku no jinken jôkyô," was published in *Beijing shuhô*, 5 November 1991, 8–41. In 1992, China published a white paper which dealt with criminal justice and the treatment of convicts in August, and another white paper which defended human rights conditions in Tibet in September. In December 1995, China published the second white paper on human rights conditions in China to publicize the progress China had achieved in the various aspects of the human rights conditions of the people since the publication of its first white paper, while reiterating China's basic arguments on human rights issues. See: *Renmin Ribao*, overseas edition, December 28, 1995.

20. This summary of its argument is based on the Japanese translation that appeared in *Beijing Shuhô*, cited above. The most detailed Japanese study on current Chinese thought on human rights is Hideo Tsuchiya, *Gendai Chûgoku no jinken: Kenkyû to shiryô* (Tokyo: Shinzansha, 1996). This writer relied on Tsuchiya, et al., *Chugoku 'kaikaku kaihô' ka no jinken* (Kobe: Kobe Daigaku Coop Print Shop, 1997), in which Tsuchiya presents a summary of his views, 7–47.

21. This writer benefited from reading Kazuko Mori's unpublished papers on human rights in China, written for a research project on human rights in Asia, coordinated by Kenichiro Hirano and sponsored by Gaimushô: "Chûgoku Ajia no jinkengaikô hihan," March 1994; "Chûgoku no jinken rongi to jiko ninshiki," March 1995; and "Chûgoku no jinken jôkyô," March 1996. A three-volume collection of research papers was printed as a reference material for the Foreign Ministry officials only. For a very pertinent observation of the paradoxical evolution of human rights conditions in China of the 1980s, see: Ann Kent, "Waiting for Rights: China's Human Rights and China's Constitutions, 1949-1989," *Human Rights Quarterly* 13, no. 1 (February 1991): 170–201.

For the recent state of human rights in China, see Kazuko Mori, "Chugoku no jinken: Tsuyomaru kokkenshugi no naka de," *Kokusai mondai*, no. 449 (August 1997): 32–44.

22. Recently the role of the most vigorous spokesman for the Asian way of human rights practice has been taken over by Malaysian Prime Minister Mahathir.

23. A Japanese translation of Fareed Zakaria, "A Conversation with Lee Kuan Yew," *Foreign Affairs* (March/April 1994) in *Chûô kôron*, May 1994, 390–408; Bilahari Kausikan, "Asia's Different Standard," *Foreign Policy*, no. 92 (Fall

1993): 24–31. Tsutomu Kikuchi, "Kokusaikankei no sôten toshite no jinken mondai," *Ajia no jinken*, 82–88; Kyoko Tanaka, "'Ajia-gata jinken' to Shingaporu," unpublished paper written for a research project on human rights in Asia, coordinated by Kenichiro Hirano, March 1996.

24. Yoneji Kuroyanagi, "ASEAN shokoku to 'jinken gaikô'," unpublished paper written for a research project on human rights in Asia, coordinated by Kenichiro Hirano, March 1995; Kuroyanagi, " 'Jinken gaikô' tai 'Ajian way'," *Kokusai mondai*, no. 422 (May 1995): 31–45.

25. "Final Declaration of the Regional Meeting for Asia of the World Conference on Human Rights, Report of the Regional Meeting for Asia of the World Conference on Human Rights," Bangkok, 29 March–2 April, 1993, at 3, A/Conf. 157/ASRM/8-A/Conf.157/PC/59. Citations here are from Cerna, "University of Human Rights and Cultural Diversity," *loc. cit.*, 740–52. There are several other articles, which critically examined "Asian Way" arguments": Minxin Pei, "Puzzle of East Asian Exceptionalism," *Journal of Democracy* Special issue (October 1994): 90–103; Yash Chai, "Human Rights and Governance," The Asia Foundation's Center for Asian Pacific Affairs, Occasional Papers, No. 1 for 1994 (September 1994): 1–22; Jack Donnelly, "An Analysis of the East Asian Debates on Human Rights," in *Changing Conception of Human Rights in a Growing East Asia* (JIIA Paper) (Tokyo: Nihon Kokusaimondai Kenkyûjo, 1995), 31–80; Koki Abe, "Ajia no jinken: Chiiki jinken kikô eno michi," *Kokusai mondai*, no. 449 (August 1997): 2–16; Koshi Yamazaki, "Chiikiteki jinken hoshô taisei to Ajia-Taiheiyô chiiki," *Kokusaihô gaikô zasshi* 96, no. 3 (August 1977): 353–387.

26. Yash Chai, "Human Rights and Governance," 8.

27. "Vienna Declaration and Programme of Action," adopted by World Conference on Human Rights on 25 June 1993, A/CONF.157/23 (12 July 1993): 4–5.

28. Takagi, " Tenanmon jiken to Nihon no jinken gaikô," *Ajia no jinken*, 194.

29. "Human Rights in the APEC Region: 1995," *Human Rights Watch/Asia* 7, no. 15 (November 1995): 30–31; Juichi Inada, "Jinken minshuka to enjo seisaku," *Kokusai mondai*, no. 442 (May 1995): 2–7.

30. *Congressional Quarterly Weekly Report* (April 30, 1994): 1372; *Public Papers of the Presidents: Clinton, 1994* (Washington, D.C.: USGPO, 1994), 991–95.

31. *Far Eastern Economic Review,* 17 March 1994, 16–17; 24 March 1994, 18–20; 26 May 1994, 16; 2 June 1994, 25–26; 9 June 1994, 14–15; *International Herald Tribune*, 13 May 1994.

32. *International Herald Tribune*, 27 May 1994.

33. "Human Rights in the APEC Region: 1995," *loc. cit.*, 31.

34. *International Herald Tribune*, 2 December 1996; 2 June 1997.

35. These are problems often noted in the State Department's *Country Report* and publications of U.S.-based human rights organizations.

Chapter 11

Asia-Pacific Economic Regionalism and U.S.-Japan Relations

Tsutomu Kikuchi

Introduction

With the rapid economic development of the Asian countries and the emerging security uncertainty in the region, together with the emergence of a new economic giant, China, the future of U.S.-Japan relations will be affected more and more by these developments in Asia. Asia will present both challenges and opportunities for U.S.-Japan relations. Asia could provide a positive basis for U.S.-Japan cooperation, but might also become a fighting ground on which both the U.S. and Japan compete so that the emerging giant could take advantage of the competition for its own benefit. In any case, Asia will be a testing ground for U.S.-Japan relations in the coming years.

Recently, calls for a multilateral approach to achieving peace and prosperity in the Asia-Pacific region have been on the rise. The deepening economic interdependence among the regional countries needs some mechanism to regulate it and reduce transaction costs. In addition, the economic dynamism is changing the distribution of power among the regional countries, thereby changing state-to-state relations. In order to manage the changing distribution of power in inter-states relations, the Asia-Pacific region would need some mechanism to "absorb" negative impacts on stable developments of regional relations. Otherwise, the changing distribution of power may cause competition and conflict rather than cooperation among the nations. The establishment of the APEC (Asia-Pacific Economic Cooperation) Forum, together with the ARF (ASEAN Regional Forum), reflects this common recognition.

This paper is intended to discuss U.S.-Japan relations in the context of this emerging regionalism. However, my discussion will be largely confined to economic relations, as there seems to be a basic consensus between the United States and Japan with regard to regionalism in the security realm. Both countries regard ARF and other security-related forums in the Asia-Pacific region as complementary to the bilateral U.S.-Japan security alliance, and neither country intends to build a highly institutionalized multilateral security mechanism in the region. As far as they are concerned, political confidence-building remains their primary motivation in supporting ARF. On larger strategic questions involving the United States, Japan, China and Russia, the Doran paper (cf. Chapter 12 of this book) provides substantial materials for discussion. In this paper I will focus my discussion on U.S.-Japan relations over economic regionalism because there are important differences in the American and Japanese approaches and to what extent they can or cannot manage such differences will have significant bearing on the future of the region as well as on the future of their bilateral relationship. In discussing the issues of economic regionalism in the region, I shall pay primary attention to APEC and related matters for underscoring the complexity of the U.S.-Japan relationship.

APEC reflects an emerging global trend toward regionalism which is taking place in various parts of the world. Regionalism has now become a major factor shaping the structure of the world economy, and, because of its enormous scale, its developments over the coming years will have an enormous impact on the shape of international political economy as well as the regional one.[1]

In the Asia-Pacific region, APEC, since its establishment in 1989, has become a key mechanism for promoting regional dialogue and economic interdependence. If APEC develops in line with the agreements adopted at Bogor, Osaka, and Manila, it could greatly contribute to the peace and stability of the Asia-Pacific region. APEC will serve several political-strategic purposes as well as economic ones:

- sustaining U.S. economic interests and thus preserving the

strategic importance of the region for the U.S., thereby contributing to the maintenance of the U.S. political and military presence in the region;
- helping to maintain harmonious economic relations between Japan and the United States, and providing a convenient regional framework for Japan to appropriate a joint leadership role in regional affairs without causing concerns for the Asian neighbors and the U.S.;
- helping to bring an emerging giant, China, into a regional arrangement within which it could play a positive role for regional stability;
- helping to create cooperative relations between the developed and developing countries, thereby contributing to the improvement of North-South relations on the regional level;
- encouraging the EU (European Union) to adopt more outward-oriented commercial policies;
- ensuring that the annual APEC summit meeting will provide an overall framework for regional confidence-building and cooperation;
- contributing to the strengthening of the global free trade principle as embodied in the GATT/WTO (General Agreement on Tariffs and Trade/World Trade Organization) system through its strategy of "Open Regionalism."[2]

Globalization and Interdependence

Economic development enables society to meet the basic human needs of its members. Societies which are not able to provide for the well-being of their members face the risk of increasing instability and confusion. Today, it is virtually impossible for countries to develop their economies without joining the complex networks of economic interdependence and thereby gaining international competitiveness by combining their comparative advantages.

In the Asia-Pacific region, a highly integrated and interdependent regional economy, mainly driven by market liberalization and export promotion, is emerging. Economic dynamism, led by multinational enterprises, is cutting across national boundaries.

Trade within the East Asian region increased faster than that of any other region over the period from 1980 to the present day. This increased economic interdependence among the countries in the East Asian region in the last decade has prompted much speculation about how governments' interests in regional trading arrangements may have changed.

As the ample literature on the international political economy shows, economic interdependence both creates and reduces conflict. On the one hand, economic interdependence can contribute to economic growth and development of the region as a whole. As peoples' well-being increases in the region, the region may become more stable and peaceful. In fact, the deepened and complex interdependence among the industrialized countries of the region appears to have helped curtail military rivalry. It is argued that mutual dependency in trade, finance and technology both raises the cost of conflict and lowers the incentives for war. Access to raw materials, finance, and markets is obtained at less cost and on a larger scale in a relatively open and liberal economy than would be possible by military control of territory or establishing a sphere of influence. Combined with the end of the Cold War, this interdependence can moderate serious conflicts in the region.

On the other hand, an increasing emphasis on economic interests in national policy agendas since the end of the Cold War may cause more serious competition and conflicts over relative (not absolute), economic gains in economic exchanges. Despite or because of increasing interdependence in the region, many East Asian countries are still involved in the military procurement race, influenced as they are by age-old political power considerations. The end of the Cold War has exacerbated this "arms race" because a large arsenal of modern weapons and weapons systems held by the major contenders of the Cold War has been made available for exportation to the Third World countries.

Economic globalization and interdependence, together with megacompetition, present many major consequences. One is that while in the past trade negotiations occurred primarily at the border, increasingly trade negotiators are concerned about what is taking place within borders, in terms of competition policy, industrial policy, etc. Discussion is now taking place about the "nature" of capitalism and the absence or presence of a "level playing field."[3] The cumulative effect of these transnational forces clearly may lead to the erosion of national sovereignty.

Globalization and the surge of foreign direct investment (FDI) also result in the enhanced role and power of the multinational enterprises (MNEs). MNEs are increasingly becoming independent actors in the international economy. MNEs are engaged in their own "foreign policy,"[4] and their alliances take various forms. For example, Motorola "allied" with the U.S. government in its battle against Japan on mobile telephone access in Japan, but allied against the U.S. government in its battle on linking human rights and most favored nation (MFN) status in China.

These new developments in the economic domain pose a serious challenge to the Asia-Pacific region where a profoundly state-centered environment prevails. In this region, states are preoccupied with the maintenance of their national sovereignty. This is sharply contrasted with the European integration process where important parts of national sovereignty are being transferred to the supra-national political authority.

Moreover, rapid economic growth has effected the character of political and social conditions within the regional countries.

Changed Economic Landscape in Asia

Previously, Asian economies had relied upon finding export markets in the United States, and they depended for their capital goods on imports from Japan. The core of their production base was provided by Japanese and multinational enterprises. The East Asian economy had a fragile relationship with the outside world, its own economic affairs heavily affected by developments in the larger economies such as the U.S. and Japan. Thus, a distinctive feature of this region was held to be its "dependent development."

The 1990s, however, has shown a dramatic change in the East Asian growth mechanism. Today the role of the United States as a primary importer of the region's goods has lost its significance, and even more important, Japan, beset by a long recession, has slowed the pace of its imports. Even so, the East Asian region has faced no decline in demand. This is because of the striking growth of exports within the region. With respect to investment, we can identify a similar phenomenon: an increased intraregional investment flow. The NIEs (newly industrialized economies) have been engaging in investments on a large scale throughout the region, especially in the Southeast Asian economies.

This means that East Asia has established an "internal circulation mechanism" of goods and capital in the region which has become the most important system supporting the region's growth. East Asia is becoming more self-reliant and resilient, rather than externally dependent.[5]

In this process, we can find different levels of engagement by Japan and the United States. Whereas in 1986, the stock of U.S. foreign direct investment in East Asia exceeded that of Japan, by 1993, it was less than half the total of Japanese investments. Two-thirds of the value of the stock of Japanese foreign direct investment in East Asia in 1993 had been added in the seven preceding years. The search for a cost advantage in East and Southeast Asia following *endaka* (appreciation of the yen), is clear in the pattern as well as in the direction of Japanese foreign direct investment during those years. Unlike the earlier emphasis on imports substituting for investments in the region, which was concentrated in manufacturing, Japanese investment served to develop a dynamic division of labor in the region. In the 1990s, Japanese affiliates in the region expanded their sales in the intraregional markets, along with developing a greater reliance on the region as a source of production inputs. In addition, the local profit reinvestment rate of Japanese affiliates in the NIEs and ASEAN (Association of Southeast Asian Nations) is above 60 percent. Japanese companies have thus gone beyond their earlier pattern of "one-way" involvement in East Asia. In other words, Japanese companies operating in East Asia have been seeking "self-containment" of their business activities within the East Asian network by looking within the region for their sales and purchases and also reinvesting their profits there. They are redeploying their resources, placing various operations, such as production, procurement of parts, technology development and sales.

The network strategy of Japanese business has strengthened the East Asian internal circulation mechanism, and the strengthening of this mechanism has reinforced the network strategy.[6]

More important than Japanese direct investment is Japanese ODA (Official Development Assistance). The bilateral aid dominance of Japan in Asia is far more pronounced than in Japan's presence in foreign direct investment. Japanese ODA is concentrated more in economic infrastructure than is the aid from most of the others industrialized countries.[7] As will be seen later, considerable attention has been directed to explicit attempts on the part of the Japanese government to link the aid program to infrastructural improvements.

The investment-ODA nexus has produced a weak set of bilateral and regional institutions such as the ASEAN-Japan Trade Ministers Meeting (AEM-MITI). The East Asia Economic Caucus (EAEC) proposal by Mohomad Mahathir might be seen as a functional response to the new Japanese production network in Southeast Asia.

In terms of trade, the more rapid increase in the rate of growth of Japan's exports to East Asia compared with its imports has generated a widening trade surplus with the region. For the United States, on the other hand, exactly the opposite has occurred: exports have grown more slowly than imports causing a deteriorating trade balance. These changing trade and investment patterns have conditioned the way in which the governments of Japan and the United States have regarded trade and investment with Asia. These views in turn have been reflected in the divergent policy agendas on trade and investment towards the region, agendas that have had an impact on the bilateral U.S.-Japan relationship.

Brief History of Asia-Pacific Economic Cooperation

Ideas for Asia-Pacific economic cooperation began to emerge only in the mid-1960s and found more elaborate expression in the 1970s. In this period, various ideas were presented, from PAFTA (Pacific Free Trade Area) to OPTAD (Organization for Pacific Trade and Development). These ideas, however, failed to gain political support from the regional countries, even when some of the political leaders were interested in them. Thus, the challenge was how to develop a structure for consultation which could accommodate the great diversity of the region. Building blocks of Asia-Pacific cooperation were constructed carefully and informally. Various consultative processes finally paved the way for the initiation of the Pacific Economic Cooperation Council (PECC) in 1980.[8]

In the process of establishing PECC, a new model for cooperation was introduced: an ASEAN model. More attention was paid to the aspect of "North-South relations" in regional economic cooperation. PECC basically focused upon confidence building through formal and informal dialogues, thereby promoting community building in the region. PECC has based its strategic assets on two factors: soft power (knowledge) and the diffusion of networks of key players, both governmental and non-governmental. In all the meetings and task forces, information and policy studies have been provided to promote the diffusion of knowledge both regionally and in the national capitals, thereby contributing to the sharing of a common political economy. Organizational flexibility and informality encouraged the diffusion of knowledge and the formation of networks of key players within the region.

Although APEC was established as an intergovernmental forum, the basic modalities of APEC were quite similar to those of PECC. The main functions were to encourage confidence and trust building among the regional countries (between the North and South), to diffuse information (knowledge), and to create human networks at the governmental level. The basic assumption of APEC is that common understandings on international political economy gained through intensive dialogue (an emergence of regional "epistemic communities") will encourage cooperation, including voluntary liberalization.[9]

Japan and Regional Economic Cooperation

Diverging patterns of economic engagement with East Asia have led to different approaches between Japan and the United States in the promotion of closer economic cooperation in the region through the APEC forum.

Governments promote and enter into regional cooperative arrangements for a variety of motives. Among the principal of these we can distinguish regionalism as a means of reducing transaction costs, as a preemptive move to forestall less desirable outcomes, as a means to attaining non-economic objectives, and, finally, regionalism as a bargaining chip.

There have been different views on to whom credit should be given for the birth of APEC in 1989. Certainly some of the Japanese MITI (Ministry of International Trade and Industry) officials claim that the credit should be given to MITI, not Australian Prime Minister Robert Hawke. Apart from the matter of who took the initiative to launch the APEC idea, let us briefly discuss the background against which the Japanese (MITI's) proposal to set up a Ministerial Conference dealing with Asia-Pacific economic cooperation in the late 1980s was made. There were three major factors behind the proposal: a system crisis, pressure in U.S.-Japan economic relations and the interests of the Japanese private sector.[10]

For MITI, Japan stood at a historic turning point. What they were most worried about was, first of all, the huge imbalances facing the world economy caused by, among other things, the huge U.S. trade deficit and its rising accumulated debt, accumulated debt issues in the developing countries, and the rising trade surplus being enjoyed by Japan, Germany and some of the Asian economies. Although there were many efforts to sustain the international economy, such as the enhancement of policy coordination among the developed countries through G5/G7, and the strengthening of the free trade system by launching the GATT Uruguay Round of multilateral trade negotiations in 1986, these imbalances would endanger the smooth developments of the world economy as a whole.

Without rectifying the imbalances in an adequate way, the international financial system would become unstable, protectionism would emerge, and the world economy might be thrown into confusion. "Black Monday" in October 1987 gave a warning via the New York Stock Exchange that these imbalances would not be sustainable.

Second, the Japanese government has faced continued strong pressure from the United States to rectify the huge trade imbalance. This demanded that Japan not only open its markets further, but also look for other ways to rectify the U.S. trade deficit; that is, to enhance the function of Asian economies as "absorbers" (strengthening the capacities of the Asian economies to import U.S. goods), thereby diffusing the pressures from the United States.[11]

Third, since the Plaza Accords in 1985, Japanese business enterprises have been rushing into the Asian markets in order to efficiently combine production factors. They have been establishing production networks throughout the region.[12] However, serious problems have remained for Asia. Among other things, the industrial infrastructure has had to be further developed in order to establish a more efficient regional network of production by Japanese enterprises.

In the Asia-Pacific context, two purposes had to be realized simultaneously: to reduce the trade deficit of the United States (i.e., to decrease the dependence of the Asian economies upon the U.S. market), and to maintain a steady increase of exports from the Asian economies in order to sustain economic growth. To realize both purposes simultaneously, first of all, Japan had to enhance its capacity to absorb the exports from other Asian economies. With the increasing enhancement of economic foundations in the Asian countries, these countries were also expected to increase their capacity to absorb exports, including those from the United States. In this regard, it was vitally important to improve the industrial infrastructure of the Asian economies.

Thus, MITI took the initiative for establishing networks for the "horizontal division of labor" in the Asia-Pacific region through its integrated use of ODA, trade and investment. This policy manifested itself in the so-called New Asian Industrial Development (NAID) Plan in 1987. The Plan called for Japan to recycle its surplus to the Asian developing countries (that is, to encourage Japanese investment in the region), to open its markets to Asian exports, to extend more ODA and technical cooperation to Asian economies, and to make efforts to transfer management resources to them (enhancement of the private sector in the region). This policy was also expected to further contribute to the construction of networks for the horizontal division of labor in the region, which had been actively pursued by Japanese enterprises, especially after the Plaza Accords.[13]

In this context, it should be noted that, given a huge trade surplus in Japan's trade with the rest of Asia, Japan has not had a strong interest in opening the Asian markets through regional cooperation, although there remained many complaints regarding Asian trade and investment practices on the part of Japanese business. For Japan, the pressing task was to rectify the huge imbalance through strengthening the "absorbing capacities" of the Asian economies by improving the industrial infrastructure.[14]

For the United States, on the other hand, its principal interest in APEC appeared to be its usefulness as a bargaining chip against the European Union in the closing negotiations of the Uruguay Round. "Playing the Pacific card" as a negotiating strategy was taken up more vigorously by the Clinton administration. In addition, given a huge trade deficit in its trade with the Asian countries, the United States viewed it as a potential lever for opening Asian markets. Especially since the Seattle meeting in 1993, the United States has made strenuous efforts to put trade and investment liberalization on the APEC agenda.

These different emphases in the interests of the Japanese and United States governments are reflected in turn in their respective attitudes towards these two views of economic regionalism in the Asia-Pacific.

Informal vs. Formal Mechanisms of Regional Cooperation

The Asia-Pacific region has been characterized by "regionalism by declaration" rather than regionalism by treaty. A lack of specificity in agreements is characteristic of the preference of many Asian economies for an informal, incremental, bottom-up approach to regional cooperation, in contrast with the "Western" preference for formal institutions established by contractual agreements.[15] Building cooperation among Asian countries has required a long period of confidence building to overcome a history of mutual suspicion and interstate conflicts. Some observers, conscious of this experience and of the sensitivities of Asian developing countries, have argued that hasty attempts to institutionalize APEC are premature and may be counterproductive to the long-term promotion of cooperation.

The Japanese government has been sympathetic to these Asian concerns. The long association of Japanese government officials and members of the policymaking community has sensitized them to the possibly counterproductive consequences of pushing too hard and too fast toward contractual obligations.

Japan has traditionally maintained a low key approach to Asia and has enjoyed a huge trade surplus. Japanese enterprises have penetrated well into highly protected Asian economies and have established production networks in the region. Thus, Japan has not had strong motivation to opening further the Asian markets. In addition, Japan has emphasized the importance of enhancing the political foundation of "internationalist groups" which have gradually been emerging in Asian developing countries and which have had great interest in maintaining close ties with the outside world. These "internationalist groups" have been regarded as the driving forces to the further opening of their respective economies. This political foundation has to be strengthened. Any hasty liberalization may produce enormous adjustment costs on the part of developing countries, thereby weakening the political basis of these "internationalist groups."

Although the Japanese government was eager to set up an official forum to discuss regional economic cooperation issues, as was shown in the report of MITI in 1988, the basic rationale for Asia-Pacific economic cooperation has not changed: steady institutionalization, gradualism, consensus-decision, emphasis on development cooperation, non-discrimination, consistency with GATT/WTO, etc.

The Logic of Reciprocity

The other principal conflict of views in the process of regional economic cooperation is between different beliefs regarding the necessity for reciprocity in multilateral trading negotiations. There is a disagreement over APEC's guiding principle of "Open Regionalism," especially on the question of whether liberalization measures within APEC should be unconditionally applied to non-APEC members, or only to those nations that have undertaken as much liberalization as member states on a reciprocal basis, as is the case with NAFTA (North American Free Trade Agreement).

Economists have long insisted that the GATT norm of reciprocity is based upon political rather than economic reasons. They argue that a lowering of trade barriers is beneficial above all to the economy that undertakes the reduction. Therefore, reciprocity is not necessary.[16] Some economists further argue that the structure of interaction between the economies in the region and the outsiders is not the "prisoner's dilemma," but what they call the "prisoner's delight."[17] Thus, the region can afford and should pursue a strategy of open regionalism under which trade and investment liberalization would occur on a non-discriminatory basis. The benefits of liberalization would be available to all members of the GATT/WTO on a most favored nation basis.

This view is, however, politically too naïve for others, especially for the U.S. trade negotiators. First of all, unilateral liberalization robs governments of valuable bargaining chips in trade negotiations. In fact, the history of international trade demonstrates that most countries play the trade game as if it was a prisoner's dilemma.[18] Thus, they insist that the benefits of liberalization in the APEC should be confined to other countries within the region. APEC should become a preferential trade bloc that discriminates against non-members. Support for this view has come from countries that have valued APEC as a bargaining chip, i.e., the United States. Consequently, this has divided Japan and the United States.

Community Building vs. Institution Building

The above arguments (differences), are closely related to how we characterize the regionalism emerging in the Asia-Pacific region: Do its members constitute a community or an association of nations (states)?

Roughly speaking, there are two processes by which countries come together to form a regional grouping: community building and institution building. The former is a gradual long-term process. This is due to the fact that shared values, history and knowledge are the foundations upon which communities are built. The latter refers to a short-term process by which political authorities deliberately establish frameworks or systems to achieve some end. Common benefits, objectives and value systems are the ties that bind together countries that pursue institution building.

Most of the government officials, academic experts and business leaders directly involved in organizing the various cooperative initiatives to date in the Asia-Pacific region (beginning with the late Saburo Okita, Australia's Sir John Crawford and the late Japanese Prime Minister Masayoshi Ohira), have tended to refrain consciously from using the term "community," judging it too ambitious. They have also shied away from talk of rapid institutionalization and have shown a marked preference for a process-oriented rather than a result-oriented approach to regional cooperation, thereby demonstrating that community building in fact occupies a central place in their thinking on regionalism.[19]

Asia is still in a post-colonial era, which is why many Asian countries are still worried about ceding national sovereignty in the name of regional cooperation and interdependence. They are suspicious of what they see as an attempt by the "big powers" to reassert influence in a new way. It is for this reason that most Asian countries are cautious about hasty institutionalization of regional cooperation.

In contrast with traditional regionalism, contemporary regionalism links countries that vary widely in their stage of development, in their political and economic systems and in their value systems. The extreme diversity of the Asia-Pacific region has boosted intraregional transaction costs far above those in regions with more uniform systems. Consensus building requires inordinate time and energy and patient diplomacy. As economic competition intensifies, the extent to which the countries concerned can bear these transaction costs—in other words, the extent to which they can reap the true rewards of cooperation, curbing the tendency to demand hasty institutionalization in the pursuit of short-term gains—will have an extremely important bearing on the future evolution of regional community building.

"North-South" Issues in Asia-Pacific Regionalism

The above arguments are also closely related to the issue on how the North-South situation can be handled in Asia-Pacific regionalism. As we have seen, one of the characteristics of contemporary regionalism is the internalization of the North-South issue in a region that encompasses both developed and developing countries. The rapid expansion of regional trade and investment has heightened what may be termed sensitivity and vulnerability to one anothers' policies. It has also created significant asymmetries in sensitivity and vulnerability among nations. The formation of cooperative frameworks with the developed countries may become a source of concern, especially among developing countries that depend heavily on the economies of these developed countries, since they fear that such links could lead to the development of dominate-subordinate relationships.

While developing countries try to secure market access and foreign direct investments within regional arrangements, they also seek, at the same time, to avoid being "caged" completely into such a regionalism that includes the major powers. Thus, developing countries try to form a coalition to maintain their autonomy and independence. The Malaysian proposal for EAEC can be understood in this context.

The developing countries within APEC also want to make regionalism as flexible as possible, to maintain economic relations with countries outside the regions, to secure market access and foreign direct investment from them, and to counterbalance politically the larger developed economies within the region. The Asia-EU (ASEM) summit meeting established in 1996 is part of this strategy.

The above arguments also highlight the need to create some form of mechanism that will enable developing countries to maintain their political and economic independence (and also cultural and social independence), from major powers. APEC provides such a mechanism, sustained by the rule of consensus decisionmaking. (This rule is based upon an assumption that mutual "learning" through intensive dialogue and consultation can lead to a common understanding among the members on international political economy, which encourages further cooperation.)

This also means that to prevent the emergence of a North-South polarization within the region, it is necessary to build frameworks (mechanisms) within regionalism that correct any economic imbalances among the member economies. In this regard, the promotion of development cooperation is a prerequisite for interaction between the North and the South. APEC is now focusing on the liberalization and facilitation of trade and investment. Yet, the hasty institutionalization of cooperation without the concomitant creation of mechanisms for development cooperation could hinder interaction and lead to relationships of domination and subordination. Japan's emphasis on the importance of development cooperation in APEC should be considered in this context.

APEC and the Regime Formation in the Asia-Pacific Region: Free Trade Agreement in the Asia-Pacific Region?

In spite of various calls for the establishment of a free trade and investment area in the Asia-Pacific region, if we look at the recent developments of regionalism, except for NAFTA, little formal regionalization dealing with deeper integration issues, such as the harmonization of national policies, has taken place between the developed and the developing countries. Regionalism does not relieve the developing countries from the basic dilemma of multilateralism and may even accelerate it. Deeper economic integration would certainly provide benefits to the developing countries. Enhanced institutional constraints on the powerful developed countries engaging in deviant behavior vis-à-vis international rules would be one of the most important gains for them. Enhanced market access to the markets of the developed countries could be provided through more institutionalized regional integration mechanisms. However, to secure those gains, the developing countries have to make greater concessions and adjustments. Given the fact that international trade and investment issues are now entering into sensitive areas (i.e., harmonization of domestic regulatory systems), which are directly related to governance and the ruling political regime, touching on these sensitive issues will certainly cause strong repercussions in the domestic politics of the developing countries.[20]

There also remain political difficulties on the part of the developed countries. First, if the regional arrangement is based upon a concept of reciprocity, the developed countries have to make concessions in return for the concessions made by developing countries on deeper integration issues. These concessions usually include sectors which are politically sensitive and highly protected, such as agriculture and labor-intensive industries like textiles and footwear. Furthermore, the developing countries may demand greater constraints on the use of "unfair" trade laws and on impartial and binding dispute settlement mechanisms. This will certainly cause serious difficulty on the part of the developed countries. (Can Japan further open its rice market? Can the U.S. give further market access to agricultural products from the developing countries? Can the U.S. give up resorting to Article 301 of the 1974 Trade Act?)

Another difficulty is related to the management of regulatory differences between the developed and developing countries. For example, if regional arrangements appear to lower standards or are not comprehensive enough in coverage, it will probably cause political controversy in the developed countries. This was demonstrated in the controversy which occurred during the process of ratifying NAFTA in the U.S.[21]

Of course, theoretically, it may be possible to formulate a free trade agreement (FTA) among like-minded countries based upon the "APEC minus X" formula, excluding such countries as China and Indonesia which appear to be having difficulty in accepting the conditions of an FTA. However, in practicality, the geopolitics of the region will not allow these countries to be excluded from such an arrangement. Even more, if Asian countries take a position that it is less problematic if "X" is the United States (an EAEC-based FTA?), the negative impact on an overall politico-military situation in the region would be enormous.

Thus, without radical changes in the Asia-Pacific region as well as the global economy, it will be quite difficult for Asia-Pacific regionalism to move toward an even deeper economic integration.

Future Scenarios and U.S.-Japan Relations

The best scenario for Japan is that APEC will develop along the line which was agreed upon at Bogor, Osaka, and Manila, contributing to the strengthening of the global mechanism as well as promoting further liberalization of the APEC economies, including the Japanese economy. This would also facilitate the strengthening of the political foundation of "internationalist groups" in those APEC economies with a strong interest in strengthening economic ties with the outside world and the further opening of its economy.

However, at the same time, we cannot deny the possibility that APEC will not work well, especially with respect to trade and investment (and over such issues as "compatibility" of economic liberalization). In fact, there is some concern among Japanese senior officials about the future prospect of liberalization based upon the principle of voluntarism, because voluntarism is apt to produce a minimum common liberalization which is insufficient for maintaining economic dynamism within the region. They see some possibility of negotiations taking place among the like-minded on specific issues of common concern.

Relating to the concept of "Open Regionalism," contrary to the U.S. position, Japan has strongly supported the non-discriminatory application of APEC liberalization to the non-members on an MFN basis. Japan is concerned about the possibility that the discriminatory application will encourage other nations, especially the EU, to favor a more inward-looking trade policy, thereby inducing the division (i.e., collapse) of the global trading system. Japan has been skeptical of the argument that reciprocal application of APEC liberalization would encourage further liberalization by non-members, thereby contributing to an enhancement of the global trading system.

However, it is still uncertain whether or not APEC could sustain its principle of "Open Regionalism," when the EU does not offer *de facto* reciprocal liberalization to the APEC economies. Given a high protection level in most of the APEC economies, voluntarism will work for the next few years. Asian economies have sufficient room for further liberalization. In addition, in order to attract additional foreign direct investment, they will have to actively liberalize their economies. For the next few years, APEC countries may allow the EU to enjoy "free-riding." Thereafter, however, if the EU continues to enjoy free-riding without reciprocal liberalization, APEC may be forced to choose a difficult policy option: formulation of an FTA.

But, at the same time, the possibility of an FTA being established in the Asia-Pacific may encourage the EU (out of fear of exclusion from the emerging markets in the Asia-Pacific), to become engaged in consultations with APEC over mutually acceptable reciprocal liberalization measures. Thus, global liberalization may be realized through consultations and negotiations between the APEC and the EU. This may be easier than through the GATT/WTO process, given the fact that most of the developing countries are reluctant to engage in new multilateral negotiations at this time.

Thus, inter-regional dialogues and consultations will play an important role in strengthening the global system as well as encouraging the APEC economies to open their markets, and enhancing the basic principle of "Open Regionalism." ASEM and the TAM (Trans-Atlantic Market) idea are good examples. The possibility of setting up an APEC-EU dialogue forum (separate from ASEM) should be seriously considered in this context. Close cooperation between Tokyo and Washington is vitally important in order to carry out this process.

The nightmare for Japan is the strengthening of the trans-Atlantic cooperation by excluding (discriminating against) Japan. The selective expansion of NAFTA to Asia would also constitute a serious threat to Japan, although the possibility is not so high, given the difficulties in reaching agreements on such sensitive issues as environment and labor standards between the U.S. and Asian economies. There is also a possibility that trade and investment liberalization in the region might be looked after through expansion or merger of the existing free trade agreements at the sub-regional levels, such as NAFTA, ANZCER (Australia-New Zealand Closer Economic Relations) and AFTA (ASEAN Free Trade Agreement).

APEC as a Regime

APEC as a regime can be described in the following way. The principles—the most important goals of APEC—are liberalization, facilitation and economic cooperation, even though the weights among them have shifted over the years and have been perceived differently depending upon its individual members. The basic norms—the rules of behavior—are that APEC is a consultative body based upon voluntarism (concerted unilateral action), not through hard negotiations, that its aim is confidence-building among the member economies, and that it should be based upon the concept of "Open Regionalism" and be GATT/WTO consistent. The set of principles which were declared at the Osaka meeting in 1995, such as compatibility, comprehensiveness and so forth, can be considered as a set of concrete norms or rules, particularly for liberalization in trade and investment.

The actual outputs of the regime are the individual commitments to liberalization and facilitation measures and varied projects of economic and technical cooperation. Since one of the basic principles of APEC is voluntarism, there is no strong mechanism in place to either promote the basic goals or enforce commitments. Constant reviews among the members and the exertion of "peer" pressure by governmental, private and academic sectors are the only ways to encourage voluntary actions.

Japanese interests in APEC were, at least at the beginning, reactive in the sense that Japan tried to utilize APEC as a means to avoid, or moderate, the external pressures arising from its huge external surplus, and at the same time, to maintain the stability of economic order in the Asia-Pacific region as well as in the entire global economy.

Japan has also pushed the traditional policies of economic cooperation within the APEC context. Japan's style in forging APEC has been rather low key and modest due partly to historical experience during the last world war and the current huge trade surplus with most of the APEC economies. The major Japanese aim, at least on the surface, has not been the market access pushed by the Japanese private sector, even though Japan appreciated the trade and investment expansion in the region. Japan could not be so aggressive in market access, basically due to its huge trade surplus vis-à-vis most of the APEC economies.

However, we may argue that Japan, as a result, has been successful in penetrating and expanding its economic presence in the region through varied means taken by the APEC process. In a sense, while Japan has, as usual, played the role of a reactive state, it has been successful in economic expansion in this region.

I may argue that the above-mentioned characteristics of APEC as a regime have been consistent with Japanese basic preferences and interests, and that Japan has been contributing to the establishment of such a regime, as exemplified by the five principles for cooperation as presented by Foreign Minister Tsutomu Hata at the 1993 APEC Seattle meeting.[22] However, as I pointed out earlier, some Japanese policymakers and officials as well as academics have begun to have doubts as to how far APEC liberalization can proceed in the future, given APEC's current set of principles. However, at this moment, they themselves do not seem to have any clear alternative ideas. They would not advocate that APEC be transformed into a free trade agreement. The most probable scenario is that, if APEC does not work well because of its members becoming more protectionist and/or the EU adopting more inward-looking commercial policies, Japan would resort to the WTO rules.[23]

Conclusion

Building a community is a lengthy process. For the moment, all we can do is to wait for the myriad processes of regional interaction and cooperation to bear fruit. It is with these considerations in mind that the proposed EAEC should be examined. Since EAEC would probably serve, above all, to improve relations among peoples in the region, participants would be well advised to use it as a forum for developing and affirming an Asia-Pacific identity, one which includes Australia and New Zealand.

As I discussed, there remain various conflicting views between the United States and Japan over the future of Asia-Pacific economic regionalism. Successfully resolving them will require patient diplomacy. If the two powerful countries view APEC as an arena in which to struggle to advance their own narrowly defined national interests, Asia-Pacific regionalism will become a hollow concept. The future of APEC depends, above all, upon whether or not its members are able to find common objectives and incentives that enlist these two countries. In this process, a practice of talking regionally but proceeding unilaterally will undermine that effort.

Notes

1. On a comprehensive political and economic analysis of contemporary regionalism, see, Yoshinobu Yamamoto, "Regionalization in Contemporary International Relations," in *Regionalization in the World Economy: NAFTA, the Americas and Asia Pacific*, ed. Van R. Whiting, Jr. (New Dehli: Macmillan India, 1996), 19–42.
2. Tsutomu Kikuchi, "Eipekku: Kyoutei-naki Jiyuu Boueki Kyotei?" (APEC: Toward a *de facto* Free Trade Area?), *Kokusai Mondai* (Japan Institute of International Affairs), no. 415 (October 1995): 46–59.
3. Arguments for creating a level playing field are troublesome. International trade takes place precisely because of differences among nations. In a fundamental sense, cross-border trade is valuable because the playing field is not level. Miles Kahler, *International Institutions and the Political Economy of Integration* (Washington: The Brookings Institution, 1995), xvii.
4. See Susan Strange's various pioneering works, including "States, Firms and Diplomacy," *International Affairs* 68, no. 1 (January 1992).
5. Toshio Watanabe, "The New Shape of East Asian Economic Development: From Dependency to Self-Reliance," *Japan Review of International Affairs* (Winter/Spring 1997): 40–51.
6. *Ibid.*
7. Jeffrey A. Frankel and Miles Kahler, " Introduction," in *Regionalism and Rivalry : Japan and the United States in Pacific Asia*, ed. J.A. Frankel and M. Kahler (Chicago: The University of Chicago Press, 1993), 7.
8. On the processes of Asia-Pacific regionalism, including both political and economic ones, see, Tsutomu Kikuchi, *APEC: In Search of a New Regional Order in the Asia-Pacific* (in Japanese) (Tokyo: Kokusai Mondai, 1995).
9. Tsutomu Kikuchi, "Asian Regionalism, with reference to APEC and ARF," paper presented at the ISA and JAIR Joint Convention on "Globalism, Regionalism and Nationalism: Asia in search of its role in the 21st Century," September 20-22, 1996, Makuhari, Japan.
10. Minister's Office, MITI, ed., *Nihon No Sentaku* (Japan's Options), (Tokyo: Tsusho Sangyo Chosakai, June 1988), 18–25.
11. Ajia-Taiheiyou Kyouryoku Suisin Kondankai, *Hirakareta Kyouryoku Ni Yoru Jidai* (Asia-Pacific Cooperation Promotion Committee, Towards an Era of Open Economic Cooperation), Ministry of International Trade and Industry, June 1989. In this report, the committee proposed to set up a ministerial conference dealing with trade and industry in the Asia-Pacific region. See also, Noboru Hatakeyama, *Tusyo Kosyo: Kokueki wo meguru Dorama* (Trade Negotiations: Drama over National Interests), (Tokyo: Nihon Keizai Sinbunsya, 1986), ch. 4.
12. Until the 1970s, most of the Japanese investment was concentrated in the manufacturing industries whose products were provided to the domestic markets

of the investment-receiving countries. Import substitution policies prevailed in Asia then. But, since the 1980s, with the introduction of an export-oriented development strategy in the Asian economies, Japanese enterprises have aggressively tried to establish more region-wide production networks to enhance international competitiveness.

13. From 1987 onward, Japanese FDI in the Southeast Asian nations rose dramatically. In the years prior to the Plaza Accords, Japan invested about $900 million annually in the ASEAN countries. After a slight drop in 1986, Japanese FDI increased sharply to peak at $4.6 billion in 1989. Altogether during the four years from 1988 to 1991, Japan invested over $15 billion in the ASEAN countries. Japanese FDI increased sharply to peak at $4.6 billion in 1989. Altogether during the four years from 1988 to 1991, Japan invested over $15 billion in the ASEAN countries.

14. For a more comprehensive analysis on the evolutionary processes of Japanese thinking on Asia-Pacific economic cooperation, see, Yoshinobu Yamamoto and Tsutomu Kikuchi, "Japan's Approach to APEC and the Regime Creation in the Asia-Pacific," in *Institutionalizing the Asia-Pacific: Regime Creation and the Future of APEC*, ed. Vinod K. Agawall and Charles Edward Morrison (New York: St. Martins Press, 1998).

15. John Ravenhill, "Economic Interdependence in East Asia: Its Growth and Effects on the Australian-U.S. Relationship," in *Negotiating the Pacific Century*, ed. Roger Bell (New South Wales, 1996), 182–183.

16. *Ibid.*, 184.

17. See, for example, Ross Ganaut, "Options for Asia-Pacific Trade Liberalization (A Pacific Free Trade Area?)," in *APEC: Challenges and Opportunities*, ed. Chia Siow Yue (Singapore: Institute of Southeast Asian Studies, 1994), 94–112.

18. Ravenhill, *op. cit.*, 184.

19. Akio Watanabe and Tsutomu Kikuchi, "Japan's Perspective on APEC: Community or Association?," *NBR Analysis* 6, no. 3 (November 1995): 23–36.

20. Stephan Haggard, *Developing Nations and the Politics of Global Integration* (Washington: The Brookings Institution, 1995), 48–49.

21. *Ibid.*

22. They are: (1) due attention given to the different stages of development and diversity; gradualism with consensus; (2) consultation rather than negotiations; (3) consistent and complementary with GATT; (4) Open Regionalism, unconditional provision on an MFN basis; and (5) intensive consultation and dialogue with non-members. Speech by Foreign Minister Tsutomu Hata at the APEC Ministerial Meeting in Seattle, November 1993, Ministry of Foreign Affairs, Japan.

23. Yamamoto and Kikuchi, *op. cit.*

Chapter 12

The United States, Japan, and the Tides of History

Charles F. Doran

What is the foreign policy landscape that Japan will face as it moves into the new millennium? In taking the long view of history, the statesman recognizes the pinnacles and gorges, the breath-taking zeniths and seemingly unbridgeable chasms of changing world power. Not flat or smooth, the foreign policy landscape is shaped by glacial movement along state cycles of power. In the short term, strategy is calculated on a flat chessboard, or series of chessboards. But, in this final decade of the century, the chessboard itself is being twisted and warped by the forces of history. Neither the rules of the game nor the identity of rivals or allies is confidently known. Not even the number of players in the central system is today a certitude.

World politics is undergoing a transformation. Although bipolarity is dead, a new international system has not yet formed. All is uncertainty as to its contours and design.

Unexpected and precipitous was the collapse of the Soviet Union. While the Ottoman Empire survived in one form or another for 600 years, the Soviet empire disintegrated in a mere 70. Equally portentous and unanticipated was the unification of the two Germanys. This much about the shifting tides of history has already become clear. What other structural surprises might await governments in this decade or the next? Japanese power continues to soar. Will Japan grow and grow like Germany at the end of the nineteenth century until Japan dominates the entire system? And what of China, whose real annual increase in GDP (gross domestic product) is more than 9 percent? What is its power trajectory, and what are its ambitions? Is Western Europe after Maastricht in a political renaissance or in eclipse, not perhaps strong enough or unified enough even to settle disturbing feuds on its own perimeter? Can Japan traverse this formidable landscape without slippage or misstep?

These problems of foreign policy that arise from changing systems structure are not historically unique. Some clues may be found in the study of state power cycles and in the historical relationship between power and foreign policy role.

"Policy-makers can if they will use history more discriminatingly," advises Ernest May. "Instead of merely projecting a trend, [they] can dissect the forces that produced it and ask whether or not those forces will persist with the same vectors."[1] In the international system, the principal source of structural change is the slow alteration in the relative power of the component states. Differing absolute levels and growth rates among the leading states set in motion a single dynamic of relative power change at the systemic level. The changing structure of the system is this single dynamic of relative power changes on the component state power cycles.[2]

For most states across long-time periods, absolute levels of power as indexed by GNP (gross national product), or wealth, or military spending, increase upwards along some faster than linear curve. Notwithstanding its absolute increases, however, a state's power relative to other leading states in the system over long-time periods follows a pattern of rise, maturation, and decline—the so-called power cycle. The periods vary. The amplitudes are different for states with bigger or smaller resource endowments, economic potential and military force potential. Although there is no inevitability to these curves, the same patterns often result.

Since relative power is a ratio, with a state's own capability in the numerator and that of its competitors in the denominator, what others do is just as important as what a state itself does. As much as fate may have something to do with the outcome, societies choose their position on the cycle by their policies and actions. On no fewer than four occasions, the Ottoman Empire reformed itself, thus sustaining its ascendancy. Throughout the communist revolution, the Soviet Union accelerated heavy industrialization and then, in the 1970s, by the same orthodoxy assured the country's demise. China, by returning land to its peasantry and freeing its markets, set loose fantastic growth. The tides of history are reflected in the ascendancy, demise, and shifting trends on the individual state cycles of relative power.

What is at issue for changing systems structure, and for international statecraft, is the dynamic of relative power. The first fundamental principle of relative power change is elegant in its simplicity: To rise in relative power, a state must have absolute growth that is faster than the average for its set of competitors. Hence the future security of a state is a function of longer-term comparative growth rates, not just immediate decisions about spending or deployment. But the full relative power dynamic is not simple, or kind. The second fundamental principle of relative power change exposes conflicting messages in absolute and relative power change that worsen the shock and surprise of history's shifting tides.

In every case, states with great, undiminished potential for absolute growth eventually bump against an upper limit to further increase in relative power. Increasing share is constrained by the "bounds of the system." Competition for share comes from other states, perhaps much smaller, whose absolute growth rate is greater. Moreover, a state that has obtained a large share of total power increasingly "competes against itself" more than against other states for share, requiring ever greater output to retain its present growth rate. This is as true for the firm in the industrial context as for the state in international relations; it is a principle of competition.

Hence, differing absolute levels and growth rates among the leading states in the system set in motion a single dynamic of changing systems structure, a single dynamic of changes in the component state trajectories of relative power. Power cycle analysis enables one to "see" systems transformation, that is, movement from one mature system to another mature system.[3] Moreover, it enables one to understand what causes the shifting tides that shape the various state cycles.

Sketched out roughly for a few selected polities in the modern system, figure 12-1 reveals something about the cycles of state power. Reflected is the contour of power in terms of how each polity actually evolved. Evident is how power accelerates and decelerates, and how the tides of history can turn against the state as the systemic bounds limit advance. Formal indexation of power (which must reflect the changing sources of power) is a matter better left for fuller discussion elsewhere.[4] But in the sixteenth century, both the Spanish-Austrian Hapsburg complex and the

Ottoman Empire felt the upper bounds to their growth in relative power. France peaked in relative power in the mid-eighteenth century. Britain peaked near the beginning of the nineteenth.

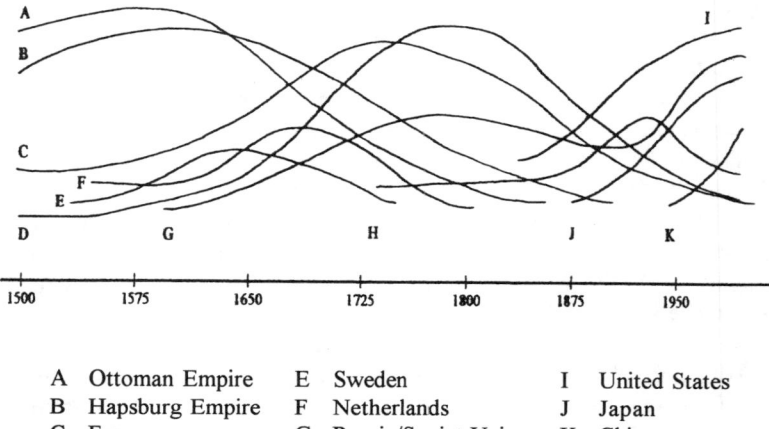

A	Ottoman Empire	E	Sweden	I	United States
B	Hapsburg Empire	F	Netherlands	J	Japan
C	France	G	Russia/Soviet Union	K	China
D	Britain	H	Prussia/Germany		

Figure 12-1. Dynamics of Changing Systems Structure: Percent Shares of Power in the Central System for Leading States (1500–1993). *Source*: Conceptualized by Doran (1965; updated 1981, 1989, 1993), based on estimations for the period 1500–1815, and data for the years 1815–1993.

Not only the leading state in the system follows the path of the power cycle.[5] Smaller actors in the central system have felt the same propulsion toward ascendancy, maturation, and entry into relative decline, often very protracted and slow. Sweden at the beginning of the seventeenth century was described as the "Swedish meteor" as it rose to historical heights and then slipped to secondary status in the face of advance by the larger industrial powers. Holland, financing the wars first against the Hapsburgs and then against Louis XIV, from a very small territorial base, flourished in commercial and in maritime terms during the same remarkable seventeenth century.

While both the United States and Japan were major powers at the end of the nineteenth century, neither state acted as through it were a member of the central system, nor was either regarded by the others as a principal state. Historians often signify the Spanish-American War (1898) and the Russo-Japanese War (1904), respectively, as bench-marks of entry into the central system. In raw power terms, however, each government was a member of the central system long before it was acknowledged to be such. The power curves depicted in figure 12-1 hold at least two major lessons for contemporary statecraft.

Myth of Hegemony

First, the power cycle notion goes far in helping to correct mistaken ideas regarding hegemony, a concept much discussed lately. A number of academic writers argue that each period of history is characterized by the "hegemony" of a single state. Accordingly, struggles between a relatively weakened hegemonic state and a rising challenger lead to the breakdown of world order. Bertrand Russell's vision of future peace invoked such a notion: "The preponderant Power can establish a single Authority over the whole world, and thus make future wars impossible."[6]

This depiction of international politics simply does not correspond to historical reality. Though the Spanish-Austrian Hapsburg Empire may have been the most powerful actor in the system in 1600, it did not write the rules of European politics, any more than Portugal or the Italian City-states had two centuries earlier. Though Paris may have been more commanding than anyone else in the eighteenth century prior to the French Revolution, France was not the arbiter of the European system.

Worse, the hegemonic thesis exaggerates, as Joseph Nye observes, the sense of present decline for principal states that are led to believe in some now-lost mythical past in which they alone established the rules of trade or of world order.[7] It also inflates the hostility and the aspirations of potential rivals, who are encouraged to dream of singular predominance. In a word, these notions of hegemony distort.

At least since the Holy Roman Empire under Charlemagne—despite evident differences in power across states as figure 12-1 illustrates—no individual state has dominated any system in the sense of ultimate control. On the contrary, power has always been shared. Sharing of power, and therefore of role (that is, of responsibility), is a plausible undertaking.[8] Pluralism is the very gist of the modern state system. Balance assures that no single state rules within the central system. Individual states employed navies for localized peacekeeping and to assure freedom of movement on the High Seas. But this is a far cry from military predominance in the central system where the essence of world order is determined.

Indeed, all of the major wars have been fought by the defenders to preserve the de-centralized character of the nation-state system. Aggressors, made abruptly aware of their declining power or otherwise shifted fate, have struck out against others, and have been rolled back by force. Hence the hegemonic theories assert just the opposite of reality. States coalesce in opposition to attempted hegemony, not in response to an effort to defend purported hegemony. Hegemonic notions and the idea of the balance of power, or of pluralism, are utterly at odds. In the conduct of diplomacy, it is well to remember this dynamic and these limits of coercive power.

This does not mean, as figure 12-1 again portrays, that all states have equal power. Far from it. The United States today is the sole military superpower. Should any state attempt to attack, this defensive strength would become quickly evident. In this sense, the United States is a Rankean great power, that is, capable of standing alone in defense against any comers. But the capacity to control—unilaterally and directly—all matters of stability everywhere in the system is quite another question, well beyond the means of any individual government. Among other things, the second Iraq war demonstrated the financial dependence upon allies of the American capacity to lead, much less to control.

Leadership is not to be confused with hegemony. The very dynamism of the system, as revealed by the power cycle perspective, suggests how virtually impossible such attempt at domination is. Of course the absence of hegemony makes leadership more difficult, if more necessary. From the power cycle perspective, leadership and adjustment are not counter-points but dual imperatives to successful foreign policy conduct.

Shocking Surprises of Shifting Trends

A second lesson drawn from the power curves involves the outbreak of major war. There are many ventured explanations for loss of security and for major war, and undoubtedly as many actual causes. A common view is that war causes the shifting tides of systems transformation. But when statecraft is viewed not as a static system—a fixed chessboard—but as a dynamic, undulating series of power trajectories, major war is seen to be an unfortunate consequence rather than a cause of systems transformation.

Over long periods of history, change in the state power cycle is rather predictable. In relative power terms, a state is in stasis, in ascendancy, or in decline. The trajectory is known because it is a linear extrapolation of past experience. And because the trajectory of future power and foreign policy role is known, it is discounted and pretty much accepted by governments.

But at certain critical points in a state's foreign policy experience, the tides of history shift and everything changes. Future expectations concerning status and security are thrown awry. In high stakes competition among governments bent on a world role, these critical points of non-linearity, where all past assessments are demonstrated to be in error, are points of wrenching invitation to anxiety, belligerence, and over-reaction. Statistical regression results for the period 1815–1975 show a high causal relationship between these critical periods and major war.[9]

In addition, gaps between power and role are squeezed to the surface in these traumatic intervals. Gaps arise because changes in foreign policy role tend to lag behind changes in power.[10] For a state in ascendancy, role lags behind power because other governments are reluctant to yield role. For the upstart, possibly rather strident government, others are not prepared to "move over." For a state in decline, role again lags behind power, but this time because allies and clients claim dependence and because internal elites are reluctant to adjust. This creates over-extension.

Germany faced this situation late in the nineteenth century as the late-comer and upstart European industrial state. So great was Germany's absolute economic output that it surpassed even Britain on every manufacturing and trade indicator, and it produced eight to ten times more output than Russia. France, Britain, and Austria-Hungary were all in relative decline, but they refused to yield status or position abroad in the colonial context or within intra-European relations. Given its militarist tradition, Germany was prone to belligerence in any case and attempted to grab through force what favorable structural change could seemingly not provide.

Focus on absolute power trends, and on the competition at the top of the system between Germany and Britain, has led to the "Mastery of Europe" thesis. So great was Germany's absolute, and thus relative, superiority in the pre-war period, and so great were the increases in its level each year, that surely Germany would have become the Master of Europe in a few years if it had not made the strategic error of going to war. In a word, it is assumed that Germany's relative power was continuing to rise in the pre-war period, and that only defeat in the war forced it onto a declining relative power path.

But according to the power cycle interpretation, what most triggered German *angst* in 1914 and German bellicosity, was the sudden discovery that the "tides of history" had shifted against it. "With no history behind it save forty years of unchallenged success in an undeviating advance to greatness,"[11] and "trust[ing] in a current that would carry [them] to [their] goal,"[12] the German Foreign Office and the General Staff were shocked to discover between 1905 and 1914 that German relative power had peaked. Notwithstanding its greatest absolute increases ever, Germany's relative power had become locked in a structural vise.

Germany and all of Europe were aware of the "underwater current," so counter-intuitive, that shattered their expectations of a continued German rise on its power cycle. The tiny absolute increments of Russia, in accelerating economic take-off at the bottom of the central system, were sufficient to halt Germany's ascent and force it onto a declining path. Germany had bumped against the upper limit to its relative growth. In the hour of its greatest achievement, it was driven onto unexpected paths by the bounds of the system.

According to this dynamic structural interpretation, the allies acted unwisely in 1914, and again, for opposite reasons, in 1939. Fearful of Germany's meteoric rise, declining Britain and France encircled Germany through the *Entente Cordiale* so as to curtail its advance in power and to preserve their superiority in status and perquisites. No serious thought was given to adjustment. Confident that its rise would continue, Germany was willing to defer its role gratification. Trying belatedly to right the wrongs of the war that followed Germany's sudden discovery of lost opportunity, the allies wrongly applied the policy of adjustment in 1939. Instead of opposing Hitler with firmness, they tried to appease. But Germany was in significant relative decline and could not legitimately claim a larger European or world role; and in no sense were Hitler's territorial ambitions legitimate. Drawing a wrong lesson from the origins of the last war, the allies failed to heed Winston Churchill's advice to oppose Hitler, and through bad strategy they made invasion possible.

Soviet power peaked in the 1980s. But instead of spilling over onto the system militarily by extending the Afghanistan intervention, as some in the communist leadership undoubtedly favored, the Soviet Union turned its trauma and anxiety inward. By trying to reform its political institutions and its economy, the Soviet Union sought to continue the upward trajectory of its power cycle. Bumping against the upper limit of its power ascendancy, it released volcanic internal turmoil that tore it apart.

In the present context, the curves of power hold another important set of insights for contemporary strategy. Will Japan grow and grow until it dominates the system as some of its critics seem to fear, or is it already in abject decline as others attest, and what are the implications for world order?

Dynamics of Japanese Power

Japan in the post-1945 period grew more rapidly than any of the other advanced industrial countries, who were members of the Organization for Economic Cooperaton and Development (OECD). Is it likely to continue this high rate of growth into the twenty-first century, eventually catching up with and surpassing the United States in terms of gross domestic product?[13] Will the absolute increments of Japan's growth become so large that it will dwarf the other leading states? This latter question involves relative comparisons. Japan's future GDP growth must be treated relative to that of the other leading economies.

When the Japanese power cycle is compared to that of the other major states, two considerations become apparent. First, the rate or increase in relative power is falling off decidedly, as of the last two decades. Internally, in keeping with some of the assumptions of the convergence hypothesis in economics, Japan's rate of economic growth, and therefore of per capita income growth, has diminished to the systemic norm.[14] Second, the *level* of Japanese relative power is second only to that of the United States today, but it is second and by a still significant margin. Though the level of U.S. power is the largest in the system, U.S. power is in nascent relative decline, further complicating the estimate of the future power level and trajectory for Japan. But one conclusion is rather certain: Japan will not tower over the other members of the central international system, including the United States. Japanese power is beginning to peak.

But is Japanese power peaking so rapidly as to enter precipitous decline? Is the disappointing (1990-96) experience evidence that Japan is sinking into sudden and steep decline? For those who are expecting this outcome, the dynamic of the power cycle contains further surprise. Japan is likely to enjoy a very long flat peak in its power cycle, maintaining the approximate level of relative power that it now experiences within the system. The capacity to maintain this level of compound growth relative to others in the central system will of course be enhanced by domestic reform of institutions and economy. Though difficult to design and implement, these reforms will serve to activate the domestic economy. Since over 80 percent of the total Japanese economy is domestic in orientation, Japan will no longer be dependent largely on its external economy for expansion. As Japanese corporations begin to locate abroad in terms of at least part of their operations, this acceleration of the domestic economy through deregulation will help compensate for the "hollowing-out" that is likely to occur and indeed is already occurring.

"Hollowing-out" is primarily the result of at least four factors.

(1) Japanese firms that are concentrated in comparatively labor-intensive industries, where additional technological innovation is nonetheless difficult, will find that the choice in many cases for them is either to relocate where labor costs are lower, or to close down. That is the principal reason for the very large inflow of Japanese investment into China and Southeast Asia.[15] Accustomed to the rules of lifetime employment, workers who put pressure on the Japanese corporation will speed this trend even faster.

(2) A response by the liberal economies to the perceived neo-mercantilist practice of Japan has encouraged them to close their economies somewhat, thereby incurring inefficiencies all around. But this action also forced Japanese firms to relocate some of their operations inside these economies, thereby creating jobs, output and tax revenue outside Japan. A case in point is the U.S. auto industry that despite a tardy push to increase its competitiveness to something that approaches Toyota standards, found that it still could not compete cost-wise with Japanese firms enjoying initial low-cost loans and other benefits from the closed Japanese capital market. The strategic response was to build barriers that forced Toyota, Nissan and others to build plants in the United States, thus hollowing-out the industry in Japan. Neo-mercantilism elicits very inefficient responses from the liberal economies that ends up hurting both the Japanese and the foreign economy.

(3) Some migration of Japanese firm operations occurs because these operations need to locate near the source of technological innovation. No longer able to merely imitate foreign product and

process, and unable to innovate fast enough at home, these firms are locating near the source of foreign innovation so as to stay competitive on the technological frontier.

(4) Hollowing-out of Japanese industry will take place because of the effect of flexible exchange rates. In order to offset a sharp strengthening of the Japanese yen, a Japanese export firm will locate some of its production abroad. Regardless of whether the yen is strong or weak, the firm is able to produce for the world market unaffected by fluctuations in the value of the yen. When the yen is low, it exports out of its Japanese plants. But when the value of the yen is high, it relies on its foreign operations to supply the world market. This form of flexible exchange rate insurance is bound to force some Japanese production abroad.

Despite all of these pressures to hollow-out the Japanese manufacturing economy, de-regulation of the domestic economy will more than offset the production losses due to the migration of manufacturing enterprise.

Another phenomenon affecting the economy and power position of Japan is the well-known effect of "bumping against" the upper bounds of the cycle. This contrasts with the movement along the cycle in other periods of history due to momentum that dampens the fluctuations around the growth curve. At the top of the cycle, there is less momentum and consequently more fluctuation up and down around mean growth. This is to be expected for some years ahead. Good and bad years will offset each other as the Japanese economy goes through major restructuring and as the overall growth rate slows down on the flat top of the power cycle.

A further question of some consequence is why Japan is peaking on its power cycle. What state in terms of the international dynamic of competition within the central system is doing the pushing? Who is responsible for causing Japanese power to reach an apex?

A common speculation is that the United States is responsible for causing Japanese power to peak. Because of the highly publicized trade disputes between the two countries, the easy judgment is that the rivalry with the United States must be the source of the problem for Japan. In actuality, the United States is having to do all it can to maintain its own position on its power cycle. It is not taking power share away from anyone else including Japan.

Instead, what is happening is that the ultra-rapid rise of China is responsible for the slowdown in Japan's upward momentum on its power curve. China's rise is pulling Japan into the relative power stasis that precedes decline (see figure 12-2). This competitive dynamic is not new to the central system. Early in the twentieth century, Russia did the same thing to the German power cycle, forcing German power to peak. Since the respective state power cycles are totally interactive, relative Japanese performance on its power cycle is not just the result of its own behavior, foreign and domestic, but the result of foreign economic performance of other states as well.

Japan and the United States

As the foregoing assessment suggests, twenty-first century Japan is likely to face a world in which its relative power position neither increases much nor decreases rapidly for quite a long time interval. Indeed skepticism regarding whether China will obtain a "dominant" place in the system is well-justified too.[16] One important qualification for Japan is the decision whether to become a military power. By doubling or tripling its military budget, it would sharply increase its apparent power through a much enlarged navy and air force. But such a sharp increase in military spending would surely upset neighbors in the region, starting with China, who would seek alliances against Japan. Likewise the global equilibrium would be upset, most specifically with Russia, China, and the Koreas. An arms race similar to that between Germany and Britain at the beginning of the century would benefit no one in the system.

Conversely, however, thinking that Japanese and American security interests are virtually identical, the United States will probably continue to request that Japan shoulder a larger share of the heavy U.S. defense cost in Asia region-wide. Insofar as the U.S. defense strategy actually carries out the same mission as a purely Japanese defense program would, the U.S. security posture will "do the Japanese bidding." The savings to Japan will not only be financial, but will be measured in avoidance of regional and global criticism as well as potentially harmful political encirclement. The potential cost is that the United States is not entirely empathetic in policy terms. By playing the American Card, Tokyo however can advance both its economic interests (through financial cost savings) and its security interests (through alliance association).

From the U.S. perspective, the Tokyo-Washington affiliation is also invaluable, not only because some of the large U.S. defense burden is covered by yen expenditures, but because the long-standing agreement,

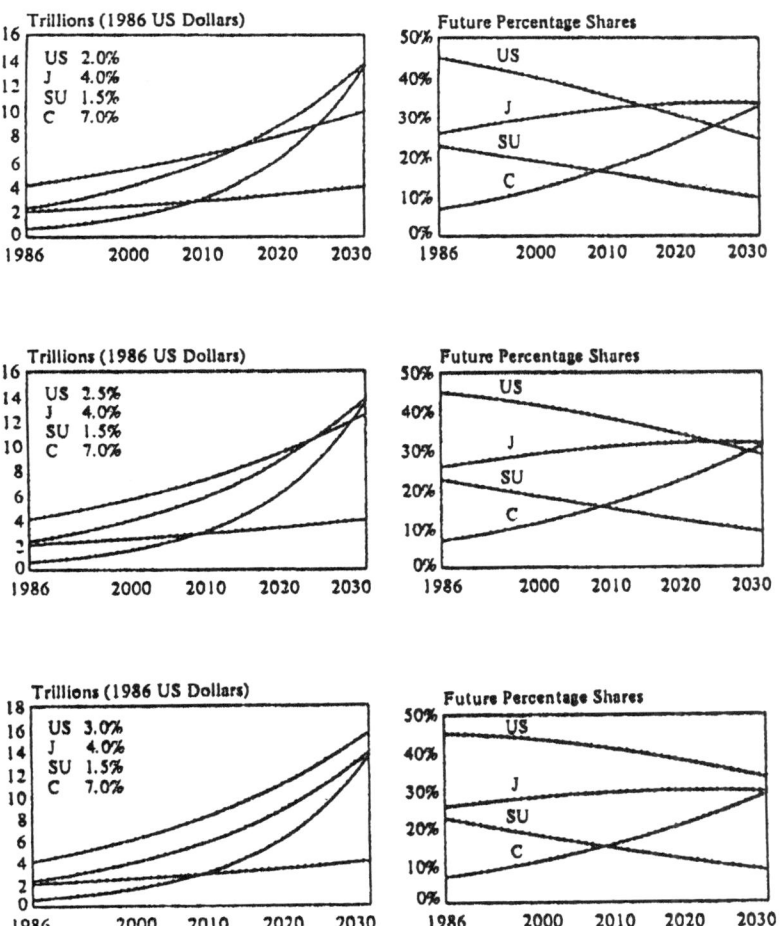

Japan slowly peaks in relative GNP under each scenario using alternative U.S. growth rates and given (unchanging) growth rates for Japan, China and the Soviet Union/Russia.

Figure 12-2. Dynamic Simulation of Absolute and Relative GNP Growth for Four Countries (1986–2030). *Source:* Drawn from Doran, *Systems in Crisis* (1991), 235.

now updated to reflect new political circumstances on each side, is potentially very reassuring both in Asia and around the world. To understand the importance of this reassurance, just consider the "opportunity costs" if this U.S.-Japanese association were severed, namely, the attitude of governments toward major unilateral Japanese military rearmament. Indeed, the Japanese strategy in economics to keep the United States involved in global economic issues and broad-based regional arrangements, such as APEC (Asia-Pacific Economic Cooperation), has a direct parallel in security.[17] But here the task is to keep the U.S. involved in firmly regional concerns inside Asia.

The Joint U.S.-Japan Economic Problem

Security and economics appear to have been separated in recent bilateral U.S.-Japan negotiations.[18] Security considerations are proceeding effectively. Economic considerations are not. The United States and Japan have an economic problem that they are not addressing.[19] Since the combined size of their GDPs is so large, the joint U.S.-Japan economic problem is fast becoming the world's problem.

The problem is sometimes characterized merely as a trade difficulty. It is that; but it is also much more. On the surface, the joint economic problem is that the United States is running a seemingly perpetual trade deficit with Japan, and Japan is encouraging a similar and equivalent trade surplus. The United States must borrow abroad largely from Japan to sustain the trade surplus since Americans refuse to save enough to cover the costs of this trade inflow from their own domestic resources. Japan provides loans and buys properties in the United States, sometimes on not very favorable terms, to keep the trade flowing toward the United States, while purposefully keeping American (and other foreign) manufactured goods and services out of Japan that would otherwise allow the United States (and other countries) to pay for and correct the trade imbalances.

There is a great irony in all of this. Japan has given the United States wise counsel on how to correct the trade problem and its deeper economic causation, but the United States has ignored the advice. The United States has provided Japan with sound advice on how to solve its portion of the joint economic problem and Japan has failed to act. Each country waits for the other to solve an economic problem that is epitomized by trade, but that is deeper than trade, and neither responds to its own deficiencies. Each appears to believe politically that it can weather the inevitable future economic storm because of sheer size and prior success. Both countries are likely to suffer from this myopia. Nor in consequence will the world economy escape either depression or slower than average growth rates.

A further irony, is that, reduced to its simplest form, the American part of the problem is the obverse of the Japanese part, and of course vice-versa. The United States has developed an economic system in which consumption is *the* economic objective. But consumption has gotten so out of hand that Americans have forgotten how to save. Japan has evolved an economic system in which avoidance of consumption is the goal. Now the techniques used to drive exports and expand savings at the cost of domestic consumption have gotten so monstrous that Japanese growth itself is threatened at the same time that its trade surplus with the United States is virtually uncontrollable.

The solution is clear. Stop denial. The United States must take steps to curb its excess consumption, increase savings, and enhance its investment, especially in areas like research and development which it has been neglecting comparatively for over a decade. Japan must open its economy to foreign-generated services and manufactured goods, especially those from the United States needed to eliminate the trade gap that is now not properly paid for or sustained. By increasing savings, ie by taking a leaf from Japan's book, the United States will correct some of its trade imbalance. By increasing consumption of foreign goods, i.e., making it possible for Japanese consumers to have access to American-made goods, Japan will encourage the domestic economic competition necessary to get its lethargic domestic industries operating and in the process will help eliminate its bilateral trade imbalance with the United States that otherwise cannot be forever financed with Japanese yen.

In the absence of these mutual corrections, the U.S.-Japan trade imbalance will cause the dollar to crash (or steeply depreciate) as well perhaps as drive the U.S. and world economies into likely severe recession. This will imperil Japanese loans in the United States and ultimately the U.S.-Japan trade and commercial relationship. More than any aspect of the security relationship, whether treated singly in negotiations or on two tracks with trade, the economic relationship—both domestically and externally since the sectors are entirely interrelated—is now so out of equilibrium that it endangers the entire future economy of each country. What could be of a higher priority for the two countries to repair?

Japan and China

From the perspective of countries elsewhere in Asia, there are two conceivable Asian structural problems ahead. First is how well Japan adapts to the international political reality of reaching the apex of its relative political power and of declining. Acknowledging relative economic decline for any country, especially a country as large and as justifiably proud of its accomplishments as Japan, is no easy matter. The shock of such adjustment is accompanied by the awareness of a disappearing world role. Knowledge of a foreign policy role foregone can be upsetting to elites bent upon maximizing the impact of their country upon the world system.

For a number of reasons, Japan is probably able to weather the stormy seas other governments and societies in the past have poorly navigated. Japan does not seek to spread an ideology that is idiosyncratic to its own cultural and political perspective. Memory of the bitter outcome of World War Two, if not overt, is latent in the Japanese political consciousness and the event itself is not to be repeated. Nuclear weapons have altered the stakes of any outcome that might result from a failure to cope with the shock of adjustment to relative decline. But relative decline itself for Japan is likely to be a very long gradual process, not subject to enormous surprises or diplomatic reversals in world affairs. A final reason why Japanese relative decline is likely to be less painful to Japan than to some other countries in the past is its long diplomatic and security relationship with the other principal "maritime power" in the international system, the United States. While never stress-free nor totally heartening, the association does provide its share of comfort, especially since the United States shall be the largest actor in the system economically and militarily for the foreseeable future.

The other potential structural problem for the Asian system is the rapid rise of China and its inevitable passage through its first inflection point, or point of abrupt, unpredictable non-linear change on the rising side of its power curve. On the one hand, this rise is unsettling for other governments as China shall inevitably elbow itself into world markets and transforms the world balance of political and military power. On the other hand, the rise of China and the momentum of growth there created becomes a matter of urgency for China itself because so much of rural China feels the pull of ascendant expectation that a sudden decline in growth rate would seem to threaten. The strain of fast development and changing values is felt both by the individual and society.[20] China must continue to grow fast in the minds of the Chinese themselves to avoid splitting apart internally over economic benefits not equally spread throughout China or broadly shared throughout a society still not entirely divorced from the ideology of equalitarianism (though perhaps of communist passion).

So China is a potential threat to itself in terms of a civil war or of a splitting apart, just as it could become a threat to others if, in the throes of passage through its first inflection point on the power cycle, China becomes militarily expansionist.

Additionally, there are two outstanding problems that confront China and its neighbors in the Asian sphere. The first is the challenge of the integration of North Korea into a stable and peaceful market system. The second is the resolution of the China/Taiwan One-China tangle. Normalization of bilateral relations between Taiwan and China is desirable, even necessary.[21] But what is involved with normalization and how can others assist in facilitating it especially in an interval when Taiwan is becoming both more democratic and attracted to affiliation with like-minded polities?[22] Each of these diplomatic snares is capable of upsetting world politics at a time when China is most sensitive about its future foreign policy role in the international system.

The most compelling Asian foreign policy issue for Japan and for the United States is to adopt a common policy for dealing with each of these threats. Behind the threats lies the reality of an emergent China attempting to become a modern advanced industrial economy and a full member of the central international system. In general, Japan and the United States have several choices, each of which involves not just themselves, or the other countries in Asia, but all of the members of the central system. That is the reality of the twenty-first century. Asian politics has become world politics. Globalization is not just a matter of commercial policy, it is more evidently a matter of international political affairs. The fate of China is a fate that will affect all of the major players including Europe and Russia as much as Japan and the United States. Somehow the West in particular must understand the earnestness of this issue and the potential scope of its impact.

To adopt the correct strategy vis-à-vis China, the other major actors need to look at the world, initially at least, through a Chinese viewpoint. China is torn between and among several worlds. It is at once a less-developed or newly developing country, painfully aware of its technological backwardness, and by weight of its GNP a major power. It is both a representative of the Third World and a member of the central system. It is both an Asian power and a world power. It enjoys a dominant role in Asia with Japan, yet it must share that role and status with its powerful neighbor. It feels itself the sole legitimate cultural expositor of Confucian civilization, yet its people are rapidly turning their backs on this traditional cultural inheritance. China is aware that it is feared by others as a potential threat to the stability of world order, yet China itself fears domination and manipulation from abroad.

Japan and the United States can pursue essentially three strategies with respect to China.

First, they can seek to forge an alliance of the Great Powers, led by the United States, against a China that is perceived as bumptious and increasingly as a military threat. Such an alliance would involve the European Union, Russia, Japan and the United States. Unable to agree on a common foreign policy of this magnitude, the European contribution might involve only Britain, France, and Germany. Such an alliance could probably only come about after something is interpreted by the West as a provocation by China, i.e., revealing hostile intent toward neighbors. It would only occur likewise after the United States took the lead in establishing such an alliance. While the United States could surely veto creation of the alliance, it could not alone bring such an alliance into being.

Russia, in some ways the weakest member of such an alliance, might be tempted by China to form its own bilateral agreement with China in a unilateral attempt to protect Russia's own security which in territorial terms, especially in Manchuria and in regions of substantial recent Chinese migration, is the most vulnerable of all the members of the central system.

Second, Japan and the United States could form one or more "collective security arrangements" in the Pacific region, emulating the Conference on Security and Cooperation in Europe (CSCE), for example. Since the problems they are designed to resolve are regional, most such arrangements are regional as well. These could be offshoots of economic associations such as APEC, or, they could be free-standing arrangements built around consultations between Tokyo, Beijing, and Washington. Arms control talks, regional reassurance measures, and common problems of peacekeeping all could receive attention inside such a framework. The object of such regional collective security arrangements would be to enhance communication among the parties to the agreement and to decrease political uncertainty including tensions. By limiting the arrangements to three-power discussions, the players most capable of resolving political-military problems would be at the table. Unfortunately, China might feel disadvantaged in such a three-way set of discussions, recognizing the close political and security ties between Tokyo and Washington. Hence, China might prefer to broaden the membership.

A sticking-point becomes the inclusion of Russia, which after all is as much a Pacific power as any of the other potential members. But to include Russia today and not to include the European Union countries is of course to create the impression that the arrangement is anti-European, an impression that both the United States and Japan and probably Russia would certainly not want to leave. Therefore, the member identification of such a regional grouping is difficult to define without alienating the very countries that in other forums and frameworks are indispensable allies.

Third, Japan and the United States alternatively could rely on the same bilateral arrangements that they have always employed. There is a two-fold difficulty here. First, it conveys the sense that Asia is too fissiparous to enjoy the same kind of amalgamated alliance structure employed in Europe. This, however, is misleading since most of those structures were created prior to the Cold War and are now being modified or amplified to reflect very different post-Cold War circumstances. Second, it could fail to meet Japan's understandable aspirations to avoid isolation. Through China's instigation, bilateral security arrangements might proliferate among other Asian countries, thereby minimizing China's own diplomatic isolation. Natural allies of Japan, such as Taiwan or South Korea, are for peculiar reasons foreclosed from allying directly with Japan. Thus, the bilateral approach is circumscribed with limitations.

For both parties inside the region, however, the alliance between Japan and the United States is primary. Sometimes compared to the Anglo-Japanese alliance, this analogy should be approached with caution for reasons that are explained by the historical purpose of the alliance and by its eventual unfortunate break-down. The U.S.-Japanese alliance in contrast has more substance than it has formalization and status. It is more militarily useful than politically visible. Ironically, for each partner, it is more valuable when it is least discussed at home or by neighbors abroad. In many respects the U.S.-Japanese alliance is unique. Structurally, it is without parallel because of the respective security needs of its two members. At the turn of a new century, the U.S.-Japanese alliance continues to serve a purpose, now more broadly defined.

Which of these three types of arrangements—(a) a multilateral alliance treaty, (b) a collective security arrangement, or (c) bilateral military alliances—best undergird world order in the Asia-Pacific? In trying to answer that question, the United States and Japan need to reflect not only on the goal that they wish to achieve, namely security and peace within the region, but on the political implications of the strategies that they believe will get them there. The right goal but the wrong strategy could be disastrous. Generally, when considering China, the United States and Japan must choose between a strategy of *containment* and a strategy of *engagement*.

Containment appeals because of success vis-à-vis the Soviet Union during the Cold War. Containment also sounds safe. It is equated with military security and thus with a feeling of certainty. Containment involves orchestrated policy among a number of countries.

Engagement, on the other hand, seems wishy-washy. It appears to have no military component. It evokes memories of appeasement and of Munich. Engagement, thus at first glance, looks dangerously unreliable as a strategy for dealing with an effervescent China.

However, certain historical and strategic realities ought to be brought into the discussion. Rising power in the long-run cannot be halted; nor can declining power, and therefore a declining foreign policy role, be artificially bolstered. This means that China will increase its power relative to rivals, and therefore its foreign policy role, whatever other governments may think about this or try to do. The challenge is not to constrain the Chinese foreign policy role, or its power, for that is politically impossible, but to deter any expansionist proclivities. Containment involves encirclement, precisely the policy that alienated post-Bismarckian Germany and prepared the conditions for World War One. Containment is an overt effort to encircle and to constrain in terms of role and power. It is bound to transmit hostility to a recently ascendant state.

China is currently a threat neither to Japan nor to the United States.[23] That is the simple political truth. Its army and navy are not a match for that of either country. Where China will be twenty years from today is another story. Depending upon its leadership, it could be a threat or it could be a fully satiated actor. But to alienate China today through a containment policy that is unneeded because of fear regarding where China might be two decades away is scarcely sound strategy. Better a strategy that seeks to integrate China more fully into the present international system, both economically and politically. This is not a strategy to undermine the present regime in China, or to try to alter its ideological preferences, whatever Beijing may suspect. Rather, engagement is a strategy to allow China to acquire the status and perquisites that its economic achievements have earned it.

But engagement is also not appeasement. China must respect the borders and the sovereignty of the states around it, including Taiwan, whatever the mythology of its association with the Mainland. No compromise in security terms here can be tolerated. Both Japan and the United States have sufficient military strength to guarantee this equilibrium, provided that the respective powder kegs in the Asian arena are kept away from open flames.

What does the commitment to a strategy of engagement mean for the United States and Japan? It means convincing other governments, namely Russia and those in Europe, that China ought to be integrated gradually into the network of governmental and non-governmental agencies. It means thinking about how China could become a more prominent member of the economic organizations that shape commercial and trade policy. Engagement also involves according China the diplomatic status that its rise in power incrementally earns.

When engagement is opted for, instead of a containment policy that is bound to feed Chinese paranoia, certain of the institutional arrangements previously considered become more attractive, others less so. A multilateral defensive alliance aimed at surrounding China is obviously not necessary, whatever the absence of such a framework may mean for comparison with Europe. But likewise collective security arrangements involving all of the principal Pacific states also are not likely to put China or Russia or both in a less than tenable diplomatic position. At the same time collective security arrangements may induce a false complacence about security that discourages realistic preparedness. Ad hoc discussion and continued communication among Japan, China, and the United States is practical and potentially beneficial, however.

By elimination, the U.S.-Japan alliance remains critical to the defense interests of each state and to political harmony in Asia. It ensures that the United States will remain involved and committed in a direct and effective way to Asian security.

From a structural perspective, at least, there is no reason why Japan and the United States ought not to continue their strategic partnership since these two "maritime powers" are not likely to undergo substantial change in their underlying capability and foreign policy outlook. Long-term power trajectories of the United States and of Japan, though not at the same level of capability, are beginning to move in sync. Additionally, poll results show in both countries a high degree of support for the joint security treaty. "Any drastic restructuring of Japan's foreign relations away from ties with the United States," concludes Takashi Inoguchi, "seems virtually impossible to the majority of Japanese."[24] A majority of Americans feels the same way about Japan.

Russia will rebuild its prestige as its economy strengthens but overall it will have difficulty in increasing its base of relative power. But analysts should not underestimate its still very significant level of military power potential. Europe is beginning to acquire a marginally more centralized and "imperial" form of political organization. China is rapidly climbing the power hierarchy. On the outskirts of the great Eur-Asian land mass, then, the two large maritime states, Japan and the United States, can exercise a balancing role, sustaining the international political equilibrium within the central system in the face of inevitable structural change and political reorientation.

While foreign policy roles may continue to shift somewhat, each country has similar long-term goals of enhanced prosperity for its people and political stability within the region and the global system. For the most part, these goals are shared within the Asian region.[25] The U.S.-Japan alliance is a cornerstone of that security. Although security and economics appear to have been separated in recent negotiations, whether on one track or two, these matters will continue to receive attention in tandem.[26] Already one of the most lasting alliance relationships in history, that between the United States and Japan, will continue to endure so long as it meets the interests of the respective democratically-elected governments, and of their elites and publics.

Notes

1. Ernest May, *Lessons of the Past: The Use and Misuse of History in American Foreign Policy* (New York: Oxford University Press, 1973), xii.

2. Charles F. Doran, *Systems in Crisis: New Imperatives of High Politics at Century's End* (Cambridge: Cambridge University Press, 1991); and "Quo Vadis: The U.S. Cycle of Power and Role in a Transforming World," in *Building a New Global Order* ed. David Dewitt et al. (Toronto: Oxford University Press, 1993),

12–39.

3. Power cycle analysis differs from Waltzian neo-realism (see Kenneth Waltz, *Theory of International Relations* (Reading, Mass.: Addison-Wesley, 1979)) regarding systems transformation, in that the latter considers static systems that abut each other in time, while the former conceives of systems as continually changing and undergoing sometimes protracted intervals of adjustment before another new, mature international system becomes established. Likewise power cycle analysis is completely different, in terms of theoretical assumption and empirical operationalization, from "long cycle analysis" that is associated with Kondratieff waves in prices of capital, commodities, and labor passing through the world economy as a whole.

4. Doran, *Systems in Crisis*.

5. Charles P. Kindleberger appears to accept the reality of the power cycle, calling it instead the "national cycle." He does not, however, probe the all important difference between relative and absolute change in a systematic way. Nor does he recognize that many states, not just the largest state at any point in time, pass through a cycle of power (*World Economic Primacy: 1500-1990* (Cambridge: Cambridge Univ. Press, 1996), 14–36).

6. Bertrand Russell, *The Impact of Science on Society* (London: Unwin Hyman, 1952), 106–107.

7. Joseph S. Nye, Jr., *Bound to Lead* (New York: Basic Books, 1989).

8. Hideo Sato, "Prospects for Global Leadership Sharing: The Economic Dimension," submission to the Symposium on U.S.-Japanese Relations, 1997, 4.

9. Doran, *Systems in Crisis*, and "Quo Vadis: The U.S. Cycle."

10. See Gustav Schmidt and Charles F. Doran, eds., *American Option Fuer Deutschland und Japan: Die Position and Rolle Deutschlands und Japans in regionally un international Strukturen* (Bochum, Germany: Universitaetsverlag Dr. N. Brockmeyer, 1996).

11. L.C.B. Seaman, *From Vienna to Versailles* (New York: Harper and Row, 1963), 143.

12. Ludwig Dehio, *The Precarious Balance: Four Centuries of the European Power Struggle* (New York: Vintage Books, 1965), 233.

13. Herman Kahn, *The Emerging Japanese Superstate* (Englewood Cliffs, N.J.: Prentice Hall, 1970).

14. James R. Golden, "Economics and National Strategy: Convergence, Global Networks, and Cooperative Competition," *The Washington Quarterly* 16, no. 3 (Summer 1993): 91–113.

15. Hiroshi Ouchi, "Business Concerns toward China," submission to Symposium on U.S.-Japanese Relations, 1997, 4.

16. Yu Chung-Hsun, "China's Economic Development Model," submission to Symposium on U.S.-Japanese Relations, 1997, 8.

17. Katsuhiko Mori, "Networking Regionalism and Japan-U.S. Relations," submission to Symposium on U.S.-Japanese Relations, 1997, 4.

18. Tomohito Shinoda, "Japan's Political Changes and Their Impact on U.S.-Japan Relations," submission to Symposium on U.S.-Japanese Relations, 1997, 24.

19. See Lester C. Thurow, *The Future of Capitalism: How Today's Economic Forces Shape Tomorrow's World* (New York: Penquin, 1996), 194–231.

20. Satoshi Amako, "Political Trends and Stability in China: with Focus on the Fourth Conference of the Eighth Session of National People's Congress," submission to symposium on U.S.-Japanese Relations, 1997, 251.

21. Satoshi Amako, "China in Transition and its Outlook for the Future," submission to Symposium on U.S.-Japanese Relations, 1997, 19.

22. Kunio Takahashi, "Taiwan and its Impact on Japan-U.S. Relations," Submission to Symposium on U.S.-Japan Relations, 1997, 4.

23. Consider, for example, the recent exchange on this matter in Richard Bernstein and Ross H. Munro, The Coming Conflict with China (New York: Knopf, 1997); *idem*, "The Coming Conflict with America," *Foreign Affairs* 76, no. 2 (March/April 1997): 18–32; and, Robert S. Ross, "Beijing as a Conservative Power," *Foreign Affairs* 76, no. 3 (March/April 1997): 18–44.

24. Takashi Inoguchi, *Japan's International Relations* (London: Pinter, 1991), 173.

25. Akio Watanabe, "Changing Security Environments and Their Impacts on the U.S.-Japan relations," Submission to the Symposium on U.S.-Japan Relations, 1997, 3.

26. Shinoda, "Japan's Political Changes and Their Impact on U.S.-Japan Relations," 24.

Index

A

ABM. *See* Anti-Ballistic Missile Treaty
Acquisition and Cross-Servicing Agreement 19
ACSA. *See* Acquisition and Cross-Servicing Agreement
ADB. *See* Asian Development Bank
AEM-MITI. *See* ASEAN-Japan Trade Ministers Meeting
AFTA. *See* ASEAN Free Trade Agreement
Albright, Madeleine 121, 153
Amnesty International 170
Anglo-Japanese alliance 235
Anti-Ballistic Missile Treaty 7
ANZCER. *See* Australia-New Zealand Closer Economic Relations
Apartheid system in South Africa 165, 179
APEC. *See* Asia-Pacific Economic Cooperation
APEC-EU dialogue 211
ARF. *See* Association of Southeast Asian Nations: Regional Forum
Arrow War 130
ASEAN. *See* Association of Southeast Asian Nations
ASEAN Free Trade Agreement 211
ASEAN-Japan Trade Ministers Meeting 200
ASEM. *See* Asia-EU summit meeting
Asia-EU summit meeting 28n, 208, 211
Asia-Pacific Economic Cooperation xiv-xv, 9, 35, 37, 196–213, 230, 234
  liberalization 210–213
Asia-Pacific economic regionalism 56–57, 195–215
  North-South issues 197, 207–208
Asia-Pacific free trade agreement 209–210
Asian Development Bank xi
Asian Tigers 91–92, 96. *See also,* Four little dragons; Hong Kong; Korea, South; Singapore; and Taiwan
Asian way, the xiii, 185, 189, 193n
"Asianization" of Japanese foreign policy 1
Association of Southeast Asian Nations 9–10, 18–19, 28n, 94, 121, 140, 188, 200–201, 212, 215n
  Regional Forum viii, 9–10, 16–17, 196
Australia-New Zealand Closer Economic Relations 211
Australia-Japan security cooperation 20

B

Baker, James 40, 181
Bentsen, Lloyd 47, 48
Berger, Sandy 33
Berlin Wall 167, 180
Bilateral security arrangements. *See* United States-Japan: security
Bilateral trade. *See* United States-Japan: trade
Black Monday 203
Brezhnev, Leonid 135
Brock, Bill 37
Brown, Lester R. 64
Brown, Ron 41n
Brownlie, Ian 165
Brzezinski, Zbigniew 156n
Bush administration 9, 181, 188
Bush, George 30–32, 40, 43, 153, 167, 180

C

CAC. *See* Central Advisory Commission
Carter administration 165, 178
Carter, James (Jimmy) xii, 132, 165, 176, 178
Central Advisory Commission 138
Central Committee 103, 105, 112–113
Central Intelligence Agency 121
Central Military Commission 136, 138, 150
Chang Hsiao-yen 124
Chang-jiang (Yangtze River) 64
Chen Xitong 113, 146
Chen Yun 145–146
Chi Haotian 150
Chiang Ching-kuo 142
Chiang Kai-shek 127, 130, 142
China
 anti-Soviet focus 134–135
 Arrow War 130
 bottom level elections 108–109

China *(continued)*
 Central Advisory Commission 138
 Central Committee 103, 105, 112–113
 Central Military Commission 136, 138, 150
 centralization and spreading decentralization 110–119
 Communist Party 103, 105–114, 118, 133, 146, 149–150
 Convention of Peking 130
 Cultural Revolution 106, 132
 de-ideology 112–119
 Deng's reforms 128–129, 132–137, 144–146
 domestic situation xi–xii, 103–125, 147, 150
 economic development x, 59–82, 110–111, 131, 137, 140, 166, 219
 economic reforms 65–66
 entry into United Nations 130–131
 fang quan rang li 110, 115
 Foreign Capital Enterprise Law 111
 foreign direct investment 60–62, 71–74, 92–96, 226
 foreign policy 119–125, 127, 131, 135–136, 143, 151–156, 236
 gross domestic product 60–61, 67, 72, 77–78, 137, 140, 218
 gross national product 61, 234
 human rights issues xii–xiii, 151, 167–169, 177, 182–183, 188, 193n, 199
 international order xiii–xv, 130–132, 134, 139, 151–154, 196–197, 227–228, 232–238
 Jiang Zemin leadership 104–107, 112–114, 119–125, 144–156
 military involvement in Vietnam 131
 military modernization 140
 most favored nation status 181, 187, 199

Index 243

China *(continued)*
  National People's Congress 104–106, 108, 113, 157n
  Opium War 130, 137
  personal rule (situationalization) 114–119
  post-Cold War changes 137–151
  post-Deng Xiaoping era xi, 103–125, 144–156
  Provisional Act of State Officials 115
  rise of legalism (institutionalization) 114–119
  Sanxia-dam development project 64
  saving rate 60–61
  security issues viii, 2, 6–8, 10–11, 17–18, 20–21, 24, 52, 131
  Separate Taxation System 110–111, 115, 117, 149
  South China Sea disputes 18, 20, 121
  Soviet border disputes 157n
  State-owned enterprises 62, 80, 146
  threat xii, 7, 121–122, 128, 234, 236
  Tiananmen Square incident xii, 107–108, 112, 114, 138–139, 143, 145, 167, 180–181
  trade issues 59, 65–76, 80, 123, 135, 151
  "Villager autonomy" 108
  White Paper on Human Rights Conditions 184, 193n
China-French joint declaration 154
China-Japan
  relations 7, 21, 121–122, 154, 232–238
  trade issues 59, 65–76, 135
  Treaty of Peace and Friendship 122
China-India boundary disputes 157n
China-Republic of Korea 21, 121
China-Russia relations 8, 151, 154, 157n, 234
China-Soviet relations 134–135, 157n
China-Taiwan
  one-China issue xi, xv, 18, 76–77, 120–125, 136, 143, 152, 155, 233
  relations 77, 120–125, 131, 142, 233, 237
  trade issues 123
China-United States
  bilateral agenda 141
  human rights 169, 188
  kowtow diplomacy 181
  relations 7, 120–122, 132, 141, 153–154, 181
  trade issues 67–76, 80, 135
Chinese Academy of Social Sciences 105
Chirac, Jacques 154
Christopher, Warren 153
Chun Doo Hwan 178–179
Churchill, Winston 224
CIA. *See* Central Intelligence Agency
CIS. *See* Confederation of Independent States
Clinton administration ix–x, 9, 33–40, 41n, 44–55, 122, 128, 143, 152–153, 181, 188, 204
Clinton, William (Bill) ix, 5, 8–9, 15, 17, 20, 29, 31–40, 43–44, 47, 49–56, 121, 123, 152, 181, 187
Clinton-Hashimoto
  security declaration 2, 17–20, 173
  summit 22, 55
Clinton-Hosokawa summit 48–49, 56
Clinton-Murayama summit 50
CMC. *See* Central Military Commission
Cold War era xi, 29–30, 127, 236. *See also* Post-Cold War era.
  changes due to collapse viii, 4, 8, 39, 139–144, 154, 180, 183
  human rights 164–165, 168

Cold War era *(continued)*
  regional conflicts 16–17, 22, 55–57, 166–167
  security 3, 7, 22, 24, 44, 181
Commission on Human Rights 164–165, 181–182
Communist Party of China 103, 105–114, 118, 133, 146, 149–150
Confederation of Independent States 180
Conference on Security and Cooperation in Europe xv, 166, 236
Containment strategy xii, 153, 236–238
Contract with America 37
Convention of Peking 130
Coordination System of the Chinese Economies 80
Council of Representatives of the Coalition Parties 45, 49
Country Reports on Human Rights 174
CPC. *See* Communist Party of China
Crawford, Sir John 206
CSCE. *See* Conference on Security and Cooperation in Europe
Cultural Revolution 106, 132
Cutter, W. Bowman (Bo) ix, 33, 35–36, 41n, 48

D

Dalai Lama 120, 124
Daw Aung San Suu Ky 188
De-ideology 112–119
Declaration by United Nations on Human Rights 165, 175
Declaration on Security. *See* United States-Japan: 1996 Joint Security
Defense Cooperation. *See* United States-Japan: 1978 Guidelines

Democratic Progressive Party 124, 143, 152
Democratic Socialist Party 48
Deng Xiaoping xii, 103–108, 110, 114, 118, 120–121, 128–129, 132–134, 136–139, 144–146, 148, 150–151, 153, 155, 168, 181. *See also* China: Deng's reforms; Post-Deng Xiaoping era.
Diet 5–6, 23–24, 29, 47, 50–51, 123
DOD. *See* United States Department of Defense
DPP. *See* Democratic Progressive Party
Dulles, John F. xi
Dynamics of Japanese power 225–228

E

EAEC. *See* East Asia Economic Caucus
East Asia Economic Caucus xiv, 200, 208, 210, 213
Economic development in Asian countries x–xi, 84. *See also* Asia-Pacific economic regionalism.
Economic Monetary Union xiv
Economic Planning Agency 60
Economic regionalism xiii–xv, 204. *See also* Asia-Pacific economic regionalism.
Economic Research Institute of the EPA 61
EEC. *See* European Economic Council
EMU. *See* Economic Monetary Union
Engagement strategy xii, 155, 236–238
EPA. *See* Economic Planning Agency
Ethnic Chinese Economic Cooperative Body 77, 79–80

Ethnic Chinese economies 60, 77–80. *See also* China; Hong Kong; Macau; Singapore; Taiwan.
EU. *See* European Union
European Economic Council xiv
European Union xiv–xv, 32, 34, 197, 204, 210–211, 213, 234
Export-oriented industrialization 90–99, 215n

F

Fang quan rang li. See Releasing Rights and Transferring Interests Policy
FDI. *See* Foreign direct investment
Ford administration 166
Ford, Gerald R. 132
Foreign Capital Enterprise Law 111
Foreign direct investment 198
  China 60–62, 71–74, 92–96, 226
  East Asian countries 73, 84, 92–99, 215n
  Hong Kong 72, 92–96
  Japan 72–74, 84, 92–96, 99, 200, 215n, 226
  Taiwan 72, 92–96
  United States 72, 94, 199
Four little dragons 133. *See also* Asian Tigers; Hong Kong; Korea, South; Singapore; Taiwan
Four modernizations 132
Four power talks 10
Framework Trade Talks ix, 33–36, 44–45, 47–50, 52, 55–57
Free trade agreement 208–211, 213
Freedom House 174
French-Sino joint declaration 154
FTA. *See* Free trade agreement
Futenma Marine Corps Air Station 19, 54–55
Fuzhou Military Region 136

G

Gang of Four 104
GATT. *See* General Agreement on Tariffs and Trade
GDP. *See* Gross domestic product
General Agreement on Tariffs and Trade 32, 38, 45–46, 49, 137, 147, 151, 197, 202, 205–206, 211–212, 215n
  Uruguay Round 32, 35–37, 41n, 45–46, 57n, 202–204
Gingrich, Newt 121–122, 124
Glasnost 181
GNP. *See* Gross national product
Gorbachev, Mikhail 135, 157n
Gore, Al 40, 120–121
Greenpeace 168
Gross domestic product
  in China 60–61, 67, 72, 77–78, 137, 140, 218
  in Japan 78, 225, 230
  in United States 78, 230
Gross national product 61, 87, 94, 218
  in China 61, 234
  in South Asia 92
Guidelines review of 1978 Defense Cooperation. *See* United States-Japan: review of guidelines.
Gulf War 4, 22

H

Hanoi 152
Hashimoto Cabinet 5, 54–55
Hashimoto Ryutaro 5, 8, 15, 17, 20, 38–39, 43, 52–56, 122–123
Hashimoto-Clinton
  security declaration 2, 17–20, 173
  summit 22, 55
Hata government 36, 51
Hata Tsutomu 35, 49, 213
Hatoyama Yukio 123

Hawke, Robert 202
Hegomony
 Asian region xi, 128, 134, 140
 myth 221–222
 superpowers 18, 132
Hills, Carla 41n
Hishida Masaharu 114
Ho Chin Minh 160, 162
Hollowing-out 19, 226–227
Hong Kong 60, 67, 77–78, 80, 90–92, 122, 141
 foreign direct investment 72, 92–96
 reversion to China 76–77, 105, 120, 123–124, 137, 148–149
Hosokawa Cabinet 45–53
Hosokawa-Clinton summit 48–49, 56
Hosokawa coalition 29, 47
Hosokawa Morihiro 35–36, 45–50, 53n, 55
Howard, John 20
Hsü Hsin-liang 124
Hu Qiaomu 146
Hu Yaobang 114, 135, 138, 181
Hua Guofeng 104
Human rights xii–xiii, 120, 122, 124, 159–171, 180
 abuses 141, 165, 177, 179, 190
 Asia 173–194
 Asian way xiii, 185, 189, 193n
 China 167–170, 177, 182–183, 188, 193n, 199
 Chinese White Paper on Human Rights Conditions 184, 193n
 Commission on Human Rights 164–165, 181–182
 Country Reports on Human Rights 174
 Declaration by the United Nations 165, 175, 184
 four freedoms 163
 international aspects 179–187
 Japan 174–179, 182, 187–191

Human rights *(continued)*
 Korea, South 178–179
 post-Cold War xii, 167, 169
 South Africa 165, 179–180
 Soviet Union 164, 166, 178
 Tibet 193n
 United States 159–171, 174–176, 178–180, 187–191, 199
 Vietnam 160
 World Conference on Human Rights 180–181, 185–186
Human Rights Watch 174
Huntington, Samuel 159, 170
Hwang Jang Yop 121

I

Ikeda Yukihiko 54, 120, 122, 124
Ikenberry, G. John 171
ILO. *See* International Labor Organization
IMF. *See* International Monetary Fund
Import-subsitution strategy 90–92
Inoguchi Takashi 238
International Atomic Energy Agency 168
International Labor Organization 166
International Monetary Fund 60, 63, 87, 134, 168
International order xiii, 128–132, 134, 139, 144–145, 151–155, 195–214, 217–238
International Red Cross 170
Ito Masayoshi 17

J

Japan
 Anglo alliance 235
 ASEAN-Japan Trade Ministers Meeting 200
 Asia-Pacific interests 212–213
 bukai 45, 51
 coalition's reform 47

Japan *(continued)*
  Council of Representatives of the Coalition Parties 45, 49
  Constitution 6, 21–23
  Democratic Progressive Party 124, 143, 152
  Democratic Socialist Party 48
  Diet 5–6, 23–24, 29, 47, 50–51, 123
  economic situation 96–99
  foreign direct investment 72–74, 84, 92–96, 99, 200, 215n, 226
  Foreign Ministry 52–54
  foreign policy 1, 190, 217, 233
  gross domestic product 78, 225, 230
  human rights issues xiii, 174–179, 182, 187–190
  Liberal Democratic Party viii–ix, 6, 10, 24, 29, 43, 45, 47–48, 51–52, 54, 152
  Ministry of International Trade and Industry 9, 12, 35, 38, 52–53, 77, 202–203, 205
  New Frontier Party 24
  political reform 43, 45–47, 55
  power dynamics 225–228
  regional economic cooperation 89, 202–207
  saving rate 97–99
  Self-Defense Forces 5, 11, 19, 22, 24, 26, 50
  Social Democratic Party 6, 23–24, 46–51
  trade issues 83–92
  vertical administration 45
  zoku 45, 51
Japan-Australia security cooperation 20
Japan-China
  relations 7, 21, 121–122, 154, 232–238
  trade issues 59, 65–76, 135

Japan-China *(continued)*
  Treaty of Peace and Friendship 122
Japan Defense Agency 7, 24
Japan-Republic of Korea 3, 10, 21
Japan-United States
  1978 Guidelines for Defense Cooperation viii, 3–5, 19–24
Japan-United States *(continued)*
  1996 Joint Security Declaration 2–11, 17–20, 122, 173
  alliance viii, xv, 2–3, 6–7, 17–19, 21, 23–27, 50, 235, 237–239
  Commission on Okinawa issues 54
  cooperation in democracy and human relations 189–190
  economic regionalism 196–215
  economic relations 38, 44, 52, 83–84, 202, 230–232
  Framework Trade Talks ix, 33–36, 44–45, 47–50, 52, 55–57
  relations x, xv, 54, 189–190, 195–213
  review of 1978 guidelines 3–7, 10, 18–24
  security
    alliance 50
    defense strategy 228
    general issues viii, 7, 11–12, 15–20, 23–24, 38–39, 43–44, 52, 235
    multilateral dialogues 9–11
  Security Treaty xv, 3, 16–18, 21–22, 25
  trade issues ix, 2, 33–38, 40, 43–45, 47–50, 55–57, 75, 83–90, 97, 231, 237
    auto parts issue 34, 36–38, 41n, 52–53, 56, 226
  U.S. forces in Japan 3–4, 11, 16, 18, 22, 26, 37–38, 54
Japanese-Russo War (1904) 221
JDA. *See* Japan Defense Agency

Jiang Zemin xi–xii, 103–104, 107, 112, 122, 139, 146, 150, 154, 157n. *See also* Post-Deng Xiaoping era.
  leadership 104–107, 112–114, 119–125, 144–156
Joint Security Declaration. *See* United States-Japan: 1996 Joint Security.

K

Kadena air base 23
Kajiyama Seiroku 54
Kantor, Mickey 32, 35–36, 37–38, 48
KEDO. *See* Korean Peninsula Energy Development Organization
Kennedy, John F. 39
Kim Dae Jung 178
Kim Young Sam 3
Kissinger, Henry xii, 156n, 166
KMT. *See* Kuomintang
Kondratieff wave 239n
Kono Yohei 47, 52
Korea
  North xv, 120–121, 124, 180, 187, 233
  threat 3, 5, 8
  nuclear crisis 4–5
  South viii, 3, 5, 10–11, 18–19, 21, 24, 90–92, 94, 96, 133, 141, 166, 174, 178–179, 235
Korea-Japan relations 3, 10, 21
Korean peninsula viii, 2–5, 8, 10–11, 23, 52, 152, 228
Korean Peninsula Energy Development Organization 3
Korean War 3, 127, 131
Kowtow diplomacy 181
Kumagai Hiroshi 35
Kuomintang 124, 127, 135, 142–143, 152

L

LDP. *See* Liberal Democratic Party
League of Nations 162–163
Lee Kuan Yew 185
Lee Teng-hui 142–143, 152
Li Peng 122, 148
Li Xiannian 146
Liberal Democratic Party viii–ix, 6, 10, 24, 29, 43, 45, 47–48, 51–52, 54, 152
Life-cycle 98–99
Liu Huaqing 150
Louis XIV 220

M

Macau 77, 80
Mahathir, Mohomad xiv, 193n, 200
Mao Zedong 104, 106, 114, 127, 131–134, 136, 144, 147, 150. *See also* Post-Mao Zedong era
Marcos, Ferdinand 179
Marine Expeditionary Unit 9
"Mastery of Europe" thesis 223
May, Ernest 218
MEU. *See* Marine Expeditionary Unit
MFN. *See* Most favored nation
Ministry of International Trade and Industry 9, 12, 35, 38, 52–53, 77, 202–203, 205
MITI. *See* Ministry of International Trade and Industry
Miyazawa administration 46
Miyazawa Kiichi 32–34, 44
MNE. *See* Multinational enterprises
Mondale, Walter F. 33, 36, 39, 54
Morris, Dick 37
Most favored nation 112, 181, 206, 210, 215n
  China 181, 187, 199
Multilateral security 9–11. *See also* United States-Japan: security.

Multinational enterprises 199
Murayama Cabinet 49–53, 56
Murayama-Clinton summit 50
Murayama Tomiichi 50–51
Myth of hegemony 221–222

N

1978 Guidelines for Defense Cooperation. *See* United States-Japan: 1978 Guidelines; *see also* United-States-Japan: review of guidelines
NAFTA. *See* North American Free Trade Area
NAID. *See* New Asian Industrial Development
National Defense Program Outline 51
National Development Congress 124
National Economic Council ix, 31, 33–37, 43
National People's Congress 104–106, 108, 113, 157n
National Security Council 31, 33
Nationalist revolution 130
NATO. *See* North Atlantic Treaty Organization
NEC. *See* National Economic Council
New Asian Industrial Development 203
New Frontier Party 24
New National Defense Outline 17, 19
"New world order" 168, 180
Newly industrialized countries 94
Newly industrialized economies 63, 94, 199, 200
NFP. *See* New Frontier Party
NGO. *See* Non-governmental organization
NICs. *See* Newly industrialized countries

Nie Rongzhen 146
NIEs. *See* Newly industrialized economies
Ninkovich, Frank 161
Nixon administration 166
Nixon, Richard M. 4, 39, 132, 176
Non-governmental organization xiii, 174, 186
North American Free Trade Agreement xiv, 31–32, 35, 37–38, 168, 205, 208–211
North Atlantic Treaty Organization 30, 166
North-South issues in Asia-Pacific regionalism 197, 207–208
Northeast Asian Security Dialogue 10–11
NPC. *See* National People's Congress
NSC. *See* National Security Council
Nye, Joseph 221

O

ODA. *See* Official Development Assistance
OECD. *See* Organization for Economic Cooperation and Development
Official Development Assistance xiii, 12, 183, 186–189, 200, 203–204
Ohira Masayoshi 206
Okinawa viii, 2, 8, 19, 23, 25–27, 38, 54–56
Okita Saburo 206
Omnibus Trade and Competitiveness Act of 1988 39
One country, two systems xv, 136, 143, 152, 233
Onuma Yasuaki 177
"Open Door" policy 130
Open Regionalism 197, 205–206, 210–212, 215n

Opium War 130, 137
OPTAD. *See* Organization for Pacific Trade and Development
Organization for Economic Cooperation and Development 53, 77, 225
Organization for Pacific Trade and Development 201
Ota Masahide 25
Ottoman Empire 217, 218, 220

P

Pacific Economic Cooperation Council 201
Pacific Free Trade Area 201
PAFTA. *See* Pacific Free Trade Area
PAP. *See* People's Action Party
PARC. *See* Xerox Palo Alto Research Center
Park Chung Hee 178
Peaceful reunification campaign 142
PECC. *See* Pacific Economic Cooperation Council
Peng Zhen 146
People's Action Party 185
People's Liberation Army 136, 149–150
People's Republic of China. *See* China
Perot, Ross 32
Perry, William 8, 10, 54
Personal rule (Situationalization) 114–119
Physicians without Frontiers 168
PLA. *See* People's Liberation Army
Plaza Accords 72, 203–204, 215n
Pol Pot regime in Cambodia 165
Political Bureau 105, 113, 146
Post-Cold War era 56, 127. *See also:* Jiang Zemin: leadership; Post-Deng Xiaoping era
human rights diplomacy xii, 167, 169

Post-Cold War era *(continued)*
impact on China 137–151
international challenges 39, 127, 151–154, 168, 198
security issues viii, 2–4, 7–8, 12, 15–16, 56, 235
Post-Deng Xiaoping era xi, 103–125, 144–156. *See also* Deng Xiaoping.
Post-Mao Zedong era 128, 133, 149–150. *See also* Mao Zedong.
Post-World War II era 127, 177
Power cycle xiv–xv, 218–225, 233, 239n
China 227
Japan 225–230
Soviet Union 224–225
Swedish meteor 220
United States 225–230
PPP. *See* Purchasing power parity
PRC (People's Republic of China). *See* China
Prestowitz, Clyde 12n, 39
Prisoner's delight 206
Prisoner's dilemma 206
Provincial People's Congress 111, 114
Provisional Act of State Officials 115
Purchasing power parity 60, 77, 78, 81

Q

QDR. *See* Quadrennial Defense Review
Qian Qichen 123
Qiao Shi 105, 147
Quadrennial Defense Review 8

R

R&D. *See* Research and development
Reagan administration 135, 178–179
Reagan, Ronald 17, 32, 40, 178

Regional economic cooperation 202–207
Releasing Rights and Transferring Interests Policy 110, 115
Republic of China. *See* Taiwan
Republic of Korea. *See* Korea: South
Research and development 98
Revisionists 1, 12n, 34, 48
Rise of legalism (Institutionalization) 114–119
ROC (Republic of China). *See* Taiwan
ROK (Republic of Korea). *See* Korea: South
Roosevelt, Eleanor 164
Roosevelt, Franklin D. 163
Roosevelt, Theodore 161
Rubin, Robert 31
Russell, Bertrand 221
Russia 228, 233–235
Russia-China relations 8, 151, 154, 157n, 234
Russo-Japanese War (1904) 221

S

Sakigake 48, 50–51, 57n
Sato Eisaku 4
Saving rate
 China 60–61
 Japan 97–99
 United States 97–98
SDC. *See* Subcommittee for Defense Cooperation
SDFJ. *See* Japan: Self-Defense Forces
Security viii. *See also* United States-Japan: security.
 China 6–8, 17–18, 20–21, 24
 Cold War era 3, 7, 22, 24, 44, 181
 East Asia 1–12, 16–21
 multilateral dialogues 2–4, 7–8, 9–11

Security *(continued)*
 Post-Cold War era viii, 2–4, 7–8, 12, 15–16, 56, 235
 Okinawa 25–27
 Soviet Union 6, 15, 112, 119, 131, 141
Semiconductor Trade Agreement of 1986 34, 44
Senkaku island 112, 123
Separate Taxation System 110–111, 115, 117, 149
Shanghai 77, 110–113, 135, 146
Shanghai gang 146
Shanghai's Pudong development project 64
Singapore 77–78, 80, 91–92, 94, 133, 166, 185
Sino-French joint declaration 154
Sino-Indian boundary dispute 157
Sino-Japan. *See* China-Japan
Sino-Russian "Strategic Partnership" 8, 151, 234
Sino-Soviet relations 134–135, 157n
Sino-U.S. *See* China-United States
Smoot-Hawley Act of 1930 32
Social Democratic Party 6, 23–24, 46–51
 historical policy shift 51, 56
SOEs. *See* State-owned enterprises
South China Sea disputes 18, 20, 121. *See also* Spratly Islands
Soviet Union
 anti-Soviet focus 134-135, 143
 collapse 22, 24, 30, 127, 139–140, 145, 148, 157n, 168, 174, 180, 183, 217–219
 human rights 164, 166, 178
 power cycle 224–225
 security 6, 15, 112, 119, 131, 141
 superpower status ix, 164, 236
 threat 1, 4, 134
Soviet Union-China relations 134–135, 157n

Soviet Union-United States relations xii, 139, 141, 166
Spanish-American War (1898) 221
Spero, Joan 33
South Africa
　human rights 165, 179–180
Spratly Islands 18, 152. *See also* South China Sea disputes
State Officials Act 115–116
State-owned enterprises in China 62, 80, 146–147
Subcommittee for Defense Cooperation 21. *See also* United States-Japan: review of guidelines.
Summers, Lawrence 33
Super 301 executive order ix, 36, 41n, 52, 209
Supreme People's Court 106, 113
Supreme People's Procuratorate 106 113
Suzuki Zenko 17

T

Taft, William Howard 161
TAFTA. *See* Trans-Atlantic Free Trade Area
Taiwan 60, 80, 141, 174
　foreign direct investments 72, 92–96
　international order 131–133, 155, 235
　Kuomintang 124, 127, 135, 142–143, 152
　National Union in China 77
　presidential election 38, 123
Taiwan-China
　one-China issue xi, xv, 18, 76–77, 120–125, 136, 143, 152, 155, 233
　relations 77, 120–125, 131, 142, 233, 237
　trade issues 123

Taiwan Straits 6–7, 18, 136–137, 142, 152–153
Taiwanization of the Republic of China 124, 142
Takemura Masayoshi 57n
TAM. *See* Trans-Atlantic Market
Theater Missile Defense 7
Three-legged stool 44
Tiananmen Square Incident xii, 107–108, 112, 114, 138–139, 143, 145, 167, 180–181
Tibetan autonomy 141
TMD. *See* Theater Missile Defense
Trade Act of 1974 39
Trade issues. *See* specific country
Trans-Atlantic Free Trade Area 211
Trans-Atlantic Market 211
Treaty of Tientsin 130
Trilateral dialogues 3–4, 7, 10–11, 235
Truman administration 127
Truman, Harry S. 127
Twain, Mark 1
Tyson, Laura 37

U

U.N. *See* United Nations
U.S. *See* United States
"Uncle Ye" (Jianying) 136, 150
UNESCO. *See* United Nations: Educational, Scientific & Cultural Organization
Union of Soviet Socialist Republics. *See* Soviet Union
United Nations 130–131, 143, 163–165, 175, 179, 184
　Commission on Human Rights 164–165, 181–182
　Declaration on Human Rights 165, 175
　Educational, Scientific & Cultural Organization 163, 166
　peace-keeping activities 18, 27

United Nations *(continued)*
  Security Council 18
  World Conference on Human
    Rights 180–181, 185–186
United States
  Central Intelligence Agency 121
  Department of Defense 7
  forces 2, 4, 8–9, 11, 121, 197
    in Japan 3–4, 11, 16, 18, 22,
      26, 37–38, 54
    in Korea 4, 18
  foreign direct investment 72, 94,
    199
  foreign policy 29, 162, 174, 176,
    233
  Futenma Marine Corps Air
    Station 19, 54, 55
  gross domestic product 78, 230
  human rights issues xii–xiii, 159–
    171, 174–176, 178–180, 187–189,
    191, 199
  National Economic Council ix, 31,
    33–37, 43
  National Security Council 31, 33
  saving rate 97–98
  Spanish-American War (1898)
    221
  Super 301 executive order ix, 36,
    41n, 52, 209
  trade deficit 31, 67–76, 203, 230
  trade policy 31–39, 89
  Trade Representative 32–37, 48
United States-China
  bilateral agenda 141
  human rights 169, 188
  kowtow diplomacy 181
  relations 7, 120–122, 132, 141, 153–
    154, 181
  trade issues 67–76, 80, 135
United States-Japan
  1978 Guidelines for Defense
    Cooperation viii, 3–5, 19–24
  1996 Joint Security Declaration
    2–11, 17–20, 122, 173

Japan-United States *(continued)*
  alliance viii, xv, 2–3, 6–7, 17–19,
    21, 23–27, 50, 235, 237–239
  Commission on Okinawa issues
    54
  cooperation in democracy and
    human relations 189–190
  economic regionalism 196–215
  economic relations 38, 44, 52, 83–
    84, 202, 230–232
  Framework Trade Talks ix, 33–36,
    44–45, 47–50, 52, 55–57
  relations x, xv, 54, 189–190, 195–
    213
  review of 1978 guidelines 3–7, 10,
    18–24
  security
    alliance 50
    defense strategy 228
    general issues viii, 7, 11–12, 15–
      20, 23–24, 38–39, 43–44, 52,
      235
    multilateral dialogues 9–11
  Security Treaty xv, 3, 16–18, 21–
    22, 25
  trade issues ix, 2, 33–38, 40, 43–
    45, 47–50, 55–57, 75, 83–90, 97,
    231, 237
  auto parts issue 34, 36–38, 41n,
    52–53, 56, 226
U.S. forces in Japan 3–4, 11, 16,
  18, 22, 26, 37–38, 54
United States-Japan-China trilateral
  strategic dialogue 7, 10, 235
United States-Japan-Republic of
  Korea defense dialogues 3–4,
  10–11
United States-Japan-Russia defense
  dialogues 10
United States-Republic of Korea
  Alliance 3–4
United States-Soviet Union relations
  xii, 139, 141, 166

United States-United Kingdom
 alliance 24
Universal Declaration of Human
 Rights 164, 175, 184
Uruguay Round 32, 35–37, 41n,
 45–46, 57n, 202–204
USFJ. *See* United States: forces in
 Japan
USFK. *See* United States: forces in
 Korea
USSR (Union of Soviet Socialist
 Republics). *See* Soviet Union.
USTR. *See* United States: Trade
 Representative
Usui Hideo 54

V

Vienna Declaration and Programme
 of Action 185–186
Vietnam 140, 160, 162, 174, 180
 China's military involvement 131
 incursion into Cambodia 140
 Soviet intervention 135
Vietnam War xi, 176
Voting Rights Act of 1965 29

W

Warsaw Pact 30, 166
WDI. *See* World Development
 Indicators
Wilson, Woodrow xii, 160–162, 175
Wilsonianism 164
World Bank 134
World Chinese Entrepreneurs
 Convention 80
World Conference on Human Rights
 180–181, 185–186
World Development Indicators 87
World Trade Organization 8, 36, 53,
 56, 125, 147–148, 151, 197,
 205–206, 211–213
 Kodak-Fuji film case 38

World War I 164, 236
World War II x, 98, 130, 163, 165,
 175, 212, 224, 232
WTO. *See* World Trade
 Organization

X

Xerox Palo Alto Research Center 87

Y

Yao Yilin 146
Ye Jianying 136, 150.
Yeltsin, Boris 157n, 180

Z

Zhang Wannian 150
Zhang Zhen 150
Zhao Ziyang 114–115, 138–139, 145
Zhou Enlai 132
Zhu Rongji 147
Zoku 55, 51
Zunz, Olivier 170

About the Editors

Chihiro Hosoya, Professor Emeritus at the International University of Japan (IUJ) and at the Hitotsubashi University, is currently Special Advisor at the International University of Japan Research Institute (Niigata, Japan). He also is a member of the Japan Academy and a corresponding fellow of the British Academy. He received an undergraduate degree from Tokyo University and a Ph.D. degree from Kyoto University. He is author of *The Road to San Francisco Peace Treaty* (1984) and co-editor and co-author of *Pearl Harbor* (1993).

Tomohito Shinoda, Associate Professor at the International University of Japan, received an M.A. degree from IUJ and a Ph.D. degree from the Paul H. Nitze School of Advanced International Studies, the Johns Hopkins University. He formerly served as Tokyo Representative of the Edwin O. Reischauer Center for East Asian Studies. He is author of *The Power of the Prime Minister's Office* (1996) and co-author of *Political Parties and Democratic Development in East and Southeast Asia* (1998).

Project Participants

Security
Michael J. Green, Olin Fellow, Council on Foreign Relations
Hisayoshi Ina, Editorial Writer, Nihon Keizai Shinbun
Seigen Miyasato, Professor, Dokkyo University
Takuya Sasaki, Associate Professor, Rikkyo University
Akio Watanabe, Professor, Aoyama Gakuin University

Trade and Domestic Politics
I.M. Destler, Professor, University of Maryland
Haruhiro Fukui, Professor, Tsukuba University
Takeshi Saito, Ministry of International Trade and Industry
Noriyuki Shikata, Ministry of Foreign Affairs
Tomohito Shinoda, Associate Professor, International University of Japan

Developments in East Asia and U.S.-Japan Relations
Charles Chang, World Bank
David Fernandez, Assistant Professor, The Paul Nitze School of Advanced International Studies (SAIS), Johns Hopkins University
Yasuko Ikemoto, Economic Planning Agency
Akinori Marumo, Professor, International University of Japan
Hiroshi Ouchi, Professor, Shibaura Institute of Technology
James Riedel, Professor, SAIS
Chung-Hsun Yu, Professor, Asia University

The Chinese Domestic Situation and U.S.-Japan Relations
Tadashi Amako, Professor, Aoyama Gakuin University
Osamu Ishii, Professor, Hitotsubashi University
H. Lyman Miller, Associate Professor, SAIS
Hirokazu Shiode, Josai International University
Kunio Takahashi, Japan Institute of International Affairs
Kenji Takita, Professor, Chuo University

Human Rights
Tadashi Aruga, Professor, Dokkyo University
Fumiko Fujita, Professor, Tsuda College
Akira Iriye, Professor, Charles Warren Professor, Harvard University
Motoyuki Takamatsu, Professor, Toyo Eiwa Women's University

International Order
Charles F. Doran, Andrew W. Mellon Professor, SAIS
Chihiro Hosoya, Professor Emiritus, International University of Japan
Tsutomu Kikuchi, Professor, Aoyama Gakuin University
Katsuhiko Mori, Associate Professor, International University of Japan
Hideo Sato, Professor, Tsukuba University